11-8-76

STUDIES IN HISTORY, ECONOMICS AND
PUBLIC LAW

Edited by the
FACULTY OF POLITICAL SCIENCE
OF COLUMBIA UNIVERSITY

NUMBER 89

TRANSPORTATION AND INDUSTRIAL DEVELOPMENT
in the
MIDDLE WEST

BY

WILLIAM F. GEPHART

TRANSPORTATION AND INDUSTRIAL DEVELOPMENT

IN THE

MIDDLE WEST

BY

WILLIAM F. GEPHART

OCTAGON BOOKS

A DIVISION OF FARRAR, STRAUS AND GIROUX

New York   1976

Reprinted 1976
by special arrangement with Columbia University Press

OCTAGON BOOKS
A DIVISION OF FARRAR, STRAUS & GIROUX, INC.
19 Union Square West
New York, N.Y. 10003

Library of Congress Cataloging in Publication Data

Gephart, William Franklin, 1877-
    Transportation and industrial development in the Middle West.

    Originally presented as the author's thesis, Columbia University.

    Reprint of the ed. published by Columbia University, New York,
    which was issued as no. 89 of Studies in history, economics and
    public law.

    Bibliography: p.
    1. Transportation—Ohio. 2. Transportation—United States—
    History. 3. United States—Economic conditions. I. Title. II.
    Series: Columbia studies in the social sciences; no. 89.
HE209.G4   1976   380.5′09771   76-18909
ISBN 0-374-93027-9

Manufactured by Braun-Brumfield, Inc.
Ann Arbor, Michigan
Printed in the United States of America

PREFACE

THE following pages are the result of an effort to trace the industrial development of a section of the Middle West, as it was affected by transportation. It is intended to be primarily a study in transportation, and the object has been to correlate the development in transportation with the industrial development.

Every effort has been made to avoid the usual errors in collecting, recording and organizing the numerous facts which have been drawn from many scattered sources. No apology is offered for the extensive use of newspapers as sources of material for certain parts of the study; for while the chief source has been the official documents, yet these only state results. In order to discover what the people were thinking about various policies of the state and local governments and the different phases of their industrial and transportation development, no better source of information is known to the writer than the newspaper. In many cases official reports have been found unsatisfactory, and an investigation of the original documents has been necessary.

In the preparation of the study the writer has been assisted by the funds of the Carnegie Institute of Washington, D. C. Thanks are due to Dr. Edwin R. A. Seligman, of Columbia University, and to Dr. M. B. Hammond, of Ohio State University, for valuable aid and suggestion in the preparation and arrangement of the material.

WM. F. GEPHART.

COLUMBIA UNIVERSITY, *April, 1909*.

TABLE OF CONTENTS

CHAPTER X

The Development of the Railway System

CHAPTER XI

The Improvement of the Ohio Rivers and Harbors

CHAPTER XII

The Development of Highways, 1850-1906

INTRODUCTION

THE present period is one of widespread interest in improved means of transportation. It is differentiated from any of the numerous periods of the past by the fact that the present agitation is not for any particular method of transportation, but for better and more adequate means of transportation. In the past there was a distinct period of agitation for canals and improved rivers, for turnpikes and railroads; but the present movement has for its object to provide for the reduction of the cost of transportation both by land and by water. Although more attention seems to be given by the public at large to the improvement of waterways and highways, this results from the fact that these improvements will be made at public expense through the agency of government. The railways controlled by private individuals are with less attention, but with no less energy, continuing that wonderful and difficult task of keeping railway transportation abreast of the industrial demands. There are doubtless few who fully recognize the real merit of the work which has been done by the railroads in developing the resources of the country, for it has been the widespread practice to emphasize the evils of railway management rather than the constructive work which they have done. However, when their work is dispassionately viewed, and when the extent of the area and the diversity of interests of the United States are considered, we shall realize that it was the railway, more than any other one agency, which made these many geographical units within the limits of the present United States a common country of a people, united in fact as well as in name. Now that the railways are no longer able to meet the demands for transporting the products of the country, many believe that they were wholly responsible for the loss of traffic by the canals and rivers and the subsequent disuse of these waterways, which are now sought to be made efficient means of transportation. As a matter of fact, a careful investigation will disclose that the unfair competition of the railways has not been the chief cause of the traffic leaving the waterways, but rather that the transportation business on the waterways was not organized in such a manner as to meet the growing industrial demands.

In spite of the low cost of shipping by water, the shipper preferred the railway because it was quicker, more certain and, above all, because he could ship at any time and in any amounts. The waterways developed little systematic organization in their business and gradually lost the carrying trade to the railways. Those enthusiastic supporters of canal and river navigation who think that cheapness in rates alone will secure freight for the improved waterways will be disappointed, if this cheapness is coupled with a haphazard conduct of the business. The day has long since passed when a single individual can conduct profitably for the public a transportation business on a railway, a highway, a canal, a river, or even a street. It is a business which demands systematic organization on a large scale, and it is safe to say that centralization rather than decentralization will be the order of the future development of the transportation business, whether on railways, highways or waterways.

There have been few, if any, examples in the history of the world, where such an extensive area of land with such great natural resources has awaited exploitation by man, as that of the United States. It is difficult to realize how extensive these resources were as compared with the limited population to exploit them. Riches awaited all and the inducements to use temporary means for their exploitation were very great. There was so much to divide and so few to share it, that the good of their successors did not appeal to those who did the pioneer work in the industrial conquest of the country. Make-shift principles in the transportation and industrial work were adopted, for that plan which would yield the greatest return in the shortest time was preferred. If canals and rivers did not transport products to the markets at any time and in any quantities which were desired, and railways promised to do this, then the latter were to be favored. Would individuals build highways, railways and bridges? If they would not, then the public must, for markets must be reached. Would individuals construct manufacturing plants? If they would not, then the state must encourage such construction by exempting them from taxation and by paying a bounty for the production of such raw products as would be manufactured in the state. Should one be surprised that evils developed in thus forcing transportation and industrial enterprises? Or was it to be expected, when such rewards were promised, that any other than a forcing process would be adopted?

The task of describing accurately the wonderful industrial development of the United States is one which it is probably too soon to essay; but when the economic history of the country is written, it will be found that the Middle West has been a

very large factor in making this history. In these
states agriculture first secured a large development.
The abundance of fertile land promised great returns,
and the need of transportation facilities was very keenly
felt. The mineral resources were great and awaited exploitation. Manufacturing become profitable as soon as
a larger population was present. It was a region of
great distances and, although the natural waterways supplied in part the early demands for transportation, the
industrial needs soon necessitated something more than
the highways of nature. Harbors must be improved,
streams must be dredged, canals must be constructed
and land routes must be built. In all this region no
other state reflected so accurately what was occur-
ring in all the states of the region, as did Ohio. The
geographical position of this state between the east and
the west caused her to experience the industrial evolu-
tion in all its phases. The topography of the region and
the natural waterways on the north and the south of the
state made Ohio the transportation valley between the
east and the west and the north and the south. Population in its western movement passed through Ohio and
much of it stopped for a time in this state. The center
of population gradually moved through it; then the center of railway mileage, and, at the present time, the center
of manufacturing is moving across the state. If statistics could be collected, it would be found that many
other centers, illustrating the industrial development of
the United States, moved, or are moving, through Ohio.
Such centers for example as the center of improved farm
area, the center of the packing industry, the center of
wheat production and the centers of the manufacture of
vehicles and farm machinery.

The producers of the state struggled for markets to

the east and to the south. The people of the state, in their efforts to reach markets, constructed at public expense canals, railways and highways. They encouraged in various ways the development of the manufacturing industry. They passed through the period of contest between the waterways and the railways for the carrying trade and saw the latter usurp this business. The people witnessed the wonderful development of the lake commerce. They passed through the various phases of highway construction. As a state, they attempted the various means of regulating the numerous industrial enterprises. We are probably too little removed from the latest phases of this regulation to judge properly of the merits of the methods used, but if one can trace the efforts made to lessen the friction due to the industrial changes of the past, adjustments to future changes may be more successfully made.

It has been with the view, then, of contributing something, however small, to a better understanding of the economic history of our country and of performing a service, however slight, to the people of my native state, that this study has been undertaken.

There is such a widespread interest at the present in improved highways and waterways and the regulation of industrial corporations that it is hoped that this attempt to correlate transportation and industrial development will be timely. Ohio has experimented with canals on a wide scale and there is now a movement to rehabilitate these artificial waterways; but to suppose that they can occupy the same field of usefulness, as they once did, is to expect the progress of fifty years of industrial development to be removed. It is believed that in pointing out their real field of usefulness in the past, a proper place in the transportation business may be indicated for them in the future.

The Ohio river is in process of improvement but it can not perform the same service in 1909 that it did in 1809. There is sufficient traffic for both water and land routes but transportation facilities in the future must be provided not simply for local needs, as has been largely the practice in the past, but also for interstate and international needs.

Markets are now world markets, and the producers of the Ohio valley are interested in reaching London, Panama, Hong Kong, as well as Pittsburgh, New Orleans, New York and Chicago. So intimate and complex have become the interests of all the people of the state, that good roads are demanded for all sections. The necessity for economies in production are becoming too pressing for transportation to make up such a large element in the cost; but this cost will not be reduced so much by the legislative enactment of two-cent rate laws, as by developing improved methods of land and water transportation. Both the industrial and the transportation business have long since become interstate in their operation and it is hoped that an account of their development and the attempts at their regulation will be of interest to those who are laboring with the difficulties involved in their proper control. How to preserve the advantages of centralized control of industrial and transportation corporations for the public at large is a problem which is demanding the thought of many serious men. If progress in material welfare is to continue under our present system of ownership and the fruits of this progress are to be shared among its creators, some more adequate solution of this problem must be found than has yet been advanced.

We are undoubtedly upon the eve of a period of large expenditures by the states for improved highways, the rehabilitation of artificial waterways and the inspection of industrial plants and industrial products. The expenditures have already begun in several states.

The experience of the states in this activity has not been encouraging, and partly because of the political party system, which made such activities a means of furthering party organization. The same party system still prevails, and it can hardly be said, notwithstanding our recognition that this public work is of such a technical character as to require for its proper performance trained officials and employees, that we have ceased to prostitute this work to base party purposes. There was some excuse for the mistakes of the past, for the people had no experience to guide them. Such ignorance we can not plead. Official records of bankrupt cities and states, of repudiated debts and of responsibilities shifted to future generations are the mournful reminders of overzealous enthusiasm in constructing public works and of ignorance and dishonesty in their management. If we are to prevent history from repeating itself, as it so often does in a democracy, we must see to it, among other things, that public work does not mean an opportunity for public plunder and political party financiering. Ohio has had a sufficiently varied experience in public work to give her a wealth of wisdom, which, if her sister states are lacking, she may well share with them for the benefit of all. If we will but act upon the basis of what that experience has been, all may well approve of this second period of large expenditures by the states for public works.

CHAPTER I

Primitive Routes of Travel and Trade

THE character and the development of the transportation system of Ohio have been so determined by the topographical and economic relation of the territory to the surrounding regions that, long before the advent of the white man, the basis of the system of communication had been laid out in harmony with these natural conditions. The position of Ohio in relation both to the north and the south and to the east and the west is a most strategic one, as regards transportation whether by land or by water.

To the north are the Great Lakes, which by their proximity to the early settled east served in early times as an easy and cheap means of bringing those manufactured products and other articles that were to be had only from a region which had for some time been settled. In later times, these same Great Lakes afforded a way of transporting to the east those abundant raw products of Ohio which were still exchanged for finished goods. In our own times this Great Lakes system reaches a more extensive region of raw products,—the northwestern and central states—and although the exchange of products between these regions is now more diversified, it is even yet largely what it was in early times—the exchange of raw products for worked-up material. These Great Lakes extend from tide water on the St. Lawrence and at New York fourteen hundred miles into the heart of the continent through an area over which population moves freely eastward and westward and in which the climatic conditions are favorable to a large return for labor and capital.

The Ohio river with its source far to the east forms not only all the southern but also a part of the eastern boundary. It afforded to the first settlers an easy means of reaching the territory and after settlement an inexpensive method of importing the manufactured articles from the long settled regions along the Atlantic seaboard. By its position and numerous state tributaries the Ohio river supplied to these early settlers a valuable transportation route for local purposes, while in the west it connected with the Mississippi,—the great commercial waterway of the central fertile valley of the United States,—and formed a through route to the ocean on the south. The numerous large and navigable tributaries of the Ohio and Mississippi gave the people of Ohio access to many regions, so that as a result of the water transportation facilities on the south and north, they could come into commercial relations with a large part of the United States.

The water-shed which separates these north and south water-ways extends practically east and west across the far northern part of the state, thus causing the largest rivers to flow to the south and leaving only a few miles of portage between the north and south rivers. This condition is not so important in recent times with the north and south railroads and canals, but in the early history of the state it was a fact of great industrial and social importance. So much for the condition of Ohio as regards water-transportation. Her position in reference to land transportation is scarcely less advantageous. The same Great Lakes system which contributes to the prestige of Ohio in water transportation also gives her an advantage in land transportation, for the southern extensions of Lake Michigan and Lake Erie force all east and west interstate routes of communication to bend to the south and pass through Ohio. The mountainous region to the south makes construction, operation and maintenance of land routes so difficult and so expensive, that all interstate east and west routes tend to swerve to the north and pass through Ohio. As a result the greater portion of east and west traffic, whether it be between the east and middle west or of a transcontinental character, passes through Ohio. Ohio is indeed the transportation valley between the east and west.

There was then little occasion for dispute over the location of the general state transportation routes, for natural conditions had marked out their location. Routes must be built to connect the two natural waterways on the north and the south, and some assistance must be given in constructing through east-and-west routes, although these in a large part would be supplied by the demands of other states. Lastly, there must be constructed many shorter routes to weave together the north and south and the east and west routes. The Ohio river was the first extensively used route of the region, for here, as in all regions, man first used that way which nature had supplied. By means of this stream the first settlers reached Ohio, and indeed before the coming of the white man, it was extensively used by the Indian tribes of the interior, who frequently sent representatives or traders to the English in Virginia and Pennsylvania and to the French in Lower Canada and at Fort Duquesne. Down this stream came the English and French traders and trappers to the mouth of the Muskingum, Scioto and Miami rivers and to other trading points on the Ohio river, and thence up the state streams to the Indian centers of population in the fertile valleys.

Along the Scioto were the Shawnee Indians; along the Muskingum, the Delawares; along the Miami, the Miamis; and around Lake Erie, the Wyandots, Ottawas and Iroquois. Although the Indian often preferred a water route, for most purposes he used a land route, and thus the Indian trails originated. The more important of these trails ran north and south and followed in a general way the course of the state rivers, although there were several important east and west trails.[1] While it is probable that these trails were originally made by animals, they became through a process of adaptation first Indian trails, then roads of the early settlers, and later the commercial highways of the state. Although it is true that they were valley trails, they were located far enough from the streams to reach in most places the high ground, and were from this fact properly called highways.[2] However, it must not be concluded that the highways and railways of the state were located here simply because there had been trails. The roads of the civilized man were located on these trails because they were the natural highways from a topographical and economic point of view. The Indians and animals located these paths on the high, dry ground, along the watersheds and streams, through and connecting productive areas, and for this reason they were suitable for the basis of commercial routes of the white man. It will be observed from the map how closely these trails followed

[1] *Cf. Ohio Archaeological and Historical Society Publications*, vol. viii, pp. 264–296, for a detailed description of these trails.

[2] *Ibid.*

the water divides and also how their origins at those points on the Ohio river which communicated with the settled portions of Kentucky, Maryland, Virginia and Pennsylvania afforded a convenient and ready route to the North-West Territory.

Pittsburgh, Cincinnati, Marietta and Detroit were the earliest points settled in the west and became important points of vantage in conquering and settling the territory through which the trails passed. It is interesting and significant to note that the routes of all the main trails are to-day occupied by important railway lines. The New York Central and the Lake Shore follow the old Lake Shore trail; the Pennsylvania follows the old Mahoning Trail; the Toledo and Ohio Central, the Monongahela Trail; the Baltimore and Ohio, the Great or Big Trail; another Pennsylvania line, the Moravia-Scioto-Beaver Trail; the Hocking Valley, the Sandusky-Richmond Trail; the Norfolk and Western, the Scioto Trail; the Cincinnati-Hamilton and Dayton, the Miami Trail; the Lake Erie and Wheeling, the Muskingum Trail. It is also worthy of note that these were among the first railways constructed in the state and were suited, as the trails were, to form the basis of our modern state railway systems, since these locations were topographically, economically and socially justified.

After the territory was conquered from the Indians and opened for settlement, thousands of people flocked into the region. It is probable that the greater number of the settlers came over-land, for the Ohio River did not become an extensively used route until after 1800. This was due chiefly to the difficulty of constructing boats to sail or to float down the river, and the snags, sand-bars, islands and other impediments which made navigation very dangerous. The overland route of the

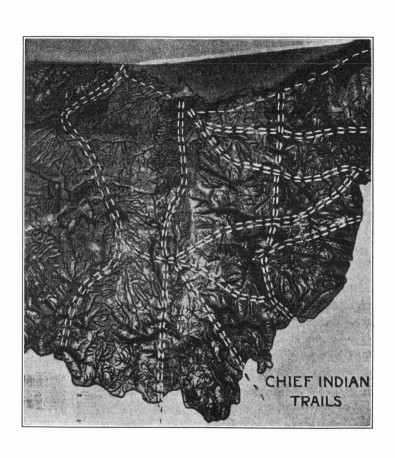

CHIEF INDIAN
TRAILS

Wilderness Road and other semi-roads was preferred.
The Wilderness Road was laid out in 1775 by Daniel
Boone upon order of the Transylvania Company. It
passed through the Cumberland Gap and the Wilds of
Kentucky to the Ohio river, where it connected with the
trail which ran through Ohio to Lake Erie. Because
the Ohio river became later such an important carrier of
passengers and freight (especially the latter), there is
danger of error in concluding that it was from the first
the chief route for travel and traffic. These old trails in
many cases also determined the location of towns, which
often grew up at the intersection of trails or where two
or more trails converged. It will be seen by referring
to the map that some point near the present Columbus
was destined to be the site of a city of the white man.[1]
The location of Sandusky, Cincinnati, Marietta, Portsmouth, Pittsburgh and other cities also illustrates the
same point, since at all these places there were natural
breaks in transportation. To these points the trapper
and the trader came to meet the Indians and to establish the rude market places of early Ohio. The mission-
ary and the settler followed, and soon the nucleus of a
town was started. In some cases stockades were built,
but more often the settlement depended upon its collective force to protect it from the Indians. The first step
in the improvement of the trails was to widen them.
Except in a few cases, where trails ran to salt wells or to
maple-sugar camps, the Indians had no occasion to widen

---

[1] Later the act which provided for the permanent site of the capital
required that it should be located within a radius of twenty-five miles of
the geographical center of the state, and this added to the natural
causes made Columbus an important transportation center, although its
real manufacturing history did not begin until the railroads had reached
the coal regions of the southeast and south.

them, since upon their long journeys, as in war or hunt-
ing parties, they traveled single file. By this manner of
traveling not only was there less effort required to make
the way, but there was also greater protection to the
group since only the one in front was continually exposed to approaching dangers and this one could readily
warn those in the rear. The desire to travel side by
side is a demand of civilized man with his developed
economic and social wants. The process of widening
these paths was begun by the pack-horse of the early
settler, whose burden on each side broke off and brushed
aside the overhanging brush and branches. As these
important trails became thus widened, other minor ones
were discontinued and became wholly overgrown by
bushes and shrubs. Even the military roads, which
were constructed by Braddock, Washington and Forbes,
soon became impassable on account of the fallen trees
and overgrown brush, so that the narrow paths continued
for many years to be the only routes of travel, and were
limited to foot-passengers and pack-horses. These pack-
horses have been well called the industrial agents between
the East and the West for they were the only means of
transportation which could be used. In Doddridge's
Notes we have an insight into the character of the traffic
when he says : [1]

The acquisition of the indispensable articles of salt, iron
and castings presented great difficulties to the first settlers of
the western country. Coined money was practically unknown
and their medium of exchange was fur, ginseng and other

---

[1] Joseph Doddridge, *Notes on the settlement and Indian Wars of the
western posts of Virginia and Pennsylvania, together with a view of
the state of society and manners of the first settlers of the western
country.*

local productions. Each family collected what peltry and furs it could obtain throughout the year for the purpose of sending them over the mountains for barter; in the fall of the year, after seeding time, each family formed an association with some of its neighbors for starting this caravan. The horses, with bells and collars around their necks, were further fitted out with pack-saddles, to the rear part of which was fastened a pair of hobbles made of hickory withes. The bags, provided for the conveyance of salt (on the return trip), were filled with feed for the horses, and large wallets well filled with bread, jerk, boiled ham and cheese, supplied the drivers with provisions. Each horse on the return trip carried two bushels of alum salt, which weighed 84 pounds to the bushel.

The foremost horse in each group was led by the driver and each successive horse was tied to the saddle of the one in front. Bars of iron were often fastened on the backs of the horses and then bent around their bodies, and barrels and kegs were fastened on the sides of each horse. The paths were in many places scarcely more than two feet wide and led over hills and through valleys. These bridle paths were for years the only means of communication with the East, but, when the region became more densely settled, the wants of the settlers more varied and numerous and their production for the market greater, the old bridle paths gave way to the improved roads.

CHAPTER II

The Settlement of Ohio and the West.

It is the purpose of this chapter to show how the settlement of various regions in the present state of Ohio and adjoining states accelerated the development of transportation routes in order not only to connect these often widely separated settlements, but also to give all regions communication with the old settlements in the East. If the first settlements had been made near the established ones in Pennsylvania, Virginia, New York and Kentucky and then had gradually spread westward and north, until the whole territory had been settled, there would doubtless have been a better and a more systematic development of the transportation routes, since the demands for these routes would have been made gradually and, consequently, the wealth of the people would have been more nearly adequate to supply them. As it was, the people of Ohio, as well as those of all the states of the Middle West were almost forced to follow the "make-shift" principle in building their means of transportation. As states, they burdened themselves heavily in constructing inharmonious and expensive ways of communication, which they have been compelled to reconstruct in part on account of original carelessness or developed indifference.

Through the efforts of Dr. Manasseh Cutler, who was the prime mover in the organization and development of the Ohio Company, it was decided at a meeting of the

directors in Boston, November 23, 1787, to send out the
first settlers to the Ohio country.[1]

This party traveled overland from Ipswich, Massachusetts, to the Youghiogheny River, at present West
Newton, Pa., where it was joined by a second party
which had come overland from Hartford. This second
party had been four weeks in making the journey, which
now could be made in less than four days. At this point,
a "fleet" was constructed which consisted of a "large"
boat, the Mayflower, forty-five feet long and twelve feet
wide with sides thick enough to prevent the Indian
bullets from passing through it, a flatboat and several
canoes. This fleet sailed down the Ohio and reached the
mouth of the Muskingum, April 7, 1788. The wonderful fertility of the West had been widely advertised
throughout the East and in many parts of Europe. The
most extravagant reports of the resources of the region
were current, such as : that grapes from which wine,
superior to European brands could be made, were abundant ; that cotton, a much desired European product
could be produced; that mulberry trees were plentiful;
that there was but little poor land and although there
were hills, yet they were not high and were covered with
a deep rich soil, which was suitable for the growing of
wheat, rye, indigo and tobacco.

This particular location at the mouth of the Muskingum, first called Adelphia but later changed to Marietta,
has been much criticised. Even granting that the first
settlers had an exaggerated idea of the region in general,
it would seem evident that the upper fertile valley would
have been preferable for a settlement to the hilly region
around Marietta. However, there were good reasons

---

[1] Henry Howe, *Historical Collections of Ohio*, vol. ii, pp. 777 *et seq.*

for selecting the location besides that of fertility of the soil. Among these may be mentioned: first, the Marietta settlers would have the protection of Fort Harmar, a government military post just across the Ohio River; second, no Indian tribe had a fixed habitation here and although exposed to the periodic Indian raids, yet the danger was much less than if the settlement had been made in the distinctive Indian territory; third, it was near to the already settled region in Virginia from whose considerable population the Marietta settlers could expect assistance; fourth, the Marietta settlers believed that the commercial route between Lake Erie and the Ohio River would be by way of Cuyahoga and Muskingum Rivers and that they were thus securing a favorable location to secure the profits of this trade. In passing, it may be remarked that, in this particular, they were in great part correct, for this was for many years the chief route of traffic between these two water-ways. When the state water-ways were made available for commercial purposes by the construction of the Ohio canals and the improvement of the inland rivers, and particularly by the improvement of the Muskingum River by the national government, this route was a very important commercial way. However, the commerce for many years after the settlement of the state did not reach the proportion anticipated by the Marietta settlers, for the Lake commerce was of little importance until after 1825.

The settlers of Marietta began immediately to provide themselves with the necessities of life, and, in the first year, one hundred and thirty-five acres of corn were planted. Although nature was kind, the first settlers soon began to realize the absence of many conveniences to which they had been accustomed in the East. There were no roads nor bridges for land travel and consequently they used the waterways as much as possible, and especially the Ohio River which by its eastern extension brought them some of the products of the East and also afforded them an easy means of communication with the other settlements to the south and those which were later established at lower points on the Ohio River. If we view the state as a whole and describe in a general way the sources of immigration, the following characterization is sufficiently accurate for our purpose. Between the Great and the Little Miami rivers, the Symnes Purchase, the people of New Jersey predominated; between the Little Miami and the Scioto rivers, the Virginia Military District, the people of Virginia predominated; in the Marietta region, the Ohio Company's purchase, the people of Connecticut, Massachusetts, and of other New England States predominated; in the Connecticut Reserve, many from Connecticut settled, but, in the upper part of the Seven Ranges, the people of Pennsylvania predominated. The village of Columbia, now a part of Cincinnati, was laid out in 1788, and, soon afterwards, a settlement was made at (present) Cincinnati, on land purchased from John Cleves Symnes, who, having formed a company, had purchased a large tract of land from Congress. The first settlers of Columbia came from Limestone, Kentucky, and were given lots on condition that they raise two successive crops and build a house within two years.

When Ebenezer Zane opened up a road in 1797—Zane's Trace from Wheeling to Limestone, many points in the region between these two places were soon settled, since the road supplied a means of reaching the region not only to the people of the East but also to those of the West. Kentucky at this time had a considerable population. Several points along the Ohio had by this time been settled for almost a decade.[1] Many prospectors came to the backwoods country, for its resources had been well advertised throughout the East and a great part of Europe. The tide of imigration set in from both the East and the South but particularly from the East. The richness and fertility of the Ohio country had been well advertised in France by the enterprising agents of the Scioto Company, and a party of Frenchmen were induced to buy a tract of land. These French settlers left Havre for Alexandria, Virginia, but, when they reached this point, they were informed that the Scioto Company had forfeited its title to the land through a failure to make the required payment. Some of the party returned to France, some went to other settlements, but the majority of them remained at Alexandria until the Scioto Company was compelled by the intervention of the national government to aid them in reaching Ohio. Wagons were obtained and the party started out on its long, rough journey. They passed through the valley of Virginia to Washington, thence in a north-westerly direction to Brownsville, where they took boat for Gallipolis, the point of settlement selected by the advance party that was sent out under Major Burnham. Gallipolis was soon one of the most flourishing settlements. In an account of a journey to this settlement, by Monsieur Montelle, we find the following:[2]

I descended the river in a flatboat in 1791, which was loaded with troops commanded by General St. Clair. To migrate from the eastern states to the far west is painful

[1] Weekly mail was established from Wheeling to Limestone, Kentucky, in 1799.

[2] *Report of the Ohio Archaeological Historical Society*, vol. iii, "The French Settlement and Settlers at Gallipolis."

enough nowadays, but how much more so must it have been for citizens of a large European town. Even the farmers of the old countries would find it very hard if not impossible to clear land in the wilderness.

In the spring of 1802, Rev. James Kilbourne left New Boston, Connecticut, for the purpose of exploring the Ohio country. He traveled by stage to Shippensburg, Pennsylvania, at the foot of the Alleghanies, where the stage route ended. After reaching Pittsburgh, he continued his journey on foot over what was then the principal road in the state—Zane's Trace.[1] At this time, the chief settlements in the state were Marietta, Cincinnati, Chillicothe, Dayton, Steubenville, Zanesville, Lancaster, Hamilton, Cleveland, Conneaut, Warren and Gallipolis. Kilbourne visited many of these during the summer and later formed a company, which purchased a tract of 16,-000 acres on the east branch of the Olentangy River. In the spring of 1803 a settlement was made on this tract, which was the beginning of that numerous population now found around the capital of the state. The settlements were gradually extended up the Miami River from Cincinnati and other nearby settled regions. The Kentuckians and the Virginians crossed the Ohio and pushed up the Scioto, some by boat but more by land. Others came into this valley from the southeast, until the region from present Columbus to Portsmouth was soon settled.

Greater difficulties are presented in explaining the settlements of the eastern and northeastern sections of the state, for here the settlements were less regularly and less systematically made. In eastern Ohio a number of settlers drifted over from Pennsylvania, and it is esti-

---

[1] *Cf. American Pioneer*, 1843.

mated that there were, as early as 1788, more settlers in eastern Ohio than around Marietta. In the beginning some of these early settlers were driven out by the Indians and some were forced out by the national government for occupying this public land without purchasing it.[1] In 1785 Ensign Armstrong was sent out by Colonel Harmar with a detachment of troops into eastern Ohio to drive out the settlers who occupied the country from the mouth of the Muskingum to Pittsburgh. In 1785 Congress had published and circulated a proclamation in the territory against the "disorderly persons who have crossed the Ohio and settled upon the unappropriated lands." The proclamation further warned them to depart immediately with their families and effects. These squatters had settled chiefly in the counties of Columbiana, Jefferson, Belmont, Guernsey and Monroe. Congress early provided for the survey and sale of certain lands in the Northwest Territory and, although some of the squatters purchased land, many others did not, and the military expedition tore down the buildings of many of them in the efforts to force the squatters to leave. For various reasons many large grants of land were made in this section, as well as in other sections of the state, to soldiers of the Revolutionary War or to others. Not infrequently a tract was donated to a surveyor on condition that he would make certain other surveys, and in such cases it was but natural for the surveyor to lay out for himself large areas of land. The abundance of the land and this practice of the surveyors justified these eastern squatters, as they thought, in occupying the land, and they became very bitter when their rights were questioned by the government.

[1] W. H. Hunter, *Reports of Ohio Archaeological and Historical Society*, vol. vi, "The Pathfinders of Jefferson County."

Many of the settlers in eastern Ohio came from Pennsylvania and reached the region in a variety of ways. The pack-horse method was a very common one. Upon the horses were fastened crates in which were placed the bedding, clothes and cooking utensils, the chief and, in many cases, the only possessions of the settlers. Many of the earlier settlers in eastern Ohio were the Scotch-Irish, a people who played no little part in the development and settlement not only of this part of the state but also of the West in general. These people drifted into the territory quite early, and, although their settlements were somewhat irregular, they were perhaps justified in disputing with the settlers of Marietta the credit of making the first settlement of Ohio. It is true that the latter was an organized and unified movement, while the former was unsystematic and separate, yet the immediate territory settled by these Scotch-Irish soon had more people than the region around Marietta.

There were, in general, three main entrances into Ohio; one from Pittsburgh down the Ohio, one from Virginia down the Ohio, and one from Kentucky, Tennessee, the Carolinas and the South across the Ohio, when either the overland route was continued or the inland state rivers were used. From these last named states many of the Scotch-Irish had come. They had gone there from New York and Pennsylvania. Gist, in his travels in 1750, found a number of these people in the Ohio territory engaged as fur-traders, some of whom had come from Pennsylvania and others from Virginia and the Carolinas. In 1785 we find the settlers at Martins Ferry informally selecting Justices of the Peace, although the settlers were squatters, in that none of the land had been surveyed and consequently no legitimate title to it was held. In fact, a surprising amount of indifference in regard to the welfare of the settlers of the west prevailed on the part of many in the east. Some of it was studied indifference arising from political considerations, for there was a fear on the part of some in the east, that the west would be so thickly settled from the population of the east, that in time the west would become a political rival and possibly dominate the public affairs of the country. There were some who were not unwilling that the Ohio river should be the boundary line, and even such men as Dr. Franklin viewed with something at times approaching indifference, if not hostility, the settlement of the west. But the defeat of the Indians by General Wayne, at Fallen Timbers, in 1794, changed this sentiment, for the victory not only broke the Indian power, but also destroyed the last hope of the British of regaining the territory. Although that portion of the state extending from Pennsylvania along Lake Erie to Cleveland was settled largely by people from Connecticut and Massachusetts, the first settlers were not the zealous church and school-loving Puritans, for this class did not come till later. They were the soldier class, an adventurous element with the characteristics of pioneers, and, like the vanguard of all wilderness-conquering armies, they had little refinement and culture and for this very reason they were probably better adapted to perform well the work before them. Again, the initial material problems were so difficult and pressing that little time was left to think of religious and educational matters.

In the present counties of Tuscarawas, Stark, Wayne and Guernsey, many of the Germans from Pennsylvania settled. The Welsh from the same states came into the Mahoning Valley. In the counties of Belmont and Harrison there was, by 1790, a considerable settlement of

Quakers from North Carolina. These people like many others came through the wilderness on foot and on horseback from North Carolina to which place many had gone from the northern states. They were opposed to slavery in theory and in practice, and the Ohio country, which was free territory by the terms of its organization, offered them a place for settlement. As a result of the wide and aggressive campaign of advertisement which was carried out by various Ohio land companies, population from the New England states began to flow into the territory, until, in 1791, owing to the severe losses from the Indian depredations, it largely ceased. Although the population of the Northwest Territory in 1800 was probably less than five thousand, yet in 1810 Ohio alone had twenty-three thousand and seventy-six inhabitants. The national government, in 1800, began to sell land in Ohio on credit and this, supplemented by the hard times in the East, caused another wave of immigration to start, which, by 1803, furnished Ohio with enough people to entitle it to be admitted as a state. A period of quiescence then began to prevail, for the European wars had caused great prosperity in the East. This, however, was interrupted by the Embargo Act of 1807, which caused another period of depression in the East and again started a movement of the population to the West. The war of 1812 checked the movement to some extent, but, by 1815, it again set in with renewed vigor until it seemed as if the East was to be depopulated. The roads to the West contained numerous travelers, bound for Ohio as the first objective point, with Indiana, Illinois and Michigan as the secondary points of settlement. The unfavorable weather in 1816 and 1817 caused a failure of the crops in the East, which tended to accelerate this movement, for the fertile lands of Ohio furnished the discouraged people of the East a welcome relief.

Goodrich in his *Peter Parley's Recollections of a Life Time* gives a description in the following words of the rush to this supposed Canaan: [1]

I remember very well the tide of emigration to the west during the summer of 1817. Some persons went in covered wagons, some on foot and some crowded together under the cover of the wagon with kettles, gridirons, feather beds, crockery, the Family Bible, Watt's Psalms and Hymns, and Webster's Spelling Book. Others started in ox-carts and trudged on at the rate of ten miles per day. In several instances, I saw families on foot—the father and boys taking turns in dragging along an improvised hand wagon loaded with the wreck of the household goods, and occasionally giving the mother and baby a ride. Many of these people were in a state of poverty and begged their way as they went. Even when they arrived at their new homes, along the banks of the Scioto or Muskingum, frequently the whole family, father, mother and children speedily exchanged the fresh complexion and elastic steps of their first abodes for the sunken cheek and languid movement which marked the victim of intermittent fever.

A traveler coming down the Ohio in 1817 speaks of the great numbers of boats, arks and rafts, all bound for the great West, which at this time to a large degree meant Ohio, although in a few years this term included Indiana, Illinois and Michigan. Many of the emigrants, in fact the greater part of them, had no definite location selected. They were simply "going out west." Some because they had failed in the East, some because they had friends or relatives in the West, and some simply through a love of change and a desire for adventure, thus exemplifying that restless character of the Anglo-

[1] Samuel Griswold Goodrich, *Recollections of a Life Time*, p. 67 (1856).

Saxon, which has sent him all over the world and carried his civilization into all climes.

Immigration from Europe in this period was also very large and of a very desirable character. It is estimated that, in 1819 alone, there were fifty to sixty thousand immigrants from Europe. The greater part of them came from England, Ireland, France and Germany.[1] These industrious classes settled throughout the West and much of its industrial, commercial and educational greatness is due to them. When the population of the West was being so rapidly augmented by the great numbers from the East, the newspapers of the latter section were very active in procuring and publishing pessimistic statements in regard to the western country, in order that they might deter the eastern people from emigrating to the West. It was stated, that wheat in the West sold for only 33 cents per bushel, whereas in New England it sold for $1.23 per bushel! That land was much higher in price than in the East; that the people were rude, rough and wicked, and that murders occurred daily; that the wages were low and the cost of living was high.[2] But all this did not remove the economic causes of the westward movement. A resident of Haverhill, N. H., stated that, in one day, sixteen wagons passed his residence bound for Indiana, and that within thirteen days, seventy-three wagons had passed through Haverhill bound for the West.[3] In the Ohio legislature of 1831 there was not a single senator or representative who had been born in the state, although the region had been settled for more than thirty-three years. By 1820 the population of the state had reached nearly a half million and by 1850 it amounted

[1] *Niles Register*, September 12, 1819.
[2] *Liberty Hall and Cincinnati Gazette*, Nov. 10, 1817.
[3] *Ibid.*, Dec. 19, 1817.

to almost two millions.   Indiana had, in 1800, only 5,641 people and did not increase so rapidly in population as did Ohio, which was largely the objective point for the advancing army of settlers who were soon again on the move, and Indiana more than doubled her population between 1820 and 1830.

Illinois, which was organized from Indiana, had in 1810 a population of 12,282, and in 1820, 55,211, which indicates that the advance into this state was more rapid than into Indiana.   This was due partly to the greater pressure on the population in the rear, partly to the Mississippi River on the west and the Great Lakes on the north and partly to the character of the soil. Michigan, which was made a territory in 1805, had a very sparse population in 1810 and 1820.   This was due to the character of the soil, the climate and the possibility of an immediate industrial life.   There was at that time no de- mand for such mineral wealth as Michigan had, for trans- portation means were absent and, so far as agricultural products were concerned, other states could produce these more economically than could Michigan.   After 1830 Michigan began to increase rapidly in population, so that by 1840 this state had 212,267 people.   This was due partly to the beginning of the Lake commerce, and partly to the industrial development in the adjoining states.   Wisconsin was formed from Michigan and in- creased at first more slowly than any of the other states of the Northwest Territory.   In 1840, this state had only 30,945 people.   In 1830 there was another wave of for- eign immigration which came chiefly from Ireland, Ger- many and northern Europe.   These foreigners settled in the west and northwest, especially in Wisconsin and along the Mississippi around St. Louis.[1]

[1] *Cf.* chapter xiv, for the later movements of Ohio population to the West.

By the Louisiana Purchase of 1803 there was opened for settlement a tract of over one million square miles, and the region up to the Mississippi River and fifty miles beyond it was rapidly settled. The settlement of these regions had a direct bearing upon the development of the transportation system of Ohio, in that it made necessary the construction of means of communication to this region, not only from Ohio, but also from the East. For reasons already noted these routes must pass through Ohio. In this connection, it must also be pointed out that the purchase of the Louisiana Territory gave to the United States the control of the mouth of the Mississippi, as well as of the river itself, a fact which was from a commercial viewpoint of immense importance. Disputes over the commerce of the mouth of the river had greatly retarded the development of the territory along the Ohio and the Mississippi and, now that the latter was secure in the possession of the United States, opportunity was given for the industrial development of the regions.

Not only did this great commercial waterway extend through the wide central valley of the country to the ocean on the south, but it also had a good market at its terminus and a large tributary which extended far to the east through a well-settled region. Down the streams of the state the people of Ohio, Indiana, Illinois and Kentucky sent the farm, forest and mill products into the Ohio, and thence by way of the Mississippi to New Orleans, or, in some cases, up the Ohio to Pittsburgh and thence overland to the East. Up the Mississippi and the Ohio Rivers from New Orleans or down the Ohio River from Pittsburgh came those numerous manufactured articles and luxuries which had been sent either overland to Pittsburgh or by ocean to New Orleans. The presence of these two rivers was a fact of great industrial and commercial consequence before the era of highways and railways. In the northern part of the Northwest Territory the population did not increase so rapidly and largely because there were no Mississippi and Ohio Rivers to connect them with the East and to supply them with a market. The northern region must wait for its commercial greatness, until the steamboat was invented, until the Erie canal was constructed and until the population and industrial possibilities would warrant the people in interesting themselves in the problem of lake navigation.

It is not strange, then, that, as the region became densely populated a widespread agitation for the development of transportation routes began. However well the Ohio River answered the early needs in this particular, it must be remembered that it was on the extreme south and that it very imperfectly served the commercial needs of a numerous population which extended over a region three hundred miles to the north. More extensive tranportation means were needed, not only to reach the eastern markets, but also to secure an advantageous exchange of products between the various regions of the states, in some sections of which the beginnings of manufacturing had been made. Not only the economic reasons urged a development of routes of travel, but the social ones as well, for when the initial difficulties of pioneer life had been conquered, the settlers longed for the social institutions and intercourse which they had had in the East.

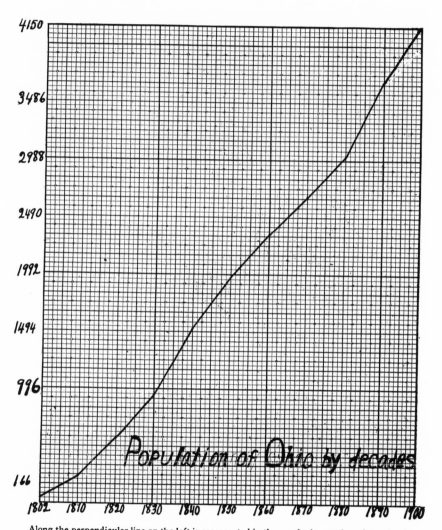

Population of Ohio by decades

Along the perpendicular line on the left is represented in thousands the number of population.

CHAPTER III

Early Roads in the West, 1788–1810.

In Ohio as in nearly all other regions the development of the means of transportation succeeded the settlement of the country instead of preceding it. There have been but few instances where the construction of transportation facilities preceded the settlement of a region, and these instances have been more apparent than real. Our great West with its transcontinental lines would seem to be a case in point, but it must be remembered that these lines were not built primarily for the purpose of opening up the West, but rather to afford means of communication between the settled regions along the Pacific coast and those of the East. In fact during the first century of our national history, the political reasons were responsible to a very important degree for whatever aid that was extended directly or indirectly in supplying means of transportation. So vast is the country, so diverse are its national resources and industrial life, that nothing short of an extensive system of transportation routes would secure that unity of interests which is necessary to make the many states one. Whatever the cost, and however great the waste in securing this system have been, the results have justified the expenditure.

In the development of the road system of Ohio, the pack-horse stage was succeeded by that of the cart and its improved form—the wagon— although the substitution of one method for another took place slowly. The transportation of goods by wagons from Philadelphia and Baltimore to Pittsburgh had become common by 1800, so that when Ohio was settled the eastern end of the route to the settled regions was already in use. One of the first methods of improving the roads was by corduroying. While this improved the condition for a time along most of the way, it had the disadvantage of contracting the route. Before and even after this improvement deep ruts were formed, which each succeeding wagon made deeper. Thus we read:

> Heavy rains would fill each rut with water and the next wagoner would push his horses into this slough, perhaps exploring it with a pole to see if a bottom was to be found. Often the driver would fill up such places with logs and brush and not infrequently he would drive into one of these ruts and be compelled to unload his wagon in order to get out. [1]

Transportation over such roads was expensive in every sense of the word—in time, labor and traction power. Since that period such miracles of transportation have been wrought, that the improvement of these old roads seems to the present generation to have been very slow and unimportant. Yet the change from a bridle path to a wagon road was fraught with enormous consequences from an economic, social and political point of view. In 1794, during the Whiskey Rebellion, the cost of shipping goods from Philadelphia to Pittsburgh by wagon ranged from $5.00 to $10.00 per 100 lb. Salt sold in Pittsburgh for $5.00 per bushel and iron and steel from 15 to 20 cents per lb. What must have been the price of these articles to the inland consumers when it is remembered that one horse carried only from 150 to 250 pounds!

[1] Archer Butler Hulbert, *Historic Highways*, vol. i, p. 52.

The freight wagon represented the growing needs of
the increasing population of the West, and the advent of
it and its companion—the stage-coach—introduced an
era, as much in advance over the old, as the later railroad was an advance over the stage coach and freight
wagon. However, just as the stage-coach men in latter
times resented the introduction of the railroad, so now
the pack-horse men opposed the introduction of the
wagon and the stage-coach. These wagon-men gradually
encroached upon the field of the bridle-men and in time
replaced them for the extensive carriage of goods. In
the process of replacement the bridle-men adjusted themselves to the new conditions of transportation by establishing routes to converging points to which they carried
the products from regions as yet inaccessible to the
wagons. At these points they would exchange their
products for those of the wagon-man and then carry in
small lots the goods from the East to the interior regions.
The wagons and coaches were overturned and the passengers ill-treated by the packhorse men. The horses
were abused and their drivers beaten. When the Cumberland Road was being constructed, the early coaches
were in danger of attack by the workmen engaged in
building the road, for many of them were in sympathy
with the pack-horse men whose employment was being
destroyed. The pack-horse men argued that the mail
could not be so rapidly carried in coaches; that the introduction of the stage-coach would throw hundreds out
of employment; that the American horse was not strong
enough to draw the heavy coach and wagon loads. Most
of the horses then used were small, but were able to
carry a few pounds a great distance over the rough and
rugged roads. When the heavier breeds from the East
and from Europe were imported to draw the heavy

wagons and coaches, the owners of these western horses did lose in the process of change.

While the introduction of the freight wagon and stage-coach was a powerful argument for the construction of more and better roads, yet as a matter of fact there were, with the exception of the Cumberland Road, no improved roads in Ohio until many years later. Some of the roads were widened and graded, yet they remained dirt roads for many years after this was done. Harriet Martineau, in writing of the American roads of this time, said:[1]

There is a variety of roads in America. There are the excellent limestone roads of Tennessee and Kentucky. There are the rich mud roads of Ohio through whose sloughs the stage-coaches go slowing sousing after rains, and gently up-setting when the rut on one or the other side proves to be of greater depth than was anticipated. There are the corduroy roads, happily of rare occurrence, where if the driver is merci-ful to his passengers he drives them so as to give them the association of being on the way to a funeral, their involuntary sobs on each jolt helping the resemblance, or if he be in a hurry he shakes them like pills in a box.

Weld in his *Travels* reports that the drivers had fre-quently to call to the passengers in the stage to lean out of the coach, first on one side, then on the other, to pre-vent it from overturning in the deep ruts with which the road abounded.[2]

Charles Dickens in his *American Notes* gives a char-acteristic description of Ohio roads and condemns in strong terms the character of the coach drivers as well

[1] Harriet Martineau, *Travels in America*, pp. 89 *et seq.*
[2] *Cf.* Isaac Weld, *Travels through North America and Upper and Lower Canada*, 1800.

as the roads.[1] In passing through the state from Cincinnati to Toledo, Mr. Dickens hired a special coach at Columbus. He says:

To insure us having horses at the proper stations and being incommoded by no strangers, the proprietor sent an agent on the box, who was to accompany us all the way through. Thus attended we started off at 6 a. m. very much delighted to be by ourselves and disposed to enjoy even the roughest of journeys. It was well for us that we were in this humor, for the road we went over that day was certainly enough to have shaken tempers that were not resolutely set at Fair down to some inches below Stormy. At one time we were all flying together in a heap at the bottom of the coach and at another we were crushing our heads against the roof. Now the coach was lying on the tails of the two wheelers, and now it was rearing up in the air in a frantic state, with all four horses standing on the top of an insurmountable eminence looking back at it, as though the would say, "Unharness us, it can't be done." The drivers of these roads, who certainly get over the ground in a manner which is quite miraculous, so twist and turn the team about in forcing a passage corkscrew fashion through the bogs and swamps that it was quite a common circumstance in looking out of the window to see the coachman with the ends of a pair of reins in his hands, apparently driving nothing, or playing at horse. Never, never once that day was the coach in any position, attitude or kind of motion to which we are accustomed in coaches. Never did it make the smallest approach to one's experience of the proceedings of any sort of vehicle that goes on wheels.

As night came on the track grew narrower until at last it so lost itself among the trees that the driver seemed to find his way by instinct. We had the comfort of knowing, at least, that there was no danger of falling asleep, for every now and

[1] Charles Dickens, *American Notes for General Circulation*, pp. 167–171, 1855.

then the wheel would strike against an unseen stump with such a jerk that he was fain to hold on pretty tight and pretty quick to keep himself upon the box.

Nor was there any reason to dread the danger from furious driving inasmuch as over that broken ground the horses had enough to do to walk and as to shying there was no room for that. The trees were so close together that their dry branches rattled against the coach on either side and obliged us all to keep our hands within.

These descriptions, although overdrawn in some particulars, give an idea of the difficulty of transporting goods and passengers over the early roads. On account of the danger and difficulty of descending, and the impossibility of ascending the Ohio River for extensive commercial transactions, this stream very imperfectly answered the demands of the time for commercial and emigrant purposes. The demand for better all-land routes was made early, and in response Zane's Trace and the Cumberland Road were laid out. Provisions were also made for the system of state roads from the three per cent fund, which will be discussed later. Until the close of the eighteenth century, the general route for mail and passengers from Cincinnati and other settled places above and below this point on the Ohio was over Boone's Wilderness Road through Cumberland Gap to the various eastern settlements. After Pennsylvania had become more densely populated and scattered settlements had been made in Ohio, the demands for roads through the Ohio country grew more pressing. The first post-road in Ohio was Zane's Trace. This was provided by an act of Congress, May 17, 1798. It ran from Pittsburgh to Limestone. Ebenezer Zane was granted three tracts of land, each not to exceed one mile square at points where the road crossed the Muskingum, Hocking and

Scioto rivers. At these points he was to establish ferries and to give surety that they would be maintained.
The road as opened was scarcely more than a blazed
trail for horsemen, and in many cases Indian trails were
doubtless used. However, this became an important
route in time and was later known as the Maysville
Road. The Court of General Quarter Sessions at its
meeting in Adamsville, Adams County, December 12,
1797, adopted a schedule of legal ferriage across the
Scioto and Ohio rivers. For the Scioto River the
charge for a man and horse was 12½ cents; for a wagon
and team, 75 cents; for horned cattle, 6¼ cents each.
Upon the opening of the road the government established a regular mail route from Wheeling to Lexington.
A road was already in use from Maysville to Lexington.
It was in connection with this road that the question of
internal improvement received a serious temporary defeat by President Jackson's well-known veto.

The enabling act for the admission of Ohio, in 1802,
provided that one-twentieth of the net proceeds from
the sale of lands lying within the state and sold by Congress should be devoted to the laying-out and building
of public roads from the navigable streams emptying
into the Atlantic to Ohio. In 1803 a supplementary act
was passed which appropriated three of this five per cent
for state roads. A committee was appointed by the
President to lay out this Cumberland Road, as it began
to be called, and after much deliberation a route was
selected in accordance with the following principles: (a)
shortness of the route; (b) that point near the end of
the route which would most nearly equalize the advantages of the portages within reach of the road; (c) that
point on the Ohio most certain of accomodating river
navigation with the road accomodation; (d) and lastly,

that route which would best diffuse benefit with the
least distance of the road. The application of these
principles in selecting a route was no easy matter, for
competition among towns and communities was very
strong. It was recognized that the road would place
the towns along it in a position to share in the profits of
the trade between the East and the West. Wheeling was
selected as the point on the Ohio because, as the commissioners said, " the obstructions in the Ohio within
the limits between Steubenville and Grave-creek lay prin-
cipally above the town and the mouth of the Wheeling
(creek)." This point was the favorite one for embarkment and departure in the dry seasons. Wheeling, it
may be stated, had the powerful influence of Henry Clay,
who made it his concern to see that the merits of Wheeling were properly placed before the commission. The
road was begun in 1811 and in 1818 mail coaches were
running between Washington and Wheeling. As soon
as the road was completed, immigrants and traffic began
to move over it, and it soon needed repairs, for in some
places only one layer of crushed stone had been used.

In 1822 a bill passed Congress providing for the repair
of the road and the establishment of toll gates, but
President Monroe vetoed this bill. However, a bill
passed in 1824 which appropriated money to repair the
road in a very thorough manner. The Ohio River had
become by this time a commercial route of great importance, and the road in its inception and later extension
was intended to be supplementary to this water route.
The numerous population of the Ohio valley was in a
position to supply the East with vast amounts of raw
products in exchange for the manufactured goods, but
up to this time this mutually beneficial exchange was
limited by the inadequate transportation facilities offered

by the Ohio River.   An overland route was needed from
the East to the West to carry to different points in the
interior regions of the state the eastern products, which
could be exchanged for the abundant raw products of
these sections.   The Ohio River served fairly well as a
commercial route for such large points as Pittsburgh,
Cincinnati, Louisville and New Orleans, but these points
could not be used as distributing centers for large areas,
because there were no roads from them to the interior
points.   It was largely due to the fact that the Ohio
River was on the south of the region that the Cumberland Road ran along a parallel line far to the north,
where it could reach a region scarcely served by the
river.   Another reason for the northern location was the
fact that Zane's road ran farther to the south.

When the question of the constitutionality of the road
was raised, the people of the West doubted that the
road would ever be extended from Wheeling.   This
was however provided by the act of 1825.   This act
was in keeping with the prevailing sentiment for internal improvements, and was especially due to the fact that
the Erie Canal had been completed in 1825.   It was a
transportation route which promised to transfer much of
the trade of the West from Philadelphia and Baltimore to
New York.   The representatives of Pennsylvania and
Maryland were instrumental in securing the extension of
the Cumberland Road, for by it Philadelphia and Baltimore would be able to retain a part of the trade of the
West.   Before the completion of the Erie Canal, the
people of the lake section of the state were largely without market facilities.   Hauling overland to Pittsburgh
was always expensive and oftentimes prohibitive.   The
road was completed to Columbus in 1833 and was later
extended to Vandalia, Illinois.   However, just as the

Cumberland Road was of less importance to Indiana and
Illinois than to Ohio, so it was less necessary to Ohio
than to Pennsylvania, for by the time it was extended
through Ohio or even to Columbus, many state roads
had been built, water transportation on the Ohio and
state rivers had been improved, canals had been constructed, and railroads had been begun.   One must not
infer that this road was not widely used, nor that it was
not a great commercial highway, but, if the national
government had not extended it westward, the state
would hardly have done so.   In any case, it would have
been only one of the many commercial highways of the
states through which it passed.   The glory of the National Road was gained before 1830, for in the latter
stages of its construction, ideas of transportation had so
changed that wagon roads were not so popular.

The railroad promised an easy solution of the transportation problem since, according to popular view, the
railroads with but little cost for repairs would last inde-
finitely, after they were once constructed.   The railroad
was to be a permanent road-bed upon which every individual would be free to haul his products by paying a
fixed charge per mile for the use of the way.   In 1832
the Committee on Roads and Canals of the House of
Representatives discussed the feasibility of various means
of transportation and in 1836 seriously considered the
question of converting the Cumberland Road into a railroad.   Later in the same year a House bill was passed,
which provided that the appropriations which were made
to assist Illinois in building the Cumberland Road should
be expended in grading and building bridges and not in
macadamizing.   This bill was so amended by the Senate,
as to provide that a railroad should be constructed west
from Columbus with all the money appropriated for the

road. A committee was appointed to investigate the comparative cost of a railroad and a highway from Columbus to the West and in its report favored the railroad, "if time of transportation, expense of repairs and political and military advantages were considered." However, the amended bill failed and an appropriation of $600,000 was made for the road. As fast as the road was completed it was turned over to the states, for President Monroe's veto indicated the unconstitutionality of any act which provided for the repair of the road by the Federal Government. Repairs must be made, so the road was transferred to the states which established toll gates with tolls varying, in 1837, from 3 cents for a led horse to 25 cents for a coach. Collection of tolls was secured by providing that the salary of the keepers of the toll-gates should be a percentage of total collections and quite naturally many abuses resulted, since the keepers had every reason to make the receipts as large as possible. The tolls in Ohio from the Cumberland Road were for some time large and averaged in the best years about $20,000. Much of the traffic moving over the road was local, and this was especially true of that moving west. The Ohio River at Wheeling offered for the through traffic a choice of routes. The river was frequently used both on account of the low cost of transportation on it and because on the overland route there were no large points to serve as distributing centers.

It is quite true that considerable through traffic moved over the road, including livestock from the interior of the state, and some of the eastern products, which came in large amounts to the few larger centers of the interior region. Up to 1850 when Ohio began to lease out portions of the national road, the state had received in tolls nearly $1,250,000. Under the plan of lease the state officials inspected the road to see that it was kept in good condition, but in 1859 the state was compelled to take over the roads, as the leases had proven very unprofitable to the holders. In 1876 the state authorized the commissioners of the several counties through which the road passed to take over and keep in repair such parts as were situated in their respective counties. Later, by consent of Congress and the people of the county, the road was made a free turnpike. The road was never a direct financial success, but the value of such works should not be judged by financial returns alone. It added enormously to the wealth of the nation and did much to make the East and the West one, just as later the transcontinental railway lines made the Pacific states a part of the United States in fact as well as in name.

In June, 1807, we find the following post roads in Ohio.[1] (1) From Chillicothe to Franklinton, thence to Washington; mail once in two weeks. (2) From Chillicothe *via* Brown's Cross-Roads, Williamsburg, Columbia to Cincinnati; mail once a week. (3) From Cincinnati *via* Hamilton, Franklin, Dayton, Stanton, Springfield, Xenia, Lebanon, to Cincinnati; mail once a week. (4) From Chillicothe *via* Wheeling to Alexandria; mail once a week. (5) From Cincinnati *via* Hamilton, Lawrenceburg, Boone C. H., to Frankfort; mail once a week.

In addition to these mail routes there were also the post roads from Wheeling to Limestone, from Marietta, Gallipolis and other points in southeastern Ohio to the East. From the political center, Chillicothe, and the industrial center, Cincinnati, the leading roads diverged. On account of the bad condition of the roads, much

[1] *Liberty Hall and Cincinnati Gazette*, June 2, 1807.

complaint was heard about the receipt of the mails.
Postmasters were frequently accused of holding the mail.
Post riders in crossing swollen streams would sometimes
lose the mail sacks and, at other times, forget some of
them, especially if the mails were heavy. However, when
the mail coach arrived many of the objections ceased, for
now greater amounts could be carried with greater certainty. These passenger and mail-coach routes were
operated in much the same way as the railroads of our
present day, in that competition and consolidation were
prominent elements. Large companies which owned
many miles of line were formed and the rivalry among
these operating companies was often very intense. Each
sought to shorten the time of the journey, to reduce the
fare, to secure better coaches, better horses, and better
drivers. The larger companies bought up the smaller
ones, and extended their lines. Although no such re-
finements as community of interests, gentlemen's agreement and present-day makeshifts of ownership were devised, yet the embryo of all these present-day plans was
found.

The first passenger coaches were long and awkwardly
constructed vehicles with the seats running cross-
wise. The chief source of revenue, however, came
from the transportation of freight. This was done in
huge wagons, called freighters, which carried the products of the eastern mills and factories to the West and
received in return agricultural products. Time tables
and tariff schedules, such as our railroads to-day have,
were published and posted, although there were no commissions to enforce adherence to published schedules, or
prevent rebates or discriminations. There were, however, many laws passed applying to the operation of the
stage coaches. For example, an act of the legislature re-

quired lamps to be placed on all coaches used at night, and subjected the driver to a fine for not providing or not lighting them.[1]   Another act required the discharge of drivers who had been intoxicated while on duty, and still another imposed a fine on any driver who left his horses unfastened while they were hitched to a coach. Passengers purchased their tickets, including all toll charges from the stage company.   A way-bill was made out and given to the driver.   This way-bill was submitted to each tavern keeper on the route, who signified, on the blank space provided, the time of arrival and of departure, just as is done at present by the local telegraph operators of railway companies.

[1] *Laws of Ohio*, First Session, Seventh General Assembly, 1809.

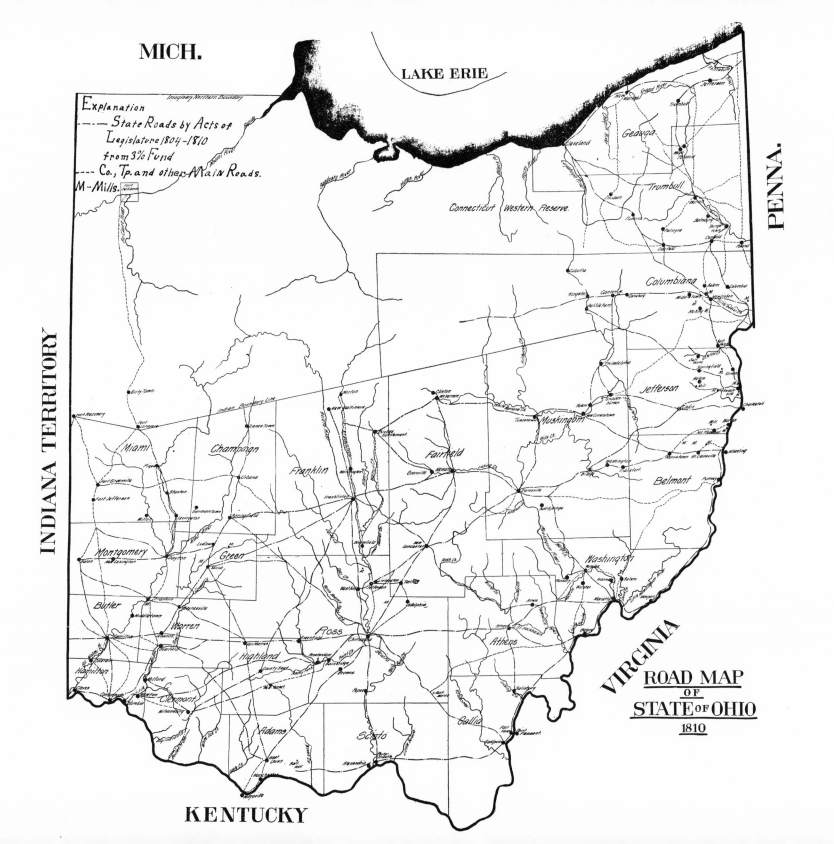

ROAD MAP
OF
STATE OF OHIO
1810

CHAPTER IV

EARLY WATER TRANSPORTATION IN THE WEST

WATERWAYS have exerted an important influence in civilizing the world, for they are highways of nature which afford an easy means of access into new regions. Other things being equal, the rapidity with which a new country becomes settled is directly proportional to its supply of navigable waterways. The fact that the Ohio, a large and navigable stream flowed westward was of vast importance in the westward spread of population in this country. Whatever dispute there may be regarding the proportion of early settlers who came to Ohio by way of water, there can be no question that this stream was the route which was most used in the general advance of population from the regions east of the Alleghanies into the territory between these mountains and the Mississippi River. The difficulties which are encountered in traveling to a new region either by land or by water are great, but the bars, snags and other impediments in the Ohio River were greater obstacles to travel than the obstructions and dangers of the overland routes. The Indian trails were nothing more than paths and many of these were so overgrown with brush that men and horses moved over them with difficulty. The military roads had deteriorated through disuse and neglect, so that scarcely a vestige of them remained. These trails were, however, soon widened and the military roads were soon restored by the emigrants who were not compelled on the land route to make the extra outlay for means of transportation, which was necessary on the water route. These well-known land routes led directly into the interior regions of the state, and the danger from Indians was not much greater than on the Ohio River. Until 1800 these land routes were therefore of greater importance than the water routes for purposes of settlement. Even after the difficulties and dangers of navigating the Ohio River were known, the land routes were more frequently used by the immigrants into Ohio. Many of these immigrants came from the adjoining states and even if they came from the more remote regions, the river could not be used to reach the interior regions. For commercial purposes and for the settlements along the river and beyond the state, the Ohio River was for many years after 1800 extensively used.

When the prospective settler of the West had reached Pittsburgh, Brownsville or Wheeling, he supposed that the most difficult part of his journey had been passed. Many of them, however, found greater troubles before them than they had left behind. To aid these immigrants and other travelers in descending the Ohio, there was published in Pittsburgh, in 1801, a hand-book called the *Navigator*, which gave directions for navigating the Ohio and the Mississippi Rivers. This hand-book, as might be expected from the place of its publication and the personal interests of the publishers, describes in glowing terms the excellence of the country along the Ohio, assuring the reader that it is not extravagant to suppose that in a few years the whole margin of the stream will form one continuous village.[1]   Between Pittsburgh and Cincinnati there were fifty-three islands and

---

[1] *Cf. Navigator*, eleventh edition, 1812.

it required caution and skill to avoid their dangers. During the time of low water, the navigation of the Ohio from its formation to Old Mingo Town, a point about seventy-five miles below, was difficult, but from this place to the Mississippi the navigation was good for keel boats or barges of one hundred to two hundred tons, except at Louisville where the falls formed for many years a great obstacle to navigation.[1] During the time of high water, boats of four hundred tons had little difficulty in descending the Ohio, except where the numerous islands and the frequent short bends in the river made it difficult to manage their unwieldy size. However, by 1810, boats of this tonnage had descended to New Orleans.

As early as 1779, the importance of the Ohio River as an agency in developing the interior part of the country had been recognized. In this year there was sent to the Earl of Hillsborough, the secretary of state for the North American Department, an address in which it was pointed out that in the development of America no part required more careful attention than this stream and its contiguous territory. This region could produce naval stores, such as corn, flour, beef, hemp, tobacco and cotton, all of which could be sent down the Ohio River in great quantities to the sea more cheaply than by the overland route to the East.[2] It was also shown that the Ohio river would offer the cheaper route over which to import the manufactured articles of Europe to the Ohio country. It was then predicted that the farmers and merchants who would settle along the Ohio, would build

---

[1] *Cf. Liberty Hall*, September 12, 1815.

[2] As early as 1806 there was a project to construct a canal around the Falls at Louisville.

ships for the purpose of carrying on this trade. This in fact they did. As early as 1775 Gibbson and Tinn, two soldiers, descended the river from Pittsburgh to New Orleans in order to procure military stores for the troops stationed at Pittsburgh. After many difficulties they succeeded in bringing back one hundred and thirty-six kegs of gunpowder in the spring of 1777, although, at the Falls of Louisville, they were compelled to unload their boats and carry the cargo around the rapids.[1]

In 1794 a line of passenger boats were started from Cincinnati. The Sentinel thus describes these boats:[2]

Two boats will travel between Cincinnati and Pittsburgh. The first boat leaves Cincinnati at 8 o'clock and returns to Cincinnati so as to sail again in four weeks. The proprietor of these boats having naturally considered the many inconveniences and dangers incident to the common method hereto adopted of navigating the Ohio, and being influenced by the love of philanthropy, and desirous of being serviceable to the public have taken great pains to render the accomodations on board as agreeable and convenient as they can profitably be made. No danger need be apprehended from the enemy (Indians) as every person on board will be under cover, made proof against rifle or musket ball; convenient port-holes for firing will be found on each boat.

Rules, regulations and time-tables were posted in the boats and in the office at Cincinnati and at Pittsburgh. There were also insurance offices at these points and at Limestone. In 1798 the two sea-going vessels, the "President" and "Senator Rose," were built at Pittsburgh, and in the same year the one hundred and twenty ton brig, "Commodore Preble" was constructed at

[1] *Cf.* Howe, *op. cit.*, vol. i.
[2] *Cf. The Sentinel of Northwest Territory*, vol. i, no. i, 1793-1794.

Marietta.[2] From this time many vessels were built at Pittsburgh and other points on the Ohio and Mississippi to carry on the traffic of these regions, for production was rapidly increasing.

The first boats which were used for navigating the Ohio were the flatboats, arks, keel boats and barges. The early boats rarely used sails and received only occasional aid from their oars but depended almost wholly upon the current of the stream to carry them to their destination. It usually took a month to go from Pittsburgh to New Orleans; but the return trip, when there was one, often occupied four months. The flat boat and the ark were used only to descend the streams, while the keel boat and barges could with difficulty be propelled up stream. The flat boat, which was for many years an important means of transportating down-stream traffic, was a roughly built boat with strong perpendicular sides and a flat bottom. When it reached its destination, it was used either to construct buildings of one kind or another for the new settlers who had traveled on it, or was sold to some other settler for a similar purpose.

Marietta was early made a clearance port. An amusing incident connected with this fact happened in 1806, when a ship cleared from this port with a cargo of pork and flour. At New Orleans this cargo was exchanged for one of cotton and the boat then sailed for St. Petersburg. When her clearance papers were examined at this place and it was found that they had been made out at the unknown port of Marietta, they were declared forgeries and the ship was forthwith seized. After minute explanations and retracing the route on the map in order to

---

[1] James Hall, *The West, Its Commerce and Navigation, passim* (1848).
[2] Hall, *op. cit. passim.*

locate Port Marietta, the ship was released. When an
emigrant to the west reached Pittsburgh, Wheeling or
Brownsville, the three main points of embarkment, he
secured a boat, and if it was not flood time, awaited this
period, unless he chose to incur the dangers of descending the Ohio during the time of a freshet. Boat building
for family and trading purposes early became an important industry at the above places. The traders first used
a canoe to carry their small stock of cider, brandy,
whiskey, groceries and dry goods, but later arks were
used. These were usually loaded at Pittsburgh and
started down the river. The arrival of a traveler at a
settlement was an occasion of great rejoicing, for he not
only brought to the settlement the luxuries of the East,
but he was also the newspaper of these early times. He
was then even more to the people than his present-day
prototype—the huckster—is to the most rural of our
communities. A family boat was from thirty to forty
feet long and cost from one dollar to one dollar and
twenty-five cents per foot, although this sum did not
include the cost of a cable, a pump and other requisites
which made the total cost about fifty dollars. Wheeling
was the safest point from which to embark during the
low stage of the river, although it did not offer so good
a market in which to purchase boats and family supplies
as did Pittsburgh, nor was it as accessible of approach
from the East until the Cumberland road was built.
From February to June and from October to December
were the best seasons for the navigation of the Ohio
River, although in the former season the floating ice
often made the trip dangerous. Head winds were
another frequent source of trouble. The river was so
crooked that a favorable wind might, within an hour,
become an unfavorable one, and these contrary winds,

contending with a strong current were not unlikely to drive the boat ashore. Boats sometimes passed from Pittsburgh to the mouth of the Ohio in fifteen days, and usually ten of these days were used in reaching the falls at Louisville. However, it was not unusual for a boat to be two weeks in reaching even Limestone, Kentucky. Much depended upon the condition of the river and the character of the weather which prevailed. Keel boats soon came into extensive use, since they were stronger, more rapid and drew less water than did the other boats. These keel boats made two or three trips up and down the Ohio and Mississippi each year, and their crew soon acquired such a knowledge of the obstacles to be met in navigating the Ohio and such skill in avoiding all dangers that many families and merchants preferred to entrust themselves and their goods to the crews of these keel boats rather than to purchase boats at the up-river points. Much loss of life and property resulted in this early period through ignorance of the stream and through failure properly to load and to sail the boats.

The first marked improvement in the character of the boats was the introduction of the barge. The barge had a capacity of fifty to one hundred tons and made annually two trips beween New Orleans and Cincinnati or Pittsburgh. The barge usually had two masts, and its chief reliance for movement was a large square sail set forward, which, when the wind was in the right direction, could be used to move the boat. If the weather conditions were not favorable, oars were used to facilitate the movement of the boat. Even then descending was easy as compared with the difficulties of ascending the river. Rowing was of little use in going up stream if the current was strong, in which case several other methods were used. One expedient was the cordelle, which consisted of tying one end of a rope to the vessel and placing the other end on the banks of the river, along which the boatman walked and pulled the boat. Another way was by "warping," for tow-paths along the banks were not always found. In warping, the yawl was sent out with a coil of rope, which was fastened to a tree along the shore or a snag in the river, and then the men on board pulled the boat up to this point, when another coil was fastened to a point further ahead to which the boat was drawn, and so on laboriously up the stream. At other times setting poles were used. This consisted in placing one end of the pole firmly in the bed of the stream, and, by leverage the vessel was pushed forward. This was a very·common method on the Ohio River where the river bottom was more solid than on the Mississippi. These methods of movement now seem very crude and expensive, yet they continued in use until the introduction of the steam boat on the Ohio and the Mississippi. The barges affected almost immeasurably the production of the Ohio region, for they reduced the freight charges from New Orleans to Cincinnati as much as five to ten dollars per hundred pounds. After their introduction most of the groceries instead of coming from the East, Philadelphia and Baltimore, came from New Orleans, since groceries and other related products constituted a light return cargo.[1]

Land transportation, especially in the case of railways, has received so much attention to the exclusion of inland water-ways, and such excellent systems have been developed that the present generation does not attach much importance to the smaller inland rivers. In the early history of the state, however, when the industrial

[1] *Cf.* James T. Lloyd, *Early Boating on the Ohio, passim.*

life was simple and other transportation facilities were lacking, the value of these streams for transportation purposes was very great. The Muskingum, Hocking, Scioto, Miami and Cuyahoga Rivers were very important aids in the early settlement and development of the region. They afforded an easy means to the settler of reaching the interior regions of the state and, after the settlements were made, they served a double purpose. They were both an outlet for the raw products of the settlers and an inlet for the necessaries such as groceries and certain manufactured goods, which came from the East or South. The Muskingum was navigable for large batteaux without serious obstacle for one hundred and ten miles, and for small boats, a further distance of forty-five miles. From the extreme upper navigable point of the Muskingum, the Cuyahoga was reached by a portage of only one mile, thus practically forming an all-water route between the Ohio River and the Great Lakes. The early settlers thought that the commerce of of the North and the South would be conducted over this route, and it behooved all who wished to enjoy the advantages of this north-and-south traffic to settle along the route. At the mouth of the Muskingum the first ferry in Ohio was established in 1790. The boat was moved by means of a rope which extended from bank to bank. At Marietta there was constructed, in 1798 or 1799, by Commodore Preble, the first sea-going vessel built on western waters.[1] This was a brig of one hundred and twenty tons which descended the Ohio and the Mississippi to New Orleans and thence sailed to Havana and, from there, to Philadelphia where it was sold. The Hocking River was navigable for small boats for seventy

[1] Hall, *op. cit.*

miles and was much used in its lower courses. The
Scioto was navigable as far as Franklinton (Columbus),
for keel boats of ten tons, and boats of smaller size went
many miles further. This stream was much used, for
this valley early produced large quantities of agricultural
products. The Miami had a stony bed and rapid waters,
and for these reasons was not so valuable for transportation purposes, although small boats could ascend it for
seventy-five miles. The Cuyahoga could be navigated
by boats to the Muskingum portages and was often used,
not only by the early settlers in reaching this region, but
also with the Muskingum River in carrying on a state
and interstate traffic.

In the settlement and development of the northern and
eastern sections of the state, Lake Erie played an important part, for it afforded, as did the Ohio River on
the south, an easy means of access to the new region,
although like the Ohio River it was not without its dangers. The first settlers who came to the Western Reserve—the surveying company of the Connecticut Land
Company under the leadership of Moses Cleveland—
arrived from Buffalo by open boat.[1] This party laid out
much of the Western Reserve into townships and also
plotted Cleveland, which began its history in 1796,
although this point had been for many years an important trading center to which the Indians of the surrounding regions came to meet the fur traders of the Lakes.
Many other settlements were soon made in this region.
Some of them exceeded Cleveland in population, but the
latter continued to be the leading trade center from
which many goods by pack-horse and other methods
were carried to the homes of the settlers. An important

[1] *Cf.* Harvey Rice, *Pioneers of the Western Reserve*, pp. 46–56, 1888.

trail ran from Buffalo along Lake Erie through Cleveland
to Detroit. This trail later became the Upper Ridge
Road and still later the general route of the New York
Central Railway. Another important trail from the
Ohio River had its terminus at Cleveland and this trail
followed what was later the water route formed by the
Ohio, the Erie Canal and the improved Muskingum
River, and still later the general route of the Wheeling
and Lake Erie and Zanesville and Marietta Railroads.

Cleveland, thus, from a transportation standpoint occupied a strategic position. A post-road from Cleveland
to Pittsburgh was opened in 1801. As early as 1765
Benjamin Franklin advised the construction of a military
post at the mouth of the Cuyahoga, and Washington, in
discussing the question of water routes from the Great
Lakes to the Chesapeake Bay, pointed out the practicability of a route from Lake Erie by way of the Cuyahoga,
Tuscarawas and Muskingum rivers to the Ohio River.
In 1769 Rev. John Heckwelder also emphasized the advantages of this Cuyahoga–Muskingum route and stated
that the former stream was navigable and had a good
harbor at its mouth, while the latter had connections
with the east, west and south. Furthermore, this route,
he said, would be intersected by the land route from
Pittsburgh to Detroit.

Many methods of transportation were used by the
settlers in reaching the north-eastern section. However
the greater number of them did not use the lake, but
came overland on horseback, in carts, wagons or on foot.
In fact the Lake did not become of any great importance until the introduction of the steam-boat in 1818, and
not of commanding significance as a commercial route
until the opening of the Erie Canal in 1825.

Such, in brief, is the history of the early water transportation in Ohio, before the improvement of the navigable water-ways. As the population increased and the natural resources of the territory were developed, there arose a demand for the improvement of the water-ways and for the construction of land routes.

CHAPTER V

THE EFFECT OF THE STEAM-BOAT UPON THE INDUSTRIAL DEVELOPMENT OF THE MIDDLE WEST.

IN 1811 the first steam-boat descended the Ohio River from Pittsburgh to New Orleans, a fact that was due to the perseverance and courage of Mr. Nicolas J. Roosevelt.[1] The success of Robert Fulton's steam-boat on the Hudson and other earlier steam-boats on different waters of the country did not by any means prove that this style of boat would be successful on all inland bodies of water, and especially on the Ohio River, which had many muddy and whirling currents, dangerous channels, snags, islands and rocks. Roosevelt was authorized by Livingston, the capitalist, and Fulton, the inventor, to make an investigation of the currents and conditions of the Ohio and the Mississippi Rivers, and if, in his opinion, they were found suited to steam-boat navigation, these men agreed to supply the capital for the construction of the boat. Roosevelt descended the rivers in 1810 and stopped at towns and settlements along the streams to discuss the project with the settlers and rivermen, but from neither class did he receive much encouragement. They considered the project decidedly visionary on account of the currents and obstacles to navigation in these rivers, and were quite certain that the falls at Louisville and other numerous obstructions

[1] *Cf.* J. B. Latrobe, *First Steam-boat Voyage on the Western Waters.*

in the Ohio River would prevent the use of the steamboat on this stream. However, so sanguine of success was the investigator that he stopped at various points along the Ohio River to open coal mines and to pile up coal along the banks of the river for the use of the steamboat, which he felt certain would soon descend this stream. His report was duly made and readily accepted by Livingston and Fulton, who thereupon authorized him to go to Pittsburgh and to build a boat.

This boat was one hundred and sixteen feet long and cost about $38,000. The people of Pittsburgh with doubts and misgivings watched the boat depart on its journey down stream and in the same state of mind was Roosevelt received and entertained at various points along the rivers. The people could not deny that the boat was moving, but this was down stream, and the boat did no more than rafts. They felt quite certain that it could not go up stream, for had not all boats been laboriously pulled or pushed up stream for years? At Louisville where Roosevelt was compelled to stop a month, to await the rise of the river so that he might pass over the falls, he invited a number of citizens on board and steamed up to Cincinnati and returned, in the hope of dispelling the last doubt of the people. Doubtless many of the people thought it really too good to be true, for they had been waiting many years for a solution of their transportation problem. Although the soil had long invited them to large production, they had often seen the fruits of their labor go to waste for lack of a market, and the promise of this rapid and easy means of shipping goods in either low or high water seemed to many too unreal. The seemingly unreal did in time prove true, yet, so far as the large industrial and commercial interests of Ohio were concerned, it was to continue for almost a decade an unreality. This was due to two facts : first, the falls at Louisville, and second, the monopoly of Livingston and Fulton. The falls at Louisville made impracticable the use of steam-boats to Pittsburgh, until greater traffic between these points had developed. This very fact however caused measures to be taken for the construction of a canal around these falls. Even before the canal was completed, steam-boats were plying between Pittsburgh and Louisville and other intermediate points. The through-route from Pittsburgh to New Orleans was generally divided into two routes, *viz.:* the Pittsburgh to Louisville, and Louisville to New Orleans routes. It might be supposed that, when this method of transportation was introduced, the rafts, flat-boats, and barges would cease to be used ; but the immediate result was just the opposite, for their numbers increased. This was a natural consequence of the great increase in production which was now made possible by the reduced cost in reaching a market. Greater quantities of the old products and a rapid increase of new ones resulted. Large quantities of flour, pork, corn, whiskey, cider, potatoes, lumber, coal, iron and wheat began to move down the river, and trade became active for seller and buyer alike. The passenger fare from Pittsburgh to New Orleans was sixty dollars in 1800, and the freight rate was six dollars and seventy-five cents per hundred pounds for general merchandise, but were decreased by more than one-half when the steam-boat was introduced.[1] However, not all these results followed at once the experiment of Roosevelt in 1811.

The first boat had two masts, for the builders expected

---

[1] *Liberty Hall and Cincinnati Gazette*, June 24, 1816.

to use sails.[1] The second boat—the Comet—was built on a plan for which French had obtained a patent in 1809, but after making a trip to Louisville in 1813, and New Orleans in 1814, this boat was taken apart and her engine was placed in a cotton factory. This was done partly because her machinery had not proved successful and partly because of the enterprise of Livingston and Fulton in securing and enforcing their monopoly of using steamboats on the lower Mississippi. The Vesuvius was built by Livingston and Fulton in 1814 and was used on the lower Mississippi. The Enterprise was constructed in the same year under the patent of French and ascended from New Orleans to Louisville in twenty-five days, but, as the river was so high that "cut-offs" were used to evade the current, the people were not yet convinced that steam-boats could be commercially used for the up-river traffic. The Washington appeared in 1816 and brought about a change in conditions. This boat was built under the supervision of Captain Henry Shreve and differed from the former boats in several important particulars. The Washington had two decks with the cabin placed between them and the boilers were on the deck instead of in the hold. Instead of upright stationary cylinders, as in Fulton's engine, or vibrating cylinders as in French's engine, the Washington had her cylinders placed in a horizontal position with a vibrating pitman. Livingston complimented Shreve very highly but assured him that their monopoly would drive him out of business, as in time it did. In 1817 the Washington made the trip from Louisville to New Orleans and returned in forty-one days. From this date the era of steam-boat

[1] *Cf.* James T. Lloyd, *Steamboat Directory and Disasters on Western Waters, passim.*

navigation on the Ohio and Mississippi Rivers really begins.

Many people thought at first that steam-boats would be confined to towing other boats and carrying passengers. The people soon realized that flat-boats and barges would continue to be used, since they could transport on the down-river trip many times the tonnage of the early steam-boats. There was also much dispute over the question as to which inventor was entitled to patent-rights on steam-boats. It was uncertain whether this honor belonged to Fulton, Fitch or Evans. The legislature of Ohio was petitioned in 1816 to pass a law which would provide that the state would defend any of its citizens against prosecution and would pay all costs for damages incurred in using patent rights on steam-boats, until the right to the patent was determined.[1] Feeling became very bitter against "any quack" who could secure the right to monopolize what was almost "a public necessity to the people of a large section of the country."[2] Meanwhile notices were published in the newspapers by the different claimants of the patent-right which warned all intending builders of steam-boats to secure permission from this or that individual, if they did not wish to subject themselves to prosecution for infringing these patent rights. The enterprising company of Livingston and Fulton secured from the state of Louisiana the exclusive privilege of navigating the waters of that state with boats moved by steam. The charter provided among other things that certain fixed rates for freight and passengers should be charged. The situation then was that the owner of a

[1] *Liberty Hall and Cincinnati Gazette*, March 4, 1816.
[2] *Western Spy*, March 4, 1816.

boat must pay a royalty to Livingston and Fulton, if he operated a steam-boat on the Mississippi, since if the shipper could not reach the only available market—New Orleans—it was useless to place the boat on the river. Even if the royalty was paid, he ran the risk of being prosecuted by one of the rival claimants. As a result of this hindrance and that of the falls at Louisville, Ohio received but little value from the steam-boat for a number of years. Livingston and Fulton placed on the river the number of boats which would bring them the largest net return on their investment, and, if others desired to place steam-boats on the river, the sheriffs of Louisiana seized them, and Livingston and Fulton prosecuted the owners of the boats for infringing their state granted privileges. The General Assembly of Ohio in 1816, passed a resolution which stated that inasmuch as the people of the state of Ohio had been deprived of the advantages of steam-boats on account of certain disputes, the senators and representatives of Ohio should use their influence to obtain a "legal exposition" of these conflicting claims and, further, that inquiry be made as to the right of Louisiana to grant such exclusive rights as had been given to Livingston and Fulton.[1]   It was felt that Louisiana by her act had greatly injured the commerce of her sister states, for she had practically closed the Ohio and Mississippi to steam-boat navigation. So many were the complaints of alleged injuries which had resulted to the people of the Ohio and the Mississippi valleys, and so frequent had become the official remonstrances, that Louisiana appointed in 1817 a commission to investigate the advisability of revoking the charter of Livingston and Fulton. This committee in its report emphasized the

[1] *Senate Documents*, 1816.

heavy losses which had been incurred by Livingston and Fulton through the wrecking and the burning of the first and the second steam-boats placed on the river, the zeal of the company in building new boats, the low fares resulting from the use of these boats, and the fidelity with which the company had observed the terms of the charter.[1] They further pointed out the advantages to the people of Louisiana from having a monopoly of the steam-boat carrying trade of the West. They said:

Have we not every reason to hope, that in a few years hence we shall have a sufficient number of them (steamboats) to allow us to carry on with the western states a trade which cannot fail to be extremely advantageous to us. Nobody can entertain a doubt that if the number of steamboats were sufficient to enable us to supply regularly the countries situated on the western streams those countries would soon abandon their connections with the Atlantic states and draw all their wants exclusively from New Orleans. The specie which the people of the western country carry home and send afterwards to the northward would remain here.

Lack of specie in the West was indeed a serious hindrance to commerce and complaints were often made when it was sent out of the states, for each section begrudged every other section any specie which it had to give up. Since the company was strictly obeying the terms of its charter and since nothing but gain was resulting to the people of Louisiana, there appeared no reason for the legislature to repeal the grant, even if the advantage to this state was secured at the expense of many other regions. The legislature therefore adopted the report without a dissenting vote. This called out

[1] Cf. *Report of the House of Representatives of Louisiana*, June 18, 1817.

from other states along the Mississippi and Ohio rivers a protest that this was an arbitrary use of power and an infringement of the rights of other states. These states denied the right of Louisiana to prohibit them from using their natural passageways to the ocean—for it amounted to this—since "the legislature might as well have extended the restriction to a total interdict of the navigation of the Mississippi within the border of the state or shut the port of New Orleans against us."[1] Since the legislature had thus determined its course of action, relief was sought from the courts. The Washington was seized by the sheriff upon a warrant from Messrs. Livingston and Fulton, and the case was tried in the District Court of Louisiana in 1818. This court decided that Louisiana had no right to grant such a privilege; but before this case reached the Supreme Court, the New York case of Gibbon vs. Ogden had been decided in 1824. This case was of such importance in its effect on transportation that a brief summary is given.[2] The legislature of the state of New York had also granted to Livingston and Fulton the exclusive privilege of navigating all waters within the jurisdiction of that state with boats moved by fire or steam. Livingston and Fulton had assigned their rights to Ogden, and Gibbon was the possessor of two steam-boats. Ogden secured an injunction to prevent Gibbon from using the boats, which the latter claimed were licensed under the act of Congress, providing for the licensing of ships and vessels employed in the coasting trade and fisheries. Inasmuch as the Gibbon boats operated between Elizabethtown, N. J. and New York City, he claimed

[1] *Liberty Hall and Cincinnati Gazette*, Nov. 17, 1817.
[2] *Ninth Wheaton*, p. 1.

the right to use them under the clause of the Federal
Constitution which gives Congress the right to regulate
commerce between states. The lower courts all held
adversely. Connecticut had granted a similar privilege.
New Jersey by an act provided that, if any citizen of that
state were restrained by the New York act, he should be
entitled to an action for damages in New Jersey with
treble costs against the party who thus restrained him.
Georgia had made similar grants in 1814, Pennsylvania
in 1813, New Hampshire in 1816, and Massachusetts in
1815. In 1822 Ohio passed a retaliatory measure against
New York. This prohibited any owner of a boat moved
by steam or fire under patent or ownership of Livingston and Fulton from landing any passenger on the
shores of Lake Erie except in case of life being endan-
gered and except, when the privilege of navigating the
waters of Lake Erie that were in New York state had
been granted to citizens of Ohio. A fine of one hundred dollars for each and every passenger on the boat
was fixed as the penalty for disobeying this act.

These acts indicate the general confusion which was
resulting from the conflicting claims and at the same
time the growing commerce that was made possible by
the use of steam-boats. The boats were suited to make
long interstate voyages, but each state wished to reap
all the advantages of their use. It would seem that it
was the duty of the national government to investigate
these claims and seek to protect the people since its purpose is to secure the protection and promote the general
welfare of citizens in the United States and not those of
any particular state. Mr. Webster in his argument for
the defendant said, that one of the chief powers granted
to the national government was the regulation of commerce between the several states and foreign nations.

It was intended that the commerce of the states should be a unity and to secure this unity it would be necessary for the national government to establish a uniform and complete system of regulation. This was being attempted by the states in question, and again the defendant was clearly within his rights by the congressional act which licensed ships engaged in the coasting trade and fisheries. For these two reasons, no act of the national government establishing a uniform system of regulating commerce was necessary to make the New York act null. It was void from the beginning, for it could not be assumed that the state had a right to exercise a power which was granted to the federal government, even if the national government had not yet exercised its right. The argument of appellant was based on the following points: first that the grant was not opposed to that clause of the Constitution which authorized Congress to regulate commerce; second, that it was in keeping with that other clause which authorized Congress to promote the progress of science and useful arts by the granting of patent rights and copyrights; and third, that the state had concurrent powers with the national government. Chief Justice Marshall held for the court that the laws of New York granting to Livingston and Fulton these rights were in collision with the acts of Congress regulating commerce and that the state law must yield to the supreme law. This decision was handed down in 1824, and the steam-boat industry began to develop immediately although Livingston and Fulton had practically abandoned their monopoly on the Mississippi and Ohio in 1820.

The simple fact that the steam-boats reduced the time from New Orleans to Pittsburgh from one hundred to thirty days, more than annihilated two-thirds of the distance, for it made possible a wider market and a great increase in the productions of the regions. Steam-boats in 1820 began plying between Pittsburgh and Louisville and other intermediate points.[1] Although the steamboats were not very numerous on the Ohio and Mississippi before 1818, they accelerated the trade and industry of that region. The situation in 1815 was expressed as follows:

The improvement of our barges and steamboats insure within two years the total supply by the Mississippi and Ohio Rivers of many articles, which are now wagoned from Baltimore and Philadelphia and our exports will be then commensurate with our imports. Our flour, pork, tobacco and whiskey will return in calicoes, hardware, coffee, cotton, sugar, bartered for at New Orleans. There was never such a prospect for improvement and trade at one time on any portion of the globe as that which is now exhibited to western America. Ohio has acquired celebrity during the war which has pushed her forward in wealth and population.[2]

The commercial and industrial advantages of the Ohio country were made known by the general advertisement which the region secured during the war, and this produced favorable conditions for a period of great commercial and industrial activity, which immediately succeeded. The people of Ohio were urged to improve the Ohio River, before the channel of trade was turned in another direction, as in a measure it was, after the Erie and the state canals were completed.[3] In 1819 there were sixty steamboats plying between New Orleans and Louisville, for as yet they did not reach Cincinnati and

[1] *Cincinnati Gazette*, May 17, 1820.
[2] *Telegraph* [Brownville], Aug. 14, 1815.
[3] *Liberty Hall and Cincinnati Gazette*, August 21, 1815.

Pittsburgh except in the few cases when the river was in a flood stage and they could pass over the Falls.[1] Cincinnati began to build steamboats in 1819, and a few were constructed at other points along the Ohio. Most of the boat-building took place at Pittsburgh on account of the iron, lumber and established manufactures which gave her the lead in ship-building.

The following table shows the number of boats built in different years on the Ohio. It will be observed that the number began to increase after 1818, when the monopoly powers of Livingston and Fulton were weakened.[2]

1811....	1	1817....	7	1821....	5	1825....	27
1814....	1	1818....	25	1822....	13	1826....	56
1815....	2	1819....	34	1823....	15	1827....	36
1816....	3	1820....	10	1824....	16		

The early losses suffered by fire and sinking were very heavy, for previous to 1826 forty-one per cent. of all the steamboats constructed had either been lost or destroyed and twenty-eight per cent. of these losses was due to other causes than fire—a sad commentary on the obstructions to navigation in the Ohio and Mississippi Rivers. The inland rivers of the state were not navigable for steamboats with the exception of the Muskingum, which after some improvement was often used by this class of boats. Zanesville was a center not only for agricultural products, but also for many manufactured goods among which iron products were especially important.

It was not until 1818 that the first steamboat appeared in Cleveland, although Cleveland at this time had no

[1] *Cincinnati Gazette*, March 30, 1819.
[2] Lloyd, *op. cit.*

harbor except for very small craft. In 1822 a schooner of forty-four tons was built at Cleveland and her first cargo was a load of provisions for the garrison at Mackinac. In 1824 the first steamboat was built at an Ohio port on Lake Erie. It will be observed how much later the trade and industry in the northern section of the state developed, for at this time there were on the Ohio River hundreds of vessels, including steamboats which transported thousands of tons of produce from the southern and central regions of the state to southern markets. The report of the collector of the port of Cleveland showed that in 1809, between April and October, the months in which most of the trade was carried on, the receipts of goods amounted only to fifty dollars. In the same year the collector's report from the Maumee District showed that there were sent out three thousand dollars' worth of coon, bear and mink skins. This indicates the absence of developed industrial life.[1]

When the Erie Canal was completed, the state canals and some state highways constructed, and the canal around the falls at Louisville built, Ohio began to furnish more products for the steamboats than they could carry, and the agitation commenced with renewed vigor for the improvement of the Ohio River. The improvement of this river would mean that the improved boats which had the great merit of cheapness could be used throughout the year.

[1] *Cf.* Charles Whittlesey, *Early History of Cleveland, passim.*

CHAPTER VI

INDUSTRIAL LIFE IN THE EARLY WEST 1788–1830.

THE present great wealth of Ohio is largely due to the amount and variety of her natural resources which, even in the early history of the state, tended to make the industrial life of the settlers one of varied productions. The character of the soil made it possible to grow a variety of agricultural products and, since the first settlers of a region must produce their own food supply, the Ohio settlers were in a position not only to do this but also to make rapid advances toward the utilization of the other great natural resources, such as the wealth of the mines, and the forests. One of the earliest commercial products of the settlers was the ashes which were obtained by burning the trees and underbrush from the cleared spaces. These ashes, as a by-product obtained in connection with the main task of making a clearing, were bleached and the lye obtained from them was boiled into black salts, which were sent back to the East to be exchanged for the manufactured goods of that section. The sugar which was obtained from the maple tree was another early product, although only for local consumption except in the northeastern section of the state where it was produced in commercial quantities. Wheat soon became a product of great value, but at first, through absence of mills and transportation facilities, the yield was very limited. For many years but little machinery was used, and milling entailed such great expense that inducements of almost every kind were offered by the first settlers to persuade individuals to establish flour and corn mills. The wheat was sown by hand, reaped with a sickle and threshed with a flail. Corn was more easily worked up, for without much expense the settler could produce an abundance of lye to convert it into hominy, and the hand-grinding of corn, although a somewhat tedious and irksome task, was yet done to some extent. Moreover corn could be raised in such large quantities at such a low cost that it could be profitably used to fatten hogs and cattle, which could be driven to market and thus solve the problem of transportation.

The flour mills established at Venice on the Sandusky River were the first to make a cash market for the wheat of the state, although before this time flour mills had been established in the southern part of the state. The first Ohio flour to reach New York came from the Venice mills in 1833 and occasioned much comment. [1] Previous to 1840 most of the Ohio flour went to market by way of the Ohio River or by overland routes to inland centers of population, which by this time consumed considerable quantities. In 1836 Oliver Hewberry purchased in Cincinnati five hundred barrels of flour at eight dollars per barrel which he transported by way of the Ohio and Mississippi Rivers and the overland route to Chicago, then a frontier town, where the flour was sold for twenty dollars per barrel. [2] Detroit was another early market for limited quantities of Ohio flour and wheat. In 1789 the first mill of any kind in Ohio was built on Wolf's Creek. This was a corn mill and a few

[1] Howe, *Historical Collections, op. cit*, vol. i.
[2] *Annals of the Early Settlers of Cuyahoga County.*

years later a saw mill was located near the same place. [1] In 1791 the settlers at Belfre constructed a floating mill which consisted of two boats firmly fastened together with the water wheel between them. The wheel was turned by the current of the stream and the mill could grind from twenty to fifty bushels of corn per day, the amount depending upon the strength of the current.

The Hudson Bay Company furnished a market to the producers of corn in the northern section of the state, but even as late as 1824 corn sold for ten cents per bushel and wheat for thirty cents per bushel. When the Erie Canal was completed a year later the prices of these articles had doubled, for the eastern markets were now opened to Ohio. However, the regions which could produce large quantities of corn at a low cost, such as the Scioto and Miami valleys, were too remote from the great centers of consumption, and the cost of transportation was so great that the farmers found it more profitable to feed their surplus corn to hogs and cattle. As a result the Scioto valley became and continued for many years to be the chief center in the West for stock-raising. In 1804 the first cattle from Ohio were driven over the mountains to Baltimore, and this was the beginning of a business which grew to large proportions. Attention was given at an early period to the improvement of the breeds of livestock, for many of the settlers of the Scioto Valley had come from Kentucky and Virginia, the two regions in the United States which had been interested for many years in high-grade stock. The production of pork was distinctively a domestic industry, which required but little capital and easily adjusted itself to changing conditions without great loss

[1] Howe, *op. cit.*, vol. ii.

and hence received much attention from the early settlers. Many hogs were slaughtered on the farm, and the product went into the markets of the country, as smoked and cured meats, a form which could not only bear the heavy charges for transportation, but which would also not suffer from the length of time that was necessary to market it. Packing centers were established later, and Ohio became the leading source of pork products, until the cheaper corn-producing region in and around Illinois caused the industry to move westward. After 1870 Chicago instead of Cincinnati was the chief center of this industry.

Another early product was flax which, together with cotton from the regions south of the Ohio and wool mixed with some of the finer imported wools, supplied the clothing of the people.[1] Tobacco was raised in large quantities in the Miami Valley and in the southeastern section of the state around St. Clairsville. In many other parts it was produced for local consumption. Before 1806 most of the salt was brought over the mountains on pack-horses and sold for six to ten dollars per bushel, although in a few places it was obtained from boiling the waters of saline springs. The scarcity of this article for the use of the household and the domestic animals was very keenly felt by the early settlers, and certain sections of land where salt wells and springs were thought to exist were never sold by the national government but were ceded to the state. In 1806 the salines of the Big Kanawha were opened and these

---

[1] In 1869 there was produced in Ohio 980,000 lbs. of flax, the greater part of which was worked up in the state; but in 1870, when the tariff upon similar imported Indian cloth was removed, the flax mills soon disappeared. It must be mentioned, however, that other causes besides the tariff contributed to their decay.

afforded for some time a source of supply for the settlers of the southern part of the state. Salt for the northern section of the state was at first obtained from the salt springs near present Youngstown, and along this route, on what was known as the Old Salt Road, many early settlers came into the state. Others purchased their salt at Pittsburgh and brought it overland. Some purchased the salt at Onondaga, New York, and brought it from Buffalo by boat and thence by ox teams to Ohio.[1] At Onondaga in 1808 there were in operation fourteen furnaces, and salt sold from two dollars and fifty cents to three dollars per bushel. As transportation facilities developed, the Kanawha and New York regions became the chief sources of supply for the state, but later the fields of Michigan and north-central Ohio largely replaced them.

The abundance of wood, which supplied the settlers with fuel, and the absence of manufacturing, which could not exist until a more numerous population had arrived and better transportation facilities had been secured, tended to retard the mining of coal, although the existence of this mineral was well known. Captain John Fink began the mining of coal for commercial purposes in 1830 at Bellaire.[2] The first load was taken on a flatboat to Maysville and this was the first coal to be transported any distance on the Ohio. Thus a trade began, which has reached such enormous proportions that thousands of tons of coal, not only from Ohio but also from Pennsylvania and West Virginia, are annually floated down the Ohio and Mississippi Rivers to the industrial centers

[1] *Cf. Tracts of the Western Reserve Historical and Archæological Society, passim.*

[2] *Cf.* Howe, *op. cit.*, vol. i, second edition, 1900.

between Pittsburgh and the Gulf. The first coal which reached New Orleans[1] came in flat-boats and was sold to the sugar refineries. It was soon found that this kind of fuel was superior to wood in securing the more equal heat, which was necessary to make a good grade of sugar. The facilities for handling the coal however were very rude, and consequently much time and labor was used in loading and unloading the boats.[2] In the northeastern section of the state the mining of coal began about the same time as in the southern part. The first boat-load arrived at Cleveland in 1828 by way of the Cuyahoga River and was used on the Lake steamers. In the Mahoning Valley the coal-mining industry began in 1845. Although the amount of coal and the thickness of the veins in the Hocking Valley exceeded that of any other region, these mines were not opened until the construction of the Ohio Canal, because up to this time no market could be reached. Later when the railroad reached this section coal mining became and has continued to be the chief industry.[3]

In certain sections of the Western Reserve, the dairy industry became important quite early, and this region has continued to the present as the chief center of dairy-

---

[1] *Cf.* Hall, *The West, Its Commerce and Navigation.*

[2] At first coal was wheeled out of the mines in wheel-barrows and shipped down the river in barrels. By fastening ropes to each end of the barrel the coal was easier to handle, since the barrels could be rolled or carried. Each barrel held 2¼ bushels and sold for $1.50 per barrel.

[3] *Liberty Hall*, June 20, 1818. Until 1850 the coal from Pittsburgh in most cases was floated down the Ohio in flat-bottomed boats, but owing to the competition of the railroads and use of steamboats the tow system was introduced. The steamer as well as the towed flatboat was built so as to use a very low-water stage. In 1818 a merchant of Cincinnati estimated the amount of coal used between Pomeroy, Ohio, and Louisville, Kentucky, as 116,000 bushels.

ing in Ohio. The settlers had learned the art of cheese and butter-making in their old Connecticut homes, and since they settled in a region which had good grazing land and many springs, it was but natural for them to continue the industry. Cheese and butter were made at first for domestic use, but commercial routes were soon developed and these products were carried into other regions. The dairy industry continued largely a domestic industry until 1862 when the present creamery system effected a revolution in the industry. This permitted large-scale production and greatly benefited the section. It relieved the families of the drudgery of the former system, and at the same time secured for them a wider market for the product.

The northeastern section of the state was a region of small farms with a comfortably large population which consumed its own products to a large extent and hence did not feel so keenly as did the other sections of the state the absence of transportation facilities. What products they did place on the market were articles of little bulk and great value. Contrasted with this section was the southeastern section with its coal, lumber, grains and meats, the central part with its grains and meats, and the southwestern part with its grains, tobacco and manufactured articles. Each of these sections soon became aggressive in securing transportation routes. When the Erie Canal was opened and the possibilities of interstate traffic became apparent to all sections, the northeastern sections became equally aggressive. Previous to this time, their efforts were largely directed to securing local roads.

Land was so plentiful that in some localities, especially in the Virginia Military District, large holdings by single individuals became quite common. These doubtless retarded in some ways the development of the region, for the farms were conducted on a semi-plantation system, with low grade labor. This system brought in and tended to perpetuate an undesirable class in contrast with the system of small holdings in other sections. Artisans either accompanied or followed close after the first settlers, and rude manufacturing was soon begun. The French settlers at Gallipolis had among their numbers many skilled workmen.[1] In the southern section, boats came down the river with the luxuries and necessities of the manufacturing and importing East, and it may readily be surmised how many of our present-day necessities were to these early settlers luxuries. Their necessities in addition to the food products generally meant the rude articles manufactured in the home. The forest directly or indirectly supplied a great part of their food, although the supply was supplemented by the few products raised on the small cleared areas. If there was a surplus of products raised, it was taken to the local merchant or river trader and bartered for small amounts of the few eastern products which reached the West. A list of articles brought down the Ohio River in 1805 will indicate the kind of goods which were obtainable by the early settlers. These goods according to the advertisement had arrived from Philadelphia and were for sale at a private house in Cincinnati. They included the following: "tea, coffee, chocolate, lump and loaf sugar, pepper, cinnamon, cloves, glass and enameled beads, calicoes, blankets, red white and yellow flannels, red baise, blue cloths, velvets, swansdown, German linen, stockings, looking glasses from four dollars to thirty dollars

[1] *Cf.* Mentelle, *Journey from the Upper Waters of the Ohio to the Wabash, passim* (1792).

a pair, and many other articles too tedious to mention." [1] In exchange for these articles the seller would accept furs and produce of good quality, since money, as in all new settlements, was scarce. The greater part of the business of the community was transacted without it and advertisements such as the following are very common in the early newspapers: "All persons indebted to the subscriber in the State of Ohio, and Kentucky in bond, note or book account are requested to make payment in wheat, pork, whiskey or beef. In every instance of failure the delinquent will be under the disagreeable necessity of making payments in cash." [2] The editor of the *Supporter* notified his subscribers to pay at once their subscriptions in cash, flour, wheat, corn, cornmeal, buckwheat, pork, beef, tallow, lard, butter, cheese, poultry, honey or sugar, and then added that, if any of his delinquent subscribers had none of these articles, he had better cease taking a newspaper. [3]

Factories of one kind or another began to start up in different sections of the state. Chillicothe had in 1810 a cotton and woolen factory which used 1800 lbs. of wool weekly and spun 720 dozen cotton yarns. [4] Steubenville at an early date attained eminence as a woolen-manufacturing center. A cut-nail factory was started in Cincinnati in 1805, and lumber yards and wagon factories soon appeared. On account of the great amount of timber, its quality and fitness, the cheapness of iron, paint and other materials requisite for boat-building which were obtained at Pittsburgh, this place became the center of boat-building and continued for many years to construct more boats than any other three towns in

[1] *Liberty Hall*, Cincinnati, June, 1805.   [2] *Ibid.*
[3] *Supporter* (Chillicothe), Nov. 16, 1810.   [4] *Ibid.*

the West.   At Pittsburgh in 1803 there were glass
factories, making window glass, bottles and other glassware.   The expense of securing such articles from Philadelphia or other eastern points was very great, for many
pieces were broken on the haul over the long and rough
mountain roads.[1]   Furniture-manufacturing establishments which worked up the black walnut, wild cherry
and yellow birch were soon established.   The cost of
transporting goods from Baltimore to Pittsburgh was
$4.50 per 100 lb., and this made the cost of the heavier
goods very great for the inland consumer.   Cramer's
Almanac for 1805 states that the value of the articles
manufactured at Pittsburgh at this time amounted to
$350,000, and this list included among other things the
following articles :

Glassware, bottles, windows, tumblers, etc.	$12,500
Glass cuttings	500
Tin ware	12,800
Bar iron, axes, hoes	19,800
Cutlery, augurs, chisels, etc	1,000
Cut and hammered nails	16,128
Guns and rifles	1,800
Scythes and sickles	1,500
Cut stones and grindstones	2,000
Wagons and carts	1,500
Barrels, tubs and buckets	1,150
Kentucky keel boats, barges	40,000
Windsor chairs	2,700
Spinning wheels	1,200
Carpenter works	13,500

Besides the above, many other articles were either made
at Pittsburgh or received from the East to be sent down
the Ohio or overland to the settlers in the West.   In

[1] *Cf.* Thaddeus Mason Harris, *Journal of a Tour in the Territories
Northwest of the Allegheny Mountains in 1803.*

exchange for these articles there was taken a large amount of the raw products of the West. As early as 1805, the extent of these products was as follows :

Article	Amount	Value
Whiskey	2,300 bbl.	$37,600
Linen	28,000 yds.	11,200
Lindsey woolens	4,000 "	2,000
Tow linens	9,000 "	2,250
Twilled bags		3,000
Stripped cotton	3,000 "	2,400
Raw cotton from Tennessee	36,000 lbs.	7,500
Maple sugar	150,000 "	1,800
Flax, hemp, oats, cheese		5,000

At Pittsburgh in 1808 there were four nail factories with an output of two hundred tons, while in 1810 there were six. In 1813 a rolling-mill was started. By 1810 statistics showed that there were produced in Ohio and Kentucky 127,894 lbs. of spun yarn. Hemp at this time was said to be enriching Kentucky faster than if the people had discovered a gold mine. The traffic up and down Ohio, notwithstanding the poor facilities for speedily and safely shipping goods, was constantly increasing. The following list of goods purchased by one commercial house in Pittsburgh from New Orleans indicates the character and amount of the up-stream traffic :

Sugar	365,672 lbs.
Coffee	19,604 "
Cotton	128,793 "
Spanish wool	13,244 "
Quicksilver	7,000 "
Indigo	80 "

In Adams County, by 1829, there were three blast furnaces which used the local iron ore and annually made more than fifteen hundred tons of castings besides making large amounts of bar iron, nails and other articles. The iron works at this place and in Scioto County and at Zanesville replaced the Juanita iron products of Pennsylvania and reduced the cost almost one-third on bar iron, nails and castings. But whatever there was of industrial life, travel and commerce developed in spite of wretched transportation facilities. The cost of carrying goods from New Orleans to Pittsburgh was $6.75 per 100 lbs., but this cost was proportionally lower than on the Philadelphia to Pittsburgh route, and efforts were made to direct the trade to the South.[1] When the merchants of the East complained of this attempt, the western people advised them to go to New Orleans and to invest their capital, for this city was to be the great center of trade and supply for the West. It was argued that the ships, which came to this southern port to carry cotton to Europe, would transport the goods needed for inland consumption very cheaply, since these goods would furnish ballast. Complaint was made that the West had been chained to the East long enough, and a declaration of trade independence was issued.[2] The newspapers of the time reflect the seriousness of the lack of means for transporting goods and mail. Editors are continually explaining to their subscribers why they did not receive their regular weekly paper. It was often due to the fact that the paper on which to print the news was not received. The local and national government were also criticised for not supplying better roads. The *Western Spy*, after stating that the eastern mails had not been received at Cincinnati for a week, reports that a note has been received from the postmaster at Chilli-

---

[1] *Telegraph*, Brownsville (Ky.), August 26, 1815.
[2] *Liberty Hall*, Jan. 10, 1815.

cothe which informs them that the stage driver forgot
the mail bags.   One driver explains his failure to bring
the Cincinnati mail by stating that he did not have room
for the mails of Cincinnati and the intermediate points,
so he left the former at Chillicothe.¹   Instead of asking,
as we now do, how many minutes late is the mail, the
question then was how many days late is it, or in fact,
will it ever come?   But trade was following the lines of
least resistance and by 1815 was strongly setting in from
New Orleans.   When two vessels arrived in this year at
Cincinnati direct from Liverpool, it was a subject of con-
gratulation among the people of Ohio, who flattered
themselves that conditions were now favorable for a large-
scale production of western commodities.²   From New
Orleans at this time queensware, groceries, sugars,
coffee and other products were coming, while down the
river the flour, wheat, tobacco, pork and other products
went.   Swedish iron was sold in Cincinnati in competition with Pittsburgh iron.

On December, 1817, the *National Intelligencer*, the
semi-official organ of the government, printed an article
which advocated an embargo on the export of bread
stuffs, and at once the West became angry "at this attempt to bind the Western farmer as a vassal to the
Eastern states. * * What an act it was to close the harbor
of New Orleans and our thousands of miles of navigation
until flour and corn is exactly the price, which the good
citizens of the East may like."³   Wheat was then selling
for $1.00 per bushel, corn at 50 cents per bushel, flour
from $6.00 to $7.00 per bbl., and pork from 4½ cents

¹ *Western Spy* (Cincinnati), December 26, 1816.
² *Ibid.*, December 16, 1816.
³ *National Intelligencer*, December 14, 1817.

to 5 cents per pound.[1]   Although the New Orleans market was preferable to that of Philadelphia or Baltimore, the southern market was far from satisfactory. Produce would be brought into the local shipping points along the Ohio River and a wait of weeks was often necessary before the river would rise.[2]   The rise of the river frequently meant the saving of a year's labor, and when the flood stage came joy was unbounded.   "The Ohio River had risen twenty feet" writes an editor, "and once more our boats are released."[3]   These were flat-boats, keel-boats and other crafts which had been loaded with flour, pork, lard, whiskey and other Ohio products.   New Orleans was for fifteen years after the settlement of the state in the possession of a foreign nation, which was almost continually hostile to the commercial interests of the Ohio Valley; and even after this obstacle to trade was removed in 1803, a quarter of a century elapsed before a canal was constructed around the falls at Louisville.   Even when New Orleans was reached, it was often found to be an unsatisfactory market, for the hot and humid climate of the lower Mississippi caused much of the flour, wheat, corn, pork and other perishable products to spoil in transit.   Many of these products were improperly prepared for carriage through a warm area to a distant market, since they had to be shipped when boats could be obtained and when the river permitted.   There was a lack of capital at New Orleans and consequently a dearth of elevators, storage rooms, commercial houses, and other machinery for handling a large trade in domestic and foreign goods.

[1] *Liberty Hall and Cincinnati Gazette*, 1817.
[2] *Ibid.*, February 15, 1820.
[3] *Cincinnati Gazette*, June 10, 1818.

Shipping facilities were also wanting, for steamers sailed irregularly. In consequence of these drawbacks the New Orleans market was alternately glutted and emptied, and prices fluctuated violently. Alfred Kelly in his report described the condition as follows :

> The damage sustained in consequence of delays in conveying goods to the market is of greatest magnitude. The market at New Orleans is so fluctuating, that a delay of a few days often occasions a serious diminution in the prices obtained for a cargo of provisions, since the market is liable to be over-stocked. Provisions, if long exposed on their passage down the river or in the ware-houses at New Orleans to the heat and moisture of that climate are greatly diminished in value. The obstructions to navigation prevent the surplus, produced in the upper county from being sent to New Orleans when the market at that place is best. Although the average price of flour in New Orleans is from 25 to 30 per cent. less than in the sea-port towns of the Atlantic states, yet it frequently occurs that New Orleans is supplied with that article for home consumption from those places.[1]

Much of the larger part of the surplus production of the upper country still descended the Ohio in flat boats, although the river was at that time (1829) navigated by many steam-boats. These boats could pass the falls at Louisville only at exceptional times. The cost of shipping by steam-boat was also higher. It was in 1824 one dollar per barrel for flour from Cincinnati to New Orleans. Flour which amounted in this year to over 300,000 barrels, constituted one-fourth of the value of all the products which descended the Mississippi. Ohio

[1] *Cf.* Alfred Kelley, *Report of the Acting Commissioner of the Lake Erie and Ohio Canal*, January 14, 1830.

alone shipped 200,000 barrels in 1820.[1]   It was estimated that 3,000 flat boats annually descended the Ohio River, and on account of the impossibility of ascending with them, these boats were sold at much less than their original cost, which varied from seventy to one hundred dollars. The city of New Orleans had a system of inspection and standards for most of the products. For example, pork was classified in three grades, Prime, Mess and Cargo, and what part of the animal should constitute each class was specified. It was provided that barrels must be constructed according to the public specifications of the act, and that certain amounts of salt and saltpeter with certain specified amounts of meat must be used.[2]

The people of Ohio had gladly changed from the expensive route from Philadelphia and Baltimore to the cheaper one to New Orleans and were very active in promoting plans for the improvement of the Ohio River. However when the construction of the Erie Canal began to be agitated, they encouraged the proposal in every possible way. The whole future of the state depended upon the development of those transportation facilities that would bring the people within the reach of markets, and every economic consideration urged them to encourage the construction of the Erie Canal. This route would open to them a great consuming center for their raw products and at the same time furnish a means of securing many manufactured products which were not produced in the state. Just as they had forsaken Philadelphia and Baltimore markets for that of New Orleans, so now they were prepared to forsake New Orleans for

[1] *Cincinnati Gazette*, August 26, 1820.
[2] *Liberty Hall*, August 26, 1830.

New York.   In 1819 the Ohio legislature was asked to charter a company to construct a canal from Lake Erie to the Ohio River which would open up another market for the products of Ohio as soon as the Erie Canal should be completed.   The charter was, however, at this time, refused.[1]

A selection from the lists of various commodities in various markets between 1816 and 1830 together with the prices of articles and freight already quoted for the years preceding 1816 will give some idea of the commercial difficulties.   It must be stated, however, that the price lists as given in the local papers of Ohio were of little value to sellers, for prices were largely fixed in New Orleans and fluctuated so violently that by the time the price list reached Ohio an entirely new one often prevailed in New Orleans.

Product	1816[2]	1818[3]	1822[4]	1826[5]	1830[6]
Wheat per bushel	.75	.81	.60	.50	.56
Flour per barrel.......	$5.00	$6.50	$5.00	$4.50	$3.50
Corn per bushel.......	.34	.50	.25	.15	.20
Whiskey per gallon ···	.62	.50	.40	.35	.30
Cotton per pound ·····	....	.35	.21	.18	.09

[1] *Liberty Hall and Cincinnati Gazette*, March 30, 1819.

[2] *Ibid.*, March 4, 1816.

[3] *New Orleans Chronicle*, July 16, 1818.

[4] Freight rates from New Orleans to northern cities were as follows: general merchandise, 3 to 4 cents per lb.; cotton, 1 cent per lb.; sugar, $7.00 per bbl.

[5] *Cincinnati Gazette*, June 11, 1822.

[6] *Ibid.*, January 7, 1826.

In giving these lists of prices, it is not intended to do more than to indicate the selling price of the various articles produced by the people of the Middle West or sold to them and to indicate how very unstable prices were. Demand and supply of course did govern prices, but the supply depended largely upon fortuitous circumstances. Prices were often so low that the expense of getting the product to the market equaled the original selling price. Necessity, and not desire of gain, was the prompting motive to production. In 1803 an effort was made to solve the problem of securing better prices and marketing goods by forming what was called the Miami Exporting Company.[1] This idea originated with Mr. Jesse Hunt, an experienced merchant of Cincinnati, who organized a company composed of merchants and farmers. At this time the agriculture and commerce of the West were at a very low ebb. The company at first was organized to collect raw products of the West and to secure the economy of large shipments and large sales, but it also became a banking company and as such was of great value to the West in supplying a medium of exchange. Many of its bank notes were issued and these were generally accepted throughout the West. When their paper began to depreciate and rumors of the failure of the company became rife, the people began to wonder how they could secure an equally good medium. The company had at different times over $100,000 in notes in circulation, and such a sum did much in these early times for trade and industry. The company's agents would contract for lots of raw products which they would collect and ship to New Orleans in large quantities. The company prospered for a number of

[1] *Cincinnati Mercury*, December 23, 1805.

years but difficulty was experienced in getting the
farmers to supply the amounts of goods which they had
agreed to furnish. Jealousy also arose between the
merchant and agricultural classes, the latter accusing
the former of securing undue profits. When steam-boat
traffic and other transportation improvements had been
secured and the markets were more easily reached by
the independent producer, and when the trouble arose
over its paper currency, the company went out of business. Other companies for a similar purpose had been
formed, such for example as the Commercial Exporting
Company of Marietta which was organized in 1816.[1]
This had for its object, in addition to the exporting
business, the encouragement of manufacturing, for after
the close of the second war with England the agitation
for local manufactures had become very active. Local
societies in many sections of the state were formed to
secure subscriptions to the capital stock of manufacturing companies, and prizes were offered for samples of the
best locally-manufactured goods. As early as 1808 complaint was frequently made that many manufactured
articles were brought over the mountains from the East
"which helped to drain the country of ready money,
that might as well be kept in the state by a system of
local manufacturing."[2] Many of these manufactured
articles which came from the East had been produced in
England, and after the war of 1812 the people of the
West were especially insistent that the policy of sending
"one-third of their products over the mountains to purchase British goods be discontinued." Many urged the
establishment of extensive cotton and woolen mills, and,
as presumptive evidence of the success of manufacturing,

[1] *Cf.* James R. Albach, *Annals of the West* (Pittsburgh, 1857).
[2] Cranmer's *Almanac*, 1808 (Pittsburgh).

they pointed to the fact that, in 1814, two breweries at Cincinnati had used 50,000 bushels of barley and 15,000 lbs. of hops, both of which were local products. It was pointed out that the balance of trade was heavily against the West and in favor of Great Britain. As these arguments were brought forward during the war with England and immediately afterward when much bitter feeling existed, they were of great value in securing aid from the national and the state legislatures in the establishment of manufactures and the improvement of transportation routes. Improved roads and rivers would be necessary for such a manufacturing community, not only to get the raw produce to the factory, but also to transport the finished goods to the scattered consumers. A brief review of the general status of trade and industry during the period from 1810 to 1830 will disclose the conditions that warranted the demand made at this time for improved roads and waterways. It will also indicate what effect the improvements, to be discussed later, had upon the industrial life of the state.

The Scioto Valley, as has been stated, became at quite an early period a chief source of supply of raw produce, and in 1811 the newspapers of this region rejoiced over the large amounts of raw produce which had been sent out of this valley. At Chillicothe in February, 1811, fifty boats were loaded with the products of the surrounding region. "If the rivers were improved so that a market could be reached the supply of corn, wheat, cattle, hogs and hemp which could be furnished by the region would be enormous."[1] To this end the citizens were urged to meet and to raise funds for the purpose of clearing the Scioto of impediments. By 1813 wholesale

[1] *The Republican* (Chillicothe), February 28, 1811.

houses of considerable importance were found in the largest cities of the state. Those in Cincinnati were especially important, and these houses sold articles received at that time from Philadelphia, Baltimore and New Orleans. By 1814 steam mills for grinding wheat and corn had been established at different points in the state. This fact, together with the better market conditions made possible by the use of the steamboat, caused the price of wheat to rise to seventy-five cents per bushel, whereas it had sold for ten to twenty cents per bushel six years before.[1] The water mills did not give up without a struggle, and continued to be used for local purposes. Cotton and woolen mills were found around Cincinnati, Chillicothe and Steubenville. Those at Chillicothe had a capacity of carding 1800 pounds of wool weekly and spinning 720 dozen of cotton yarn. Cincinnati had 23 cotton-spinning mules, 3300 spindles, 71 roving and drawing heads, 91 wool-carding machines and spinning machinery carrying 130 spindles. At an exhibition of American manufactured products which was held in Washington, February 25, 1825, broadcloth, cassimers and carpets from Steubenville were exhibited. Cincinnati in 1815 was manufacturing among other things the following articles: cut and rough nails in sufficient quantities to supply the demand of the surrounding region, stills, kettles, copper vessels, tinware and all kinds of fire-arms, saddlery and carriage mountings, clocks, pottery, glassware, furniture, vehicles, cooperage material, steam, saw and flouring mills, fur hats, sugar, tobacco, snuff, soap, candles, whiskey, beer and wines.[2] The export articles of greatest value were pork, bacon, lard, whiskey, brandy, beer, porter, pot and pearl ash, cheese, soap, candles, hemp, spun yarn, walnut,

[1] *Liberty Hall*, December 20, 1814.   [2] *Ibid.*, October 30, 1815.

cherry and blue-ash boards, cabinet furniture, chairs and kiln-dried meal for the West Indies.[1] The imports consisted of goods from the East Indies, Europe and the Eastern United States. From the Missouri Territory, lead and peltry were received; from Tennessee and Kentucky, cotton, tobacco, saltpetre and marble; from Pennsylvania and Virginia, bar, rolled, cast and manufactured iron, millstones, coal, salt and glassware.

Cattle and hogs were driven from some sections of the state to the eastern markets. As early as 1810 it was estimated that 40,000 head of hogs were driven to eastern markets.[2] When the War of 1812 opened there was created a demand at Detroit which was filled in the same way. In 1822 there were shipped from Circleville, which was but one of the several exporting points for the production of Scioto Valley, 21 boats loaded with 7000 barrels of miscellaneous freight, 11,000 barrels of pork, 6500 barrels of flour and 40 kegs of lard. These products were valued at $36,400, and the total river exports of this town for the year 1822 were estimated at $100,-000.[3] The producers and shippers of this valley stated that they could export ten times as much, and they did this when the Ohio Canal was completed. Cincinnati was then the greatest provision market of the West, and to reach this market the people were urged to construct roads, bridges and canals.

For several months, the editor of the *Gazette* writes, the roads have been almost impassable. Much of the produce of the country which otherwise might have reached this market must necessarily remain on the lands of the farmer to be lost or conveyed to town at an unfavorable time. The

[1] *Liberty Hall*, November 8, 1815.
[2] *Cf.* John Kilbourne, *Ohio Gazetteer*, fifth edition, 1818.
[3] *Olive Branch*, Circleville, March 18, 1822.

creeks and streams are usually without bridges and being almost always high at this season much produce is lost. Markets change with a change in weather. At one time the city is flooded with an overwhelming abundance of the choicest produce of the earth and at another time it is destitute of many of the articles of domestic consumption. These sudden variations produce the most pernicious effects, they discourage the people. Independent of the uncertainty of the markets which is produced by bad roads, and high waters, the expense attending the intercourse carried on between the city and country during winter is a great drawback to trade and industry. Double teams, the breakage of wagons, delays and loss of goods swell the amount of expense to a sum oftentimes greater than the value of the load. Money, in a great measure, has ceased to flow in from emigration, and the only means of creating and keeping a cash capital among us is through the mediums of our exportations. [1]

Cincinnati in 1826 was not only the chief point of shipment for the produce of the whole Miami Valley and parts of Indiana, but it was also the distributing center for most of the goods for the region west of the Muskingum River, for nearly the whole of Indiana and for a large part of Kentucky. A large amount of its capital was invested in commercial enterprises in order to supply the demands of this extensive region. The imports for 1826 were estimated at $2,528,590, and the exports at $1,063,560, although the latter did not include that not inconsiderable amount which went direct to market from the regions around Cincinnati without inspection at this city. [2]

In the northern section of the state while there was no extensive manufacturing or commercial enterprises prior to 1830, considerable amounts of wheat, butter, cheese

[1] *Cincinnati Gazette*, January 21, 1823.
[2] *Cf.* E. Drake, *Cincinnati in 1826*, p. 77 *et seq.*

and pork nevertheless reached the eastern markets. When the Erie Canal was completed, and especially after the Ohio Canal was opened, this region began to grow very rapidly in the variety and the extent of its industrial products. The national government was urged to assist in supplying the means of transportation for the reason that many settlers in Ohio owed the government for land. They could not pay for this land until they had a market for their goods, and these markets could not be reached until transportation facilities were constructed. It was pointed out that all the money advanced by the federal government would in this manner be returned in payment for land. Even the well-drawn political lines were broken on this question of transportation, and many of the people of the state threw aside their inherited political ideas and principles and supported the candidate who favored internal improvements. When the Jackson-Clay campaign came on, a great effort was made to show that Jackson favored internal improvements, for he was popular in the West. His friends were successful in a large degree, although many continued apprehensive, because Clay's views in respect to internal improvements were well known. The senate of Indiana passed a resolution calling upon the governor to write to Jackson to ascertain what his views were on this question, "in order that the people of this state may vote intelligently at the coming election." Intelligent voting in this case meant voting for the candidate who would give the West internal improvements.

The arguments for national aid in constructing transportation routes were generally summed up in three statements: (a) they would aid in sending the mail; (b) they would facilitate the movement of troops; (c) they would accelerate the sale of public lands. Little

emphasis was placed upon the purely social develop-
mental effects of transportation. The people were interested in securing tangible arguments on which to
base their claims for aid, for so great was the undertaking from a financial point of view that no western state
would have dared to undertake to supply itself with an
improved transportation system. The agitation before
1830 was confined to the improvement of water-ways
and the construction of highways, for, prior to 1827, the
people of Ohio knew practically nothing about railways.
In 1827 there appeared in Ohio papers an article describing a railroad, and arguments were at once advanced
to prove that it was a cheaper means of transportation
than those in use.[1] Doubt, however, was expressed
whether Pennsylvania could furnish iron enough for construction purposes at a non-prohibitive price. Questions
also arose as to whether double or single tracks should
be used. The greater number favored a single track
with numerous turn-outs. It was said that the light
freight would move as fast as ten miles per hour, while
the heavy traffic would move at least four miles an hour.
This was during the era of the state construction of
canals, and at first there was no thought that the railroad
was to be a great public road which would do much to
solve for all time the transportation problem. Some
said that funds for railway building could not be secured
in sufficiently great amount, and that even if they could,
" the roads would be built on a niggardly plan calculated
more for enriching the builders than for benefiting the
public.[2] Disputes had become so numerous among
stockholders of turnpike and canal companies, delays in
construction were so frequent and the troubles of private
ownership were so numerous, that some thought that the
only solution for the railway would be public ownership.

[1] *Cincinnati Gazette*, March 10, 1827.   [2] *Ibid.*, March 24, 1827.

CHAPTER VII

The Relation of Canals to the Industrial Development of the Middle West.

It is impossible to state just when the agitation for canals began in the state of Ohio, but the subject was discussed almost as soon as the territory was settled. The attention of the earliest settlers in Ohio was directed to the subject by the falls of the Ohio at Louisville, which, as has already been shown, seriously interfered with the marketing of the products and greatly retarded the development of the state. These falls not only interfered with the use of the early crafts but except at high water they also made impossible the use of the steam-boat along the whole course of this river. In 1817 the first steam-boat from New Orleans reached Cincinnati at a time when the river was extremely high and this event was made a subject for speculating as to the benefits that would accrue to the people of Ohio, if such boats could navigate the river at all seasons of the year.[1] It was estimated that five thousand flat-boats passed over the falls each year and that at least three thousand of them required pilots to go safely through the rapids. This meant an annual outlay of fifteen thousand dollars for this class of boats alone.[2] The losses resulting from the falls at Louisville were due to the following causes:

[1] *Cincinnati Gazette*, March 12, 1817.
[2] *Liberty Hall and Cincinnati Gazette*, Jan. 6, 1826.

(1) Drayage at seventy-five cents per ton. Ships were compelled to unload at Louisville and to have their cargoes hauled around the falls. This meant two additional handlings of the goods. (2) The injury which resulted to produce and merchandise from these additional handlings. (3) Delays which implied the continuous pay of laborers, interest on idle capital and loss of time. (4) Irregularity of trade and glutting of the market. (5) Loss of perishable goods. (6) Loss of flat-boats which could not ascend the river. (7) Loss by the detention of boats on bars, for the common way of making repairs even in the case of steam-boats was to run the boat upon the bar of an island, make the repairs and then wait for the river to rise and once more float the boat: meanwhile large quantities of goods might have been waiting to be carried to the market. (8) Losses incurred by original producers in being compelled for want of a market to hold their wheat, corn, pork, flour, whiskey and other products.

Many projects were advanced for constructing a canal around the falls, and every suggestion was enthusiastically received by the people of southern Ohio. Many of the early companies which were organized for this purpose asked for stock subscriptions and these were quickly given by the people. The first company of any importance was the Jeffersonville Canal Company which was incorporated by the state of Indiana. Shares of stock were issued and committees were appointed in Cincinnati and other cities of the Ohio valley to solicit subscriptions. There had been from the first much dispute as to the respective advantages of the Indiana and Kentucky sides of the river for a canal and although many investigations and several surveys had been made, there was no unanimity in the reports on these routes. Some favored one side and some the other, according as the friends of the one or the other side had been more influential in making the appointments. In 1820 a commission consisting of one representative from each of the states of Ohio, Virginia, Kentucky and Pennsylvania reported to the legislatures of these states, which unanimously recommended the Kentucky side.[1] Indiana immediately appropriated ten thousand dollars to complete the work on the Jefferson Canal, but Kentucky soon appropriated one hundred thousand dollars for the purpose of constructing a canal—the Portland Canal—on the Kentucky side. The people of Ohio were now urged to assist Kentucky, although previously to this they had been accusing the people of Kentucky (especially those of Louisville) of insincerity in their efforts to secure a canal around the falls, since Louisville was enriched to a great extent each year by the returns from storage, transfer and other gains from the delay and the break in the transportation at the falls.[2] Although some subscriptions had been paid by the people of Ohio to the Jeffersonville Canal Company, the greater part had been withheld. The charter of the Kentucky Company, however, did not meet the approval of the Ohio subscribers on account of its specifications as to the kind of a canal to be constructed, and the Indiana. charter was not wholly satisfactory, because it provided a bonus to Indiana, as a return for granting the charter. As a result, most of the people of Ohio, who were interested in the project, concluded that nothing further ought to be done until a competent engineer had examined the two locations and had reported upon their respective costs. They had almost concluded that the cost would be too

[1] *Cincinnati Gazette*, May 27, 1820.   [2] *Ibid.*, March 25, 1818.

great for a private undertaking and they now proposed, to prove to the national and state governments that the work could be executed and then to ask these governments to do the work. In the session of the Ohio legislature of 1820 [1] the House passed a bill which authorized the Governor to employ an engineer to make surveys on both the Indiana and the Kentucky sides and to furnish an estimate of the cost of each canal. The Senate agreed to this bill, but Governor Brown in a later message said that he had looked for such an engineer in New York "where they were having such services, but could not find one." [2] He asked that the authority to make the appointment be continued and extended to include the surveys and cost of a canal from the Ohio River to Lake Erie. Finally by aid of the national government a canal was secured around the falls at Louisville in 1828. Thus it was forty years after the settlement of Ohio before the greatest single obstruction to the successful commercial navigation of the Ohio River was removed. Before this time the people of Ohio had become interested in the state canals. The first legislative mention of canals was in 1812 when John McIntire was empowered to build a dam across the Muskingum River and to conduct the water by a canal to a point below the falls of the Muskingum. This canal secured water-power for mills and greatly improved the navigation of the stream.

In reply to a request from the Legislature of New York that Ohio aid and coöperate with New York in securing a canal from the Hudson River to Lake Erie, the Ohio legislature in 1812 passed a resolution which

[1] *Laws of Ohio*, 1821.
[2] *Executive Documents*, 1822.

expressed the opinion that Congress ought to build this canal:[1]

This means of communication would have the most extensive and beneficial effects by facilitating the intercourses between remote parts of the United States, diminishing the expense of transportation and thereby rendering the produce of our country more valuable, the price of foreign commodities cheaper, and its tendencies would be to encourage agriculture, manufactures, internal commerce, and to strengthen the bond of union between the states.[2]

This was no doubt sincerely enacted, for production had been so long retarded by the unsatisfactory market at New Orleans and the high cost of reaching the expensive markets of Philadelphia and Baltimore, that the people of Ohio rejoiced at any promise of relief. The first official mention of the Ohio-Erie Canals, was made in the message of Governor Brown in 1818, although his predecessor, Governor Thomas Worthington, had in correspondence with the Secretary of the Treasury—William H. Crawford—pointed out the feasibility and desirability of a canal between the Ohio River and Lake Erie.[3] After the receipt of Governor Brown's message the matter was taken up in both houses and in December, 1818, the Senate reported a bill to incorporate a company to construct a canal between Lake Erie and the Ohio River. This bill was not acceptable to Governor Brown and did not become a law.[4] The Senate offered a resolution in the same year providing for a joint commission of both houses to prepare a bill authorizing the

[1] *Laws of Ohio*, 1812.
[2] Congress had refused to aid New York in constructing the canal.
[3] *Journal of Senate*, 1817.
[4] *Ibid.*, 1818.

Governor to employ engineers to survey four routes for a canal between Lake Erie and the Ohio River. This bill also failed to become a law. Although the Governor, the Senate, the House, and the people wanted a canal, no bill could be passed to authorize the survey of the routes. The Governor urged the matter by frequent messages to the assembly; the Senate would pass one bill, the House another, and no agreement would be reached. Meanwhile the people were complaining on account of the lack of transportation facilities. Finally after four years of resolutions, messages and committee meetings, by a combination of the friends of the canals and supporters of an educational measure, a law was passed January 31, 1822 which authorized the Governor to employ an engineer and to appoint a commision to make surveys and furnish estimates of the cost of a canal.[1] The Senate of the United States had, however, in 1820, reported a bill:

> To appoint a commission to examine the country between the Sandusky and the Miami Bays of Lake Erie and the navigable waters of the Scioto and Great Miami Rivers of Ohio, and to ascertain whether and by what routes a canal should be laid out, and if practicable, to determine and lay out the route of such a canal.

But much opposition was encountered "to starting improvements in the back woods," and the bill was rejected by a vote of 26 to 13.[2] The people of the West said that the defeat of this bill was only in keeping with the general practice of preventing the West from deciding how any of the public moneys should be spent.[3] The same

---

[1] *Laws of Ohio*, 1822.   [2] *Senate Documents*, 1820.
[3] *Cincinnati Gazette*, May 17, 1820.

bill was again introduced in 1821 and after meeting the same objection was again defeated. The advantages which the people of Ohio thought would result from these canals are indicated by the report of the committee to which Governor Brown's message of 1822 was referred. They pointed out that because Ohio produced mainly the great commercial staples, the New York market on account of its capital, tonnage, commercial situation and climate was preferable to that of New Orleans.[1] A trader who arrived in New Orleans in the spring with a cargo of flour, wheat, pork and other Ohio products usually found the market overstocked. To leave his property would mean to loose it, and to wait for a higher price would usually involve the loss of the greater part of it through spoiling. He was thus forced to sell his products at a sacrifice, often receiving only enough, or sometimes less than enough, to pay transportation charges. During the season of 1818–19 there were received and inspected at Cincinnati alone 130,000 barrels of flour, which at this time sold in Cincinnati at $3.50 per barrel and in New York at $8.00 per barrel. The cost of shipping by canal to the latter market would be $1.70, thus making a saving of $2.80 a barrel which would mean a saving of $375,000 on the total amount sent to Cincinnati. Again it was pointed out that while the Scioto valley then produced enormous quantities of flour, wheat, corn and pork, production would be many times increased if better means of transportation could be secured. The commissioners argued that most of the imported goods and those manufactured goods of the eastern states bought for Ohio, Indiana, Kentucky, Illinois and Missouri would be purchased in New York

[1] *Journal of the House of Representatives*, 1822.

and sent by way of the Ohio Canals. Such practical arguments appealed strongly to the people of the regions affected, and the enthusiasm engendered by the prospect became unbounded. The Erie Canal was nearing its completion and this made it possible to secure the services of an excellent engineer—Mr. James Geddes—to work with the commission appointed in 1822. Later when other employees were needed, these too came from the Erie Canal.

The commission appointed in 1822 reported in January, 1823, and found each of the following routes practicable: [1] (a) the Cuyahoga and Muskingum route; (b) the Black and Muskingum; (c) the Grand and the Mahoning; (d) the Scioto and the Sandusky; (e) the Maumee and the Great Miami. They reported that canals had great advantages over any other mode of conveyance; that the agricultural produce of the country would be quadrupled; and that other bulky products, such as the gypsum of Sandusky, the fisheries of the lake, and coal would be transported by the canal; that manufacturing would rapidly increase in Ohio since coal, iron, wool and flax were either found in abundance or could be produced when needed. They pointed out that stone and lime for the construction of locks would probably be found along each of the proposed routes. The committee recommended that funds be secured by applying to Congress for the right to sell seven hundred thousand acres of school and salt lands on the condition that the funds from the sale of the school lands should be guaranteed by the state to return six per cent for the support of the schools of the state. A difficult problem was now presented for solution. Every section through which

[1] *First Report of Canal Commissioners*, 1823.

a canal could be built demanded that its interest be considered in selecting the route. Some compromise was necessary, if a canal was to be constructed. Manifestly the sections of dense population must be supplied with a canal or the project would be defeated by the votes of the neglected sections. The canals must be located not for the future needs but for the present ones, and not chiefly because of their importance as through transportation routes, but as local routes.

The three most natural routes for a canal were; (a) down the Maumee River by way of the Great Miami River to Cincinnati; (b) down the Cuyahoga River by way of the Scioto River to Portsmouth; and (c) down the Cuyahoga River by way of the Muskingum River to Marietta. The canals then authorized embraced not one of these routes, but portions of all of them. At this time the three most densely populated sections of the state were the northeastern, the central and the southwestern. At first it was proposed to start the canal in the northeastern part of the state, to run it in a southwesterly direction and to terminate it at or near Cincinnati. But this route was found impracticable and nothing was left save a compromise between the sections. In order to satisfy the northeastern and central sections, a canal was provided which was to begin at Cleveland, run south to the divide, then west to the Scioto and thence through the center of the state to the Ohio River at Portsmouth. To secure the support of the densely populated section of the southwest, a canal was located from Cincinnati to Dayton with the promise that it would be extended to Toledo. Thus the sectional interests were served and at the same time the economic demands were in a large way satisfied. It was in some respects unfortunate that such an extensive system had to be planned then, for if the state could have constructed only the one canal from Cleveland to Portsmouth by way of Columbus, it would have reached what were the chief agricultural sections of population and at the same time it would have afforded a transportation route for the through Lake Erie and Ohio River traffic. If the Muskingum and the Great Miami Rivers had then been improved, these three routes would have given to Ohio an inland water-transportation system, which would have gone far to satisfy the economic needs of the state. It was unfortunate for some of the states that New York had happily selected a route and constructed a canal, which from the first proved such a commercial success. This was due to the importance of New York as a foreign commercial port, to her manufacturing, and to the fact that through this canal she could reach the central states, which produced a great surplus of raw products. The people of other states had not learned to discriminate between canals. They assumed that what had been found true in the case of one canal could be predicted of all, and thus was started again the mania for canal construction which, before it had run its course, had placed a heavy burden on the resources of many states, for many of these canals proved financial failures.

The act providing for the Ohio canals passed the legislature in 1825 by a vote of ninety-two to fifteen.[1] The same year which saw the beginning of the work on the canals witnessed the extension of the National Road through Ohio. At the same time there began a renewal of the agitation for the building of state, county and township roads. The national government spent at this time $70,000 on the improvement of the Ohio River.

[1] *Journal of the Senate*, 1825.

MAP OF OHIO
CANALS

Explanations.
County Lines
Existing Canals
Abandoned Canals
Proposed Canals
Rivers and Creeks
Dams and Feeders

The canal around the falls at Louisville was also in the course of construction, and the outlook for the people of Ohio was most encouraging. Transportation facilities commensurate with the needs and producing ability of the region gave promise of being supplied within a few years. Yet not a few objections were heard to the canal policy of the state. Some were opposed to it, because they did not derive any direct advantages from the canals, some because they thought that the canals would injure their lands[1] and subject them to the association and annoyance of an undesirable class of citizens, just as later when the railroad came, many a town lost the railway because the " good old influential settlers lived in the past and not in the present." Some said the state would be forced to borrow so much money that the debt would never be paid : that the canal project was a sectional measure : some objected to being taxed to pay any part of the sum required for the construction of the canals. They desired that the whole cost be defrayed from the proceeds of loans to be paid by the returns from tolls on the canals, or that those who were directly benefited by them should pay the cost without any general state tax being levied.[2] In the northeastern section of the state the trade was chiefly with Pittsburgh. The wagons from Ohio would haul butter, cheese, pot and pearl ashes, bees-wax, feathers and other products to Pittsburgh and return with the manufactured goods of Pittsburgh or the foreign merchandise which had been brought there. Pittsburgh was, however, complaining in 1825, that she was losing her trade[3] and urged that a

[1] *Cincinnati Gazette*, March 12, 1825.
[2] *Western Courier and Western Public Advertiser* (Ravenna), March 22, 1825.
[3] *Western Courier*, Oct. 15, 1825.

canal be constructed from Pittsburgh through Ohio to Lake Erie. By 1826 Pennsylvania had expended sixteen million dollars on canals, turnpikes, bridges and public work, and at this time plans for additional large expenditures were being drawn up in an effort to retain a share in the growing western trade which the success of the Erie Canal was giving to New York.[1] The cost of sending goods to Ohio from New York by way of Philadelphia and Baltimore was from three to four dollars per 100 lbs., although from New York to Sandusky it was only $1.25 per 100 lbs.[2] The opening of the Erie Canal meant a wider market to the people of Ohio and this denoted an increased production and higher prices for domestic products and greater comforts and conveniences for the people of the state. After the two main Ohio canals were provided for, there were numerous projects for the construction of minor canals of which many were lateral canals to the two main routes. In 1833 the two original canals were finished, although the canal system of Ohio was not completed until 1846 when Ohio had 813 miles of canal and slack-water navigation.[3]

In 1835 there was shipped from Ohio 86,000 barrels of flour, 98,000 bushels of wheat, 2,500,000 staves and many other products to New York by way of the Erie Canal.[4] This was the first blow to the commerce of the Ohio River, for prior to this time all the heavier products had gone down the Ohio and Mississippi, and thence by sea to New York and other eastern ports. Even goods

[1] *Western Courier*, Feb. 4, 1826.
[2] *Cincinnati Gazette*, Sept. 10, 1827.
[3] *Cf.* map opposite p. 117.
[4] *Report of the Internal Commerce of the United States*, 1888. "Commerce of Ohio and Mississippi Rivers."

from western New York had found an outlet by this river route prior to the completion of the Erie Canal. However, the New Orleans trade did not seriously suffer from the canal competition of New York and Ohio, for during the period of 1825–1850 the river trade showed a greater percentage of increase than did the canal trade. This was due to the development of the regions of the Middle West. The truth of the matter was that the sections reached by the Ohio River and the canal were capable of producing enough to utilize to the fullest extent the transportation facilities of both routes. The canals of Ohio acted as feeders for both main routes, although it must be understood that it was for local reasons that the Ohio canals were constructed, and it was the local trade which sustained them during their years of prosperity. The competition between the north and south routes was scarcely felt at Cincinnati until about 1850 when a new and more powerful competitor —the railway—appeared. At the first appearance of railways, many thought they would be used to supply connections between points which had no water transportation, for the people had come to recognize the fact that canals could not be built anywhere and everywhere. The simple fact that railroads for the first twenty years of their history were composed of many short disconnected lines shows that they were looked upon as purely local transportation routes. After the canals had been opened the great benefits to the counties through which they passed began to be realized and this made the people of the counties not thus served more pronounced in their opposition to paying for them by the general state tax. Partly to pacify these sections the legislature established a permanent Board of Public Works which should "from time to time present to the consideration of the General Assembly such objects of internal improvement as they shall judge the public interest may require."

In pursuance of this direction, the first Board reports:

That the action of the legislature, authorizing the construction of a variety of works at public expense, is a response to public sentiment, and that nothing short of the extension of canal navigation to every considerable district of the state will satisfy that public will, which justly claims that benefits conferred shall be co-extensive with burdens imposed, and that in those counties where canals cannot be made, an approximation to equality shall be obtained by the aid in constructing roads.[1]

When it became evident that railways might become serious competitors of canals, various means were employed to protect the canals. As early as 1838 the Board of Public Works was instructed to report "whether in their opinion the extension of the Lake Erie and Mad River Railroad from Dayton to Cincinnati would operate to the injury and interests of the state by creating competition with, and diverting business from the Miami Canal."[2]

Whereupon this board investigated the matter and reported that

the chief products moving south on this canal were flour, pork, whiskey, and that moving north was merchandise. Practically all the pork, and a large proportion of the flour and whiskey, are brought to points along the canal to await its opening, and all the pork, one-third of the flour and one-fifth of the whiskey would move to market by rail. Since the canal did not yet afford a revenue sufficient to pay inter-

[1] *Report of the Board of Public Works*, 1837.
[2] *Journal of the House of Representatives*, 1838.

est on their investment, it would seem unwise to permit such a transportation route to be built. [1]

Notwithstanding this opinion of the Board, which was held for many years, there had already been chartered more than twenty railroad companies in addition to the fifty-five canals and eighty turnpike companies. [2] As was to be expected from the character of the work which it did, this Board of Public Works was subjected to much individual criticism and several legislative investigations and in fact the Board was for a time abolished. When a public work was to be undertaken, many districts wished to benefit from it and those which did not secure the benefits accused the successful sections of using improper influence. Party politics often joined with these sectional interests to embarrass the work of the Board. The Board was always a favorite object of attack for the party out of power, and this too often made its plans such as would prevent the criticism of politicians rather than such as would further the commercial interests of the state. In 1841, owing to the the prevalence of hard times, the Board was asked what the effect would be of a discontinuance of the public works. Upon an adverse report by the Board, work was continued until the next year. The state's financial difficulties had then become so great that work was temporarily suspended. Tolls as first established were based

[1] *Report of the Board of Public Works, 1838.* It was further argued that since the raw products of the southwestern part of the state found their market along the Mississippi River, a railroad would be no great gain, for when the river was frozen or low these products would be stored in Cincinnati instead of at the canals or at the points of production.

[2] *Files of the Charters of Incorporated Companies,* Office of the Secretary of State.

upon the value of the articles, which consisted chiefly of raw produce of the farm and certain merchandise for local consumption; but the Board by 1845 was not at all confident that this merchandise could be kept upon the canals by the readjustment of charges.[1] The Board reported in 1849 that "the toll had been reduced on merchandise and all through freight in order to compete successfully with the various rival improvements in this and other states."[2] The lower tolls which were charged on western produce by the Erie Canal tended to draw these products to the New York market; so, in 1850, the Board of Public Works of Ohio reduced tolls thirty per cent in an effort to secure the advantages which would result from having this western produce move through the Ohio canals. The railroads, however, more than met this reduction. Whereupon the Board asked for power to meet this competition instead of having tolls fixed by a general act of the legislature for "otherwise a large number of citizens who have in many cases invested all they own in boats, stock and business houses on the canals will be greatly injured and the revenues from the public works will sink into insignificance and the work ultimately decay."[2]

Laws had been passed in 1850 to regulate the charge on both railways and canals but neither obeyed these laws, although the canal interests, which were losing traffic, complained much about the violation of these

---

[1] *Report of Board of Public Works*, 1845.

[2] *Ibid.*, 1849. The opening of the Lake Erie and Mad River Railroad offered a more rapid means of transportation between Cincinnati and the Lake. The Little Miami Railroad also supplied a route to the Cincinnati markets, for produce of the southwestern part of the state. In other sections railways and highways were freeing producers from their dependence on canals.

laws by the railroads. The Board reports that "both railroads and canals are desirable and necessary but there should not be and there would not be any conflict between the two systems, if the public authorities and those who direct the affairs of railroads were at all times actuated by a sincere and enlightened desire to promote the interests of the people."[1] At this time there were those who argued that the canals should be sold, but it was the opinion of the board that the railroads would be the purchaser, and the members of it advised that canals should be maintained in order to keep down freight rates. This in itself was indicative of the fact that canals were becoming secondary transportation routes. That the canal officials recognized this is shown by the following extract from the report of the Board:

It was supposed that competition between railways would be effective in keeping down rates, but it is not likely to do so, for consolidation is the order of the day. The immense railway system of Ohio is rapidly becoming a unit over which periodical conventions of railway officials constitute a flexible, but most efficient board of control. We have felt it to be our duty to resist by all means at our disposal every intrusion by railroads upon the canals which impaired the navigation and traffic of the latter.[2]

By 1855 the Board admitted that, notwithstanding the decrease made by them in tolls, the railroads had been able to secure their share of the traffic because "as private corporations they could make individual terms, and as a result have secured the transportation of much freight which naturally should move to market by way of the canals."[3] A few years later the situation was

---

[1] *Report of the Board of Public Works*, 1850.
[2] *Ibid.*
[3] *Ibid.*, 1855.

even more apparent, and this led the President of the Board of Public Works to report that

The experience of the past nine years proves that under state control the canals cannot retain their business whenever they come into competition with railroads. This is due to an inflexible tariff of tolls and by a division of freight charges into two items, tolls and freight in the control of different parties, one of which takes no interest in the business.[1] The boat owners meet at every point active and ever watchful railroad freight agents with full control of the freight charge and ready to contract either for separate lots, for the season's business or even for years in advance at such rates as they find necessary to receive the business. The railroads have actually taken possession of the grain market at points where canals and railways compete, and require their agents to purchase grain for the storage of which they use the empty cars on the side-tracks. The canals at these points receive only the surplus, which the railways cannot carry. Even in years of abundant harvest, such as the present, the increase in the canal business is but trifling, and during the past ten years the number of boats on the canals have decreased 500 per cent.[2]

Politics as ever entered into the question and neither party dared to ask the people of the state for sufficient money to rebuild the canals, for public sentiment was opposed to them. The people were interested in cheap and quick transportation, and if the railway promised this (as they thought it did) it was unfortunate, they argued, that they had spent so much money on canals. But now that

[1] As a matter of fact this was only a secondary cause of the decrease of canal traffic, for, as we shall later learn, the industrial demands had grown far in advance of the transportation facilities of the canals and the primitive organization of the transportation business on them.

[2] *Remarks of Abner Backus, President of the Board of Public Works in 1860.*

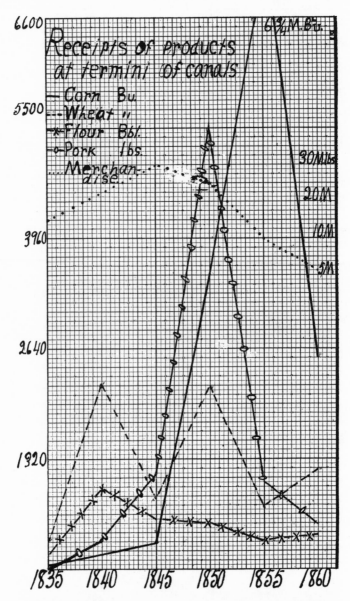

Along the perpendicular line on the left are represented in thousands of bushels, pounds and barrels respectively, the amounts of corn, wheat, flour and pork received jointly at Portsmouth, Cincinnati, Cleveland, and Toledo. Along the perpendicular line on the right is represented in millions of pounds the amount of merchandise jointly received at the same points.

the mistake was known, it would be unwise to spend more upon a means of transportation, which had been so productive of scandal and trouble and which was now inadequate. Even if some one could have shown them that by thus abandoning the canals instead of enlarging them they would pay for their negligence in increased rates during the era of railway competition, they doubtless would not have acted differently. In the midst of their general disgust with canals, the theory of present sacrifices for future blessings would not have appealed very strongly to them. The public works had been such a field for political discussion that they had come to be looked upon as a source of corruption, and every request for funds by the Board of Public Works was regarded as fraudulent, so that the decrease of an appropriation was considered by many as so much saved from corruption. Such were the fruits of the numerous accusations of dishonesty made against those who had located and managed the state's public works. Although the unprejudiced investigator explains most of these charges as due to party animosity and sectional jealousy, yet the history of the state's work in canal construction and management has not been encouraging in either its earlier or later periods.

New York State increased her canals to double their former size in order to keep pace with the increased industrial demands, but Ohio did nothing and her canals decayed. This decay was markedly accelerated when she leased them in 1861, although many people rejoiced at this event "because the eternal question of the canals was for a time solved." When the state resumed their operation in 1878, they were even less efficient transportation agencies. The railroads had secured the bulk of the traffic. No important interests in the state demanded their improvement, and they ceased to be in a large way even potential competitors of railways. The railways had increased not only in mileage but, what was of more importance, they had become interstate and had developed excellent system and organization in their business. Canals could be used only at certain seasons of the year; they were always slow; the boats were small as compared with the increased demands for transportation. The canal business lacked the energy, economy, the close and vigilant management which was the leading feature of the railway business. The later years were years of progressive decay, until now the canals of Ohio are scarcely worthy of the name of good ditches, although in a few places they do afford some valuable water power for industrial purposes, and their reservoirs furnish pleasant outing places.

It is impossible to prove just what effect the canals had upon the industrial and social life of the state. One can present evidence of the increased wealth of the regions served, remembering that the canals were but one of the causes of this increased wealth, although the most important one in the period from 1830 to 1855. The population of Ohio in 1830 was 937,903 and in 1860, 2,339,511. The effect of the canals upon the population of particular cities is more clearly seen in the following table :[1]

Population of cities	1820	1857
Cincinnati	2,602	200,000
Cleveland	400	60,000
Dayton	1,139	25,000
Chillicothe	2,416	10,000
Toledo	500	14,000
Portsmouth	500	5,000
Newark	700	4,000
Akron	700	4,000

[1] *Census Reports.*

Another method of indicating the effects of the canals, although by no means a conclusive proof, is to exhibit the increase in the value of property, as shown by the taxation returns. The thirty-seven canal counties show an increase in the value of real estate and personal property from $53,000,000 in 1835 to $486,500,000 in 1859, while the fifty-one non-canal counties show for the same period an increase from $41,000,000 to $390,000,000.[1] The producers were able by means of the canals to reach markets for their abundant raw produce, but this was considerably limited to the producers near the canals, for after all is said in favor of the canals, the fact remains that the canals of Ohio and of the Middle West were distinctively local transportation routes. The improvement in transportation as compared to that of the preceding period of mud roads and far distant rivers was a very great factor in the industrial progress of the state, and although their golden age had ended by 1855, we must not forget that it was the aid that they furnished to industries which gave many of the present industrial enterprises their real foundation, and made their development possible. It was this development which necessitated a more rapid and adequate means of transportation. They found a market for the surplus products of the forest, field and mine.[2] They established a commercial connection between the eastern seaboard and the western interior. What was actually accomplished by connecting

---

[1] *Report of Auditor.* These figures are somewhat misleading, for the counties through which the canals passed were on the whole the natural agricultural counties where a greater increase was to be expected.

[2] The graph shows in five-year periods the leading products received at the different termini.

The effect of the canals may also be seen by reference to the graphs of prices, chap. xiv.

the Great Lakes and the Atlantic Ocean with the Ohio and the Mississippi rivers exceeded all rational expectations and prophesies, irrational as they seemed in the pre-canal period. Notwithstanding the powerful aid of the state legislature, traffic left the canals, and for this result the following reasons may be assigned:

(a) The failure on the part of the canal interests to develop a systematic organization of the business to keep apace with the industrial demands.

(b) They served only local districts.

(c) They were closed a part of the year and were much slower than railways in transporting goods.

(d) Tolls were not adjusted to varying needs and conditions.

(e) The people lacked confidence in their utility and did not divorce their management from politics.

(f) The railways discriminated against them.

CHAPTER VIII

The Development and Improvement of Highways in Ohio, 1810–1850

During the past few years there has been a renewed agitation for good roads in the state of Ohio. This is a latter-day manifestation of a movement which began as soon as the northwest territory was organized. Viewed in its larger aspects, this movement is only a local expression of a national movement to secure more adequate facilities for the transportation of the rapidly increasing products of the country, which have already overtaxed the capacity of our railway system. Ohio has been more fortunate than most other states have been in regard to highways, in that she early secured a fund for their construction and gave considerable attention to the subject of devising ways and means to obtain good roads. Her road laws, so far as legal enactments were concerned, seemed to leave little to be desired. Notwithstanding all this, it cannot be said that the results have been commensurate with the means and the attention given to the subject. This is the more surprising when it is remembered that the state as a whole is well supplied with road-making materials. However easy it may be to explain the neglect, there is little excuse for the state not having developed a well-improved and modern system of state highways. What the provisions of these early road laws were, what means were employed and what use was made of the funds to secure highways, it will be our purpose to indicate briefly.

Among the laws of the Northwest Territory there was one which made provision for the opening and regulating of highways by means of a petition to the justices of the court of the general quarter sessions, who appointed, if necessary, three disinterested parties to condemn and appraise the land for road purposes. The law required every male citizen over sixteen years of age to work on the roads for not more than ten days each year, and for each day that he failed to work or "wasted the day in idleness or inattention to the duty assigned him, such delinquent shall forfeit and pay to the supervisor, who warned him to work, fifty cents."[1] The same law provided for defraying the cost of constructing bridges by the counties in which they were located. This was the first law which directly referred to roads in Ohio, and, although the provisions have been changed or modified from time to time, there is a similarity between its main provisions and those of the road laws of Ohio at the present time. Some of the first roads laid out and improved were those having their termini at mills, for it was of vast importance to the early settlers that mills should be accessible. Careful provisions governing the taking of toll by the miller was made in these laws. A higher toll was permitted when the mill was moved by horses than when it was run by water. Another road law was passed in 1799, which fixed the age limits at 21 and 50 and reduced the number of days of compulsory work on the roads from ten to two.[2] The court of the general quarter sessions under this act appointed supervisors, and the law authorized the county commissioners to levy a road

[1] *Laws of the Northwest Territory*, 1787.   [2] *Ibid.*, 1799.

tax not to exceed one-half of the tax levied for defraying territorial or county expenses. A curious provision of this act was that which fined any workman on the roads who asked travelers for money. The law provided that the justices of the court of the general quarter sessions, or a majority of them, could order any bridge to be built, and that its cost must be borne by the general district, when the justices considered the cost of the bridge too great for the local district in which it was situated. However, little resulted in the way of good roads under these territorial laws, and not until the congressional act which admitted Ohio as a state was passed, did the state secure a fund for the construction of roads. This was the famous Three Per Cent Fund. This fund made possible a system of roads for early Ohio which, if the state had been compelled to depend on her own efforts, she certainly would not have secured for many years.

The act of Congress which authorized the people of Ohio to form a state constitution, provided:

That the Secretary of the Treasury shall from time to time and whenever the quarterly accounts of the receiver of public monies of the several land offices shall be settled, pay 3 per cent. of the net proceeds of the lands of the United States, lying within the state of Ohio, which since the 30th day of June, 1802, have been or hereafter may be sold by the United States after deducting all expenses incident to the same, to such person or persons as may be authorized by the legislature of the said state to receive the same, which sums thus paid shall be applied to the laying out, opening and making roads within the said state, and to no other purpose whatever.[1]

Thus originated the Three Per Cent Fund, which made possible the early state roads. By February, 1804, $17,-

[1] *Laws of Congress*, 2d session, 8th congress.

000 was available from this source and the state legislature accordingly passed a long act that provided for the
laying-out and opening of certain roads, which in this
case numbered seventeen. The act[1] provided for the appointment of sixteen road commissioners, who should
cause the roads to be surveyed and plainly marked, with
a width of fifty-six feet. The amount of money to be
spent on each road was specified, and in order that no
part of a road should receive an inequitable amount, each
road was divided into sections from five to thirty miles
each, with an equal amount appropriated for each section. The character of the road is disclosed by the
further provisions of the act that

> All timber and brush shall be cut and cleared off at least
> 20 feet wide, leaving the stumps not more than one foot in
> height; wet and miry places shall be made passable by a
> causeway 16 feet wide, to be made of timber covered with
> earth; small streams that are difficult to be passed shall be
> bridged.

If any road had had appropriated to it less than ten dollars per mile, the commissioner was to use his discretion
in regard to width and bridging.

In April, 1803, an act provided for the appointment of
County Surveyors by the Common Pleas Court,[2] and in
1804 three County Commissioners were provided.[3] However, the duty of the commissioners was not so much to
care for roads and bridges as it was to supervise the
adjustment of claims against the county, and to assess
taxes. Their powers were later extended " to make and
enforce all orders necessary to open and regulate highways upon application." Provision was also made for

---

[1] *Laws of Ohio*, 1804.   [2] *Ibid.*   [3] *Ibid.*

petitioning the commissioners to open roads, to appoint
viewers and for boards to assess damages. A comprehensive road law following in its main provisions the
former act was passed in February, 1804.[1] This provided
for three days' work by all males between the ages of
eighteen and fifty and imposed a fine for refusal to work.
The fine was used by the supervisor in employing other
workmen on the road. As the money from the Three
Per Cent Fund was received from the national government, the state legislature provided in detail for its expenditure, specifying in each case how, when and by
whom it should be expended. The disposition of this
Three Per Cent Fund became, from the beginning, a
source of contention between the two houses of the assembly, and an occasion of log-rolling among the members, as well as a means of furnishing the small change
for political party financiering. Few of the bills providing for the expenditure of the fund ever became laws,
until a conference between the two houses had been
called, and various claims adjusted and interests satisfied.
Naturally enough each section wanted a state road and
its representative obstinately contended for it, since his
re-election then, as to-day, depended somewhat upon
what he secured for his district. As a result those districts which had no representatives suffered and those
districts which had the most influential representatives
secured the lion's share. Each time a bill was passed,
commissioners were appointed to lay out the roads and
this afforded an opportunity for the party in power to
reward its workers. No small part of this fund was
taken in paying these commissioners for a work which
might have been done by the commissioners of the

[1] *Laws of Ohio*, 1804.

counties in which the roads were located. At first all
the money was expended in laying out roads, but parts
of it were later used in constructing bridges and improving roads which had been previously laid out. In some
cases county roads were made state roads and improved
by means of this fund. At various times other sums
were available so that by 1830 the sum of $342,814.15
had been expended by the state in laying out and opening the roads. The distribution of this amount over the
several years was as follows:

1804	$17,000.00	1815	$46,000.00
1806	7,725.00	1817	60,000.00
1807	15,000.00	1820	50,000.00
1808	6,000.00	1821	3,093.62
1809	9,000.00	1823	300.00
1810	23,000.00	1825	5,576.00
1811	8,380.00	1826	19,500.00
1812	41,000.00	1830	22,239.95

After 1830 the fund diminished rapidly, but by that time
the state had so increased in wealth that it was better
able to carry on the work of building roads.[1]

Bridges in early times were few, and, as a result, ferries
were numerous. So important a part did they play in
the economic and social life of the people that the legislature made very minute provisions for their operation.
Every person who ran a ferry was required to take out
a license, and such a license was granted only upon petition of twelve householders of the township in which
the ferry was to be located.[2] The operator must keep a
" good and sufficient boat, sufficient hands to manage it,
and offer service from daylight until dusk and convey
mail and public express across it at any hour of the

---

[1] *Cf.* map, chap. iii, p. 38.   [2] *Laws of Ohio,* 1805.

night." The commissioners of the county fixed the rate of ferriage, for this monopoly at a time when the necessity for passageways was urgent and frequent might have been a menace to the welfare of the early settlers.

In 1806 another general highway act was passed which gave the county commissioners power to repair and open roads. It required them to hold four special meetings a year, which were wholly devoted to matters relating to roads.[1] The township trustees were also empowered to levy a road tax, which could be discharged by working on the roads at the rate of sixty-seven cents per day. These sums of fifty to seventy-five cents per day may seem small, but they were the ordinary payments for public work and owing to the relative higher purchasing power of money they were equivalent to the larger payments of the present time. Resolutions were frequently passed by the state legislature requesting their senators and representatives in Congress "to use their best efforts to get a bill passed whereby certain state roads" should be declared post roads. The people thought that they would secure in this way the maintenance of these roads by the national government.[2]

In February, 1809, a long act was passed which incorporated the first Turnpike Company.[3] The power of the company and its duties to the public were minutely set forth. The capital stock of the company was $10,000 divided into shares of $25 each and subscription to the stock must be open to the public. The road must "not exceed 60 feet in width and 22 feet must be bedded with wood, stone, gravel or other proper and convenient material, faced with gravel or stone pounded, or other small hard substance, so as to secure a firm and even

[1] *Laws of Ohio*, 1806.   [2] *Ibid.*, 1807.   [3] *Ibid.*, 1809.

surface." The Common Pleas Court must appoint three inspectors as soon as eight miles of the road was completed, and if the road had been constructed according to the specifications, the company was permitted to erect toll-gates not less than eight miles apart. The toll which the company could charge was fixed at the following rates:

Two-horse wagon.......................... 12½ cents.
For every additional horse............... 4 cents.
Wagon or cart drawn by one yoke of oxen.... 12½ cents.
For every additional ox................... 6   cents.
Coaches or other four-wheeled vehicles of
  pleasure................................. 20 cents.
Sulky chaise chair and other two-wheeled
  vehicle of pleasure .... 12½ cents.
Sleigh or sled............................. 8   cents.
Every score of hogs or sheep .... 10 cents.
Every head of neat cattle.................. 1   cent.
Every horse and rider, or led horse 6   cents.

"Except that all attending public worship or funerals, or jurymen going to or coming from court, armies and troops of Ohio and United States and all electors going to or coming from any election should pass free." A fine of five dollars was imposed upon any one who used a by-path around toll gates. If the company neglected to keep the road in repair for fifteen days the Justice of the Peace appointed three inspectors who examined the road as to its condition for transportation. If they reported adversely no toll could be charged and if the road was not repaired, before the next session of the Common Pleas Court was held, the officials of the company were subject to a fine of twenty to one hundred dollars each. A complete and accurate report must be made of all expenditures and receipts, and all capital stock must be paid in and expended before another issue was permitted. Dividends must be publicly declared twice a year, and every three years a financial report must be made to the state legislature. Every ten years a decennial report was made to the same body, and if the financial conditions warranted paying more than ten per cent. dividends, the surplus must be used in buying up the outstanding stock of the company. When all this stock was thus purchased, the road was to become a free turnpike. It will be observed how closely the state supervised and regulated the operation of this early company. If our later charters had followed the original in its regulative and protective features, it is probable that many evils in our later transportation history would have been avoided. The act did furnish a model for many of the later turnpike charters, but the people of the state became so anxious for transportation routes, that when more liberal terms were later demanded by the incorporators, they were willingly granted by the legislature.

The construction of improved highways by turnpike companies became after 1810 the favorite method in Ohio of securing roads, for it must be remembered that the Three Per Cent Fund was used in most cases to lay out roads. These oftentimes were not improved for many years, and the counties in most cases spent very little in improving the means of transportation. Ross County, which had been the early seat of the capital of the state, spent in 1813–14 only $89.70 for roads and bridges.[1] Much was done by the collective efforts of private individuals to secure and improve means of transportation, and something was accomplished by the federal government, which in 1814 had twenty-five post

[1] *Report of Treasurer of Ross County, Supporter* (Chillicothe), September 24, 1814.

roads in Ohio.   The rates of postage which are in a way
indicative of the transportation facilities were in 1814 as
follows:

> For any distance of 40 miles or under 12   cents.
> For any distance of 90 miles not exceeding 150. 18½ cents.
> For any distance of 150 miles not exceeding 300. 25½ cents.
> For any distance of 300 miles not exceeding 500. 37½ cents.
> Any paper if printed in the state for any dis-
>   tance not exceeding 100 miles .... 1½ cents.

The basis for the charge was purely a distance one, for
cost of carriage was almost wholly directly proportional
to distance.   During the period of Turnpike transportation the complaints about the delivery of mail were very
numerous, but this was in a large part due to the rapid
development of the Middle West.   No sooner was a mail
route laid out, than the settlement of other regions and
the consequent movement of population, together with
the changes in weather and the absence of bridges, made
the delivery of mail very uncertain.

Governor Worthington in his message to the legislature of 1816[1] recommended that the road law be so
amended as to assess the chief cost of improved roads
upon the land holders through whose land the road
passed, since he thought the adjacent owners received
the chief benefit from improved roads and waterways.
Although this recommendation was not followed, a new
road law was passed, which increased the powers of
supervisors and county commissioners and permitted the
tax levy for road purposes to be increased.   In 1817 the
governor again urged the necessity of constructing highways, and recommended the revision of the laws defining
the duties of supervisors, in as much as the existing

---

[1] *Laws of Ohio*, 1816.

ROAD MAP
OF
STATE OF OHIO
1828

laws did not fix responsibility. Governor Worthington urged that through roads should be constructed from the Lakes to the Ohio River, and from the east to the west, instead of using the Three Per Cent. Fund, and such state moneys as were appropriated to supplement this, in constructing local roads.[1] He believed that local roads should be provided by the local communities, and that what was most needed by the state in general was through transportation routes. In 1821 a state road tax was assessed and the proceeds were used to improve the highways within the state. The rates were as follows:

> On every 100 acres of first rate land············ 50   cents.
> On every 100 acres of second rate land········ 37½ cents.
> On every 100 acres of third rate land·········· 25   cents.

This act sought to place the building of roads in the hands of the township trustees and it was provided that the county treasurer should ascertain and pay to these Trustees the part contributed by the landowners of the township.[2] The auditor's report for 1823, shows that there were 226,084 acres of what was called first rate land, 6,870,920 acres of the second rate land, and 6,585,-449 of third rate land. Upon these three classes there was assessed a state tax of $141,053.71 of which $47,593.82 constituted the state road tax.[3]

In 1824 a legislative act fixed the width of state roads at 66 feet, county roads at 60 feet, and township roads at 40 feet.[4] This act for the first time defined the widths

---

[1] *Executive Documents*, 1817.

[2] *Laws of Ohio*, 1821. The United States lands were exempt from taxation for five years after purchase according to the terms of the agreement between the United States and Ohio.

[3] *Report of Auditor of State*, 1823.

[4] *Laws of Ohio*, 1824.

of the various roads and recognized the three classes of officials who might construct roads. During the early period the question of transportation was one of the chief subjects considered by the state legislature, for the state's development was retarded by the lack of roads and improved waterways. This interest in transportation is disclosed by the fact, that forty-four per cent. of all the local acts passed by the legislature of Ohio in 1825 referred to this subject and twenty-two per cent. of all the general acts referred directly to transportation.[1] This record was, however, exceeded by that of 1826 when fifty-five per cent. of all acts referred to transportation. The greater number of these acts had reference to roads.[2] By 1826 stage coaches were arriving at Columbus three times a week from Cincinnati, Chillicothe and Lancaster, and twice a week from Zanesville and Delaware. The decade of 1820 to 1830 and the one succeeding mark a period of rapid building of transportation routes in Ohio. The governor pointed out in his message to the legislature in 1827 that the location of the National Road had been decided, the routes of the state canals had been fixed, and the Erie Canal had been completed.[3] Everything in a transportation way looked encouraging and the people were urged to lay out a greater number of roads in order to make the most of the through east and west route,—the National Road—and the through north and south routes,—the canals and rivers.[4]

[1] *Laws of Ohio*, 1825.   [2] *Ibid.*, 1826.

[3] *Journal of the Senate*, 1827.

[4] *Cf. Cincinnati Gazette*, Sept. 12, 1837. "A new era in the prosperity of the city would be witnessed had we good roads to Chillicothe, Lexington, Indianapolis and Columbus. It is certain that the number of travelers between this city and Columbus would be increased tenfold, if there were any adequate provisions for getting from one point to the other without risking life. Cincinnati can be reached pleasantly

It will be recalled that the first private turnpike charter was granted in 1809 although it was not until after 1817 that these companies became numerous. The state roads laid out from the Three Per Cent Fund were not improved roads and did not supply the needs of the rapidly growing industrial society either as to number or character. These private turnpikes were well constructed, and as the terms of the charter usually provided that no toll could be collected unless the roads were kept in good repair, these were the only good roads in the state with the exception of the National and the Maumee roads and a few other roads near the large centers of population. Private capital could not be expected to build such roads unless a fair investment was clearly indicated, and for this reason improved roads awaited to a great extent the settlement and partial development of a district. But the people wanted roads to aid in this development, and when the question of constructing canals at public expense was decided in the affirmative, many people, particularly those of districts which did not secure a canal, insisted that the state should also aid in building highways and railroads. Since the sections of the state which secured canals also needed means of reaching them quickly and easily, the policy of state aid to both railways and highways was entered upon with general unanimity. This demand became expressed in the law of 1836[1] which authorized the governor to sub-

only in one way, and that is by the river. In the winter or in the wet and frosty season of the year the city is cut off from communication on every side. The farmer thinks the roads should be made by the inhabitants of the towns, for otherwise they would starve and freeze, while the inhabitants of the town think the farmer should make them because they increase the value of the land."

[1] *Laws of Ohio*, 1836.

scribe to the stocks of turnpike companies an amount
equal to that subscribed by private individuals. Previous
to this, however, the commissioners of counties had been
authorized to subscribe to the stock of any turnpike
company whose road lay within the county certain
amounts which were usually specified in the special act,
although sometimes the act authorized "the commissioners of X County to subscribe to and own any amount
of stock in X Turnpike Company that they may deem
proper."[1] When the state subscribed to the stock of such
companies, an annual report was required and subscription was prohibited to the stock of any road which would
affect the profits of one already constructed. In no case
was the road to be located within twenty miles of another
such road, nor was the total annual subscription to exceed three million dollars. In 1840 the auditor's report
showed that the state had subscribed $1,603,700 to such
companies, and by 1848 this had reached $1,921,675.71.[2]
The large amount which had been subscribed by 1837
and the pressing financial difficulties of the state caused
the auditor to report:

That the policy of the state in enacting this law (1836) was
doubtless instigated by sound views and capable of good purpose: but the extent to which it is pressing the public liabili-
ties, the abuses which it has engendered, and the present
condition of the state's finances, would seem to point with an
unerring finger to its suspension, if not to its final repeal.[3]

Some companies had secured the subscription and had
not built the roads, and, as the state's credit was becoming impaired, further expenditures were thought unwise,
until some of the past expenditures for public improve-

[1] *Laws of Ohio*, 1832.
[2] *Report of the Auditor*, 1848 and 1849.   [3] *Ibid.*, 1840.

ments had become more productive. The law was repealed in 1840 except in certain cases where the road
had been begun and part of the subscription had been
paid out. But in 1842 the auditor was directed to sus-
pend the issuing of warrants to turnpike companies for
state subscriptions, not only because there were no funds
for such a purpose but also because some of the outstanding warrants were running to protest. In 1844
the condition of the state treasury had become so serious that the board of public works, the treasurer and
auditor were forbidden to make any contract for the
extension of any public work.[1] The Three Per Cent
Fund continued to be a source of revenue for laying out
roads but this was decreasing in amount. When the
lands of the north-western part of the state were opened
for settlement by canals, road and railways the Fund
increased for a time. It is quite impossible to state
exactly what sums were subscribed by the local governments during the period of aid to turnpike companies,
since not infrequently their officials were authorized to
subscribe in any amounts which they deemed wise,
although such subscriptions could later be made only
upon vote of the people. After a careful tabulation of
the specific sums authorized, a very conservative estimate would place the sum equal to that subscribed by
the state, that is to say approximately two million dollars.

[1] Great difficulty was experienced during the early years in collecting
the land tax, and in this year the delinquent taxes amounted to one-
ninth of the total state tax levied. In many cases the return from the
land was uncertain both on account of the farmer being unable to
market the produce, and on account of the crops being more subject
than now to the condition of the weather. Then, too, the state tax
had become large, and as it was levied for a purpose from which many
derived little direct benefit, some thought there was further justification
for indifference as to payment.

Much litigation and difficulty was experienced by the state with the turnpike companies to whose stock it had subscribed. The companies not only disregarded the toll rates which the legislature had fixed but, in many cases, also refused to report either the amount of toll which had been collected or the use to which it had been put. In some cases the money from the bonds of the state issued for construction purposes was used to pay other expenses, and the state's share of the tolls was continually employed to pay company debts.[1] In an effort to secure greater uniformity and obedience to the toll laws the auditor recommended that :

Since the people of Ohio in their sovereign capacity as well as individually have expended large sums in the construction of Turnpike Roads, a commissioner should be appointed from each company which had received state aid, to meet with the commissioners of the purely private companies and the Board of Public Works to devise as nearly as possible uniform tolls.[2]

This recommendation resulted in the Turnpike Convention of 1844 which adopted a new schedule of tolls to take the place of that fixed by the law of 1817.[3] As these tolls prevailed in general throughout the Turnpike period, they are given in the following table:

[1] *Cf. Reports of Auditor*, 1840 and 1843. A fine of $500.00 was imposed in 1840 upon any turnpike official who refused to pay the dividend due the state, but when either no report or an incomplete one was filed it was impossible to determine what dividend was due. The Supreme Court of Hamilton County decided that the tolls belonging to the state could be used to pay company debts and the sum could be credited upon the drafts due from the state.

[2] *Ibid.*, 1843.

[3] However, in some cases certain special schedules had been established for companies at the time of their incorporation.

For every sheep............................ 2½ mills
For every hog 5   mills
For every head of cattle 6 mo. old and up $0.01
For every horse, mule or ass 0.03
For every horse, mule or ass with rider 0.06¼
For every vehicle of two or four wheels drawn
   by one animal............................ 0.12½
For every additional animal to such vehicle .. 0.06¼
For every four-wheeled vehicle, including
   coaches, stages, carriages, barouches, wagons,
   etc., drawn by two animals 0.25
For every additional animal to such vehicle .. 0.06¼
For every sled or sleigh drawn by one animal. 0.10
For every additional animal................. 0.05
For all wagons carrying not less than 5,000
   pounds, with a tire not less than 4 inches
   wide, a reduction of 25 per cent. from above
   rates.................................. 0.31
Additional toll was made for loads of over 5,000 pounds.[1]

As prosperity began to return in the forties and as the state had definitely ceased to aid in highway construction, the local governments began to construct free turnpikes. In 1843 these turnpikes were constructed under the act which authorized commissioners to lay out the road, receive donations and gifts and collect all tax levied on the land within two miles of the road. This plan gave the name Two-Mile Turnpikes to highways constructed under this act.[2] In 1845 the first general act for laying out and constructing highways was passed. Previous to this, special legislation was the rule in conferring authority to build a road, a railway, a bridge or to form a manufacturing company.[3] In the same year plank roads were begun, as they seemed to

[1] *Report of the Turnpike Convention*, 1844.

[2] In 1845 twenty-five such roads were authorized, and in 1846 thirty-seven.

[3] *Laws of Ohio*, 1845.

meet the demand for improved highways. These roads proved very popular for a time.[1]

It must be remembered that the West in general was a debtor class during this period, and although potentially wealthy, it needed means of transportation in order to realize on the immense natural resources. This fact will go far to explain, if not to justify, the enthusiasm of the West for state banks of issue, which gave to the people credit and an expanded currency in order to market their produce. Wheat was hauled from the north-central part of the state to Toledo, but the bulk of the farm crops, as compared with their value, limited the distance which they could be transported over the poor roads. Those districts near the National Road and the few other good roads fared better, and the transportation system as organized upon these roads was remarkably efficient.[2] There were three classes of transportation agencies: first, individual owners of six-horse teams who hauled freight east and west on contracts made for each trip; second, farmers along the line, who, during the slack farming season or when the charges were raised unduly high, went into the business temporarily; third, and by far the most important, large freight and passenger companies that owned many wagons and coaches. The first class had to conform to the regulations and charges laid down by the companies, for the "scab" wagoner was given treatment no less severe than that

[1] *Ohio Cultivator*, June 23, 1849. "Plank roads are rapidly finding favor in this state. They are constructed without steep grades and with numerous turnouts. The cost is about $2,000 per mile, and their duration, when hemlock is used, is about seven years. The advantages of this road are: (a) they can be used throughout the year; (b) heavier loads can be hauled; (c) cost of transportation is low."

[2] It was said that the farmer along the way knew the time of day from the passage of the coaches of these companies.

accorded in all trades to the present-day "scab." Charges were usually based on the hundred pounds per mile, but sometimes a general charge was made for a load. There was a certain *esprit de corps* among the regular drivers and transporters. It was a difficult matter to secure without influence a position in the transportation business on the National Road or the early turnpikes.[1] There was intense rivalry among the companies, and the particular kind of coach, the excellence of the horses, the sobriety of the drivers and the rapidity of travel were all considered fit subjects for advertisement.[2] In time as canals, railways and more roads were supplied, these companies ceased to operate in Ohio and the stage coach and freighter followed the frontier to the West until, pressed by the railway, they disappeared and their golden days are now known only in the literature descriptive of the period.

[1] Thomas Seabright, *The Old Pike.*

[2] *Cf. Cincinnati Gazette*, February 6, 1836. The chief companies were the Stockton, the Good Intent, the June Bug and the Pioneer. The fare in 1836 from Cincinnati to Wheeling via Columbus was $11.50. In 1829 the President's message was carried from Washington to Columbus in 34 hours and 45 minutes, "a performance unparalleled in the annals of traveling in this section." *Cf. Ohio State Journal*, Dec. 11, 1829. In 1846 the President's message was carried by one of these companies from Wheeling to Columbus in eight hours and one-half. *Cf. Ohio Statesman*, Dec. 11, 1846.

CHAPTER IX

Changes made in the Transportation and Industrial Problems by the Constitution of 1851

The constitution adopted in 1851 made such important changes in the policy of the state towards the subject of transportation and industry, and the debates upon this constitution so well reflected the prevailing views on these subjects, that it is worth our attention to consider briefly some of these changes and the views as expressed by the delegates. Those parts of the debates which concern our subject were upon the following points: (a) should the state continue its policy of directly aiding railroad and turnpike companies by means of stock subscriptions and by donations of land; (b) should transportation and industrial corporations be chartered under a general incorporation law or by special acts, as had been the practice; (c) what control should be exercised over such companies? The state had aided transportation and industrial corporations by donating funds and lands, by loaning its credit, by bounties and by exempting them from taxation. At this time its direct financial aid amounted to about $3,000,000, and it had by special laws empowered many local governments to subscribe a much larger sum to such companies. Much of this money had not been productively expended. Some of it had not even been expended for the purpose for which it had been appropriated, and in most cases there had been little direct financial return to the state and the local governments. Although this last result was not sufficient reason in itself why further aid should not be granted, yet this very failure to secure any adequate financial return affected considerably the decision of the delegates, since this fact and the financial policy which resulted from it had influenced unfavorably the fiscal legislation of the state.[1]

On the question of further state and local government aid to transportation companies, there were two divergent views. Each of these was an expression of the needs of the regions and interests represented. Those delegates who represented the more densely populated and wealthier sections were opposed to further state aid, inasmuch as by the past generosity of the state, the natural resources of their regions and their accumulated wealth they had satisfied at least the pressing demands for transportation. Quite naturally these delegates objected to paying for the transportation routes that were to be built in the less developed sections, since the expense of such routes would be met by general taxation, and, as their taxable property was much greater in value than that of the poorer districts, the greater part of the cost would fall upon their constituents. Again, they reasoned that although they would need more transportation facilities, it would be to their interest to leave this problem to each locality, since their increased wealth would enable them to build such routes. Whatever local tax would be raised for such purposes would be locally expended. The less populous, which were the less wealthy, sections contended that the state should continue its aid to transportation companies, since the re-

---

[1] The financial embarrassments of the state during the forties were believed by many to be the fruits of the state's policy in regard to internal improvements.

sults of such expenditures had reflected itself in the increased wealth of the regions. They had contributed according to their ability in supplying these routes to other sections, and they now demanded as a matter of justice, that the state should aid their districts or in any event should permit them as local governments to build routes upon a credit system and to subscribe to the stock of transportation companies. One of these delegates expressed this view when he said:

The people of Hamilton County (the Cincinnati district) have got the benefit of thieving, and now they want to prevent anybody else from enjoying the right of making improvements upon their own capital or capital which belongs to the state. Now these gentlemen from Cincinnati and all other points where they have railways made or where they have their roads in full progress and all their avenues of trade opened, want to shut the gate and prevent the people living in other sections of the state from constructing arms and branches to these great roads.[1]

But these districts of small wealth and small population were outvoted by the more populous sections. Another question which occasioned an animated debate was, whether the state could and should tax the holders of stocks and bonds issued to secure funds for the internal improvements. The original act which provided for the issue of these bonds declared that

the faith of the state is hereby pledged that no tax shall ever be levied by the legislature on the stock to be created by virtue of this act nor on the interest that may be payable

[1] *Report of the Debates and Proceedings of the Convention for the Revision of the Constitution of the State of Ohio*, 1850–1851. "Remarks of Mr. Brown of Carrol County."

thereon, and further, that the value of said stock shall in no way be impaired by any legislative act of this state.[1]

The object of this very liberal provision was to attract funds by which to engage upon these internal improvements, for in the midst of this period of competition among various states for funds, ready capital was not easy to obtain. The language of this provision would seem to be clear as to the intention of the legislature, but the fundamental question now up for consideration was, could the legislature of 1825 bind the action of this convention, which was the sovereign body assembled through its representatives. But if these delegates did repudiate these former obligations and tax the stocks and bonds, would this be in effect a repudiation of financial obligations or debts? This was an act which no delegate was willing to admit he favored. Yet many wished to tax these bonds, if they could sufficiently refine the phrase "state repudiation." After a time they based their argument on the ground that no former legislature had the right to barter away this attribute of sovereignty, the right of taxation. In reply to this argument numerous court decisions were cited by their opponents, which indicated that such taxation would impair a contract made by the state and would therefore be in conflict with the constitution of the United States.[2]

Until 1836 the credit of the state was good and many contended that capital was easily secured on account of

---

[1] *Laws of Ohio*, 1825. This was the act which provided for the first loan to build the canals.

[2] *Cf. 7 Cranch*, 164, State of New Jersey *vs.* Wilson. *8 Wallace*, 430, Home of The Friendless *vs.* Rouse. The Supreme Court of the United States denied to states the power of taxing bonds, issued under such conditions.

this exemption. Although the exemption clause had
not been repeated in most of the acts following the
original one of 1825, it was doubtless assumed to apply
both by the borrower and the lender. From 1836 to
1846 many financial devices were necessary to keep the
state government in operation, and many of the delegates
remembering this experience were disposed to prevent
the state from engaging in internal improvements. In
the constitutional convention it was stated:

Every railroad that the people of Ohio have made with
their own money, everything that tends to render of less value
any of the improvements of the state might be called impair-
ing the original value of these bonds, as well as the proposed
taxation. It is strange that vested rights can only be seen in
that species of property that finds its sympathies in men's
pockets. The state of Ohio engaged in speculation in internal improvements in 1825. Lobbies of capitalists and
those interested in the particular improvement secured the
further aid. The state became the victim of the speculator
and the capitalist. All the original bondholders sold out at a
sacrifice. The state has since made up the deficits of this
period by taxation, or in other words, the generation of the
present, whose money has been spent by the previous generation without its opinion having been asked upon the expenditure, is now ready to pay a principal and interest, upon the
debt, asking only that since it was a joint error, that the implied joint risk be assumed by the bond-holder as well as the
people. I wish Ohio would pass a law removing her register
office from New York, depriving the stock market of that city
of its nourishment. The state of New York has lured her
sister states by false appearances into egregious financial
blunders. It is her system of internal improvements, decep-
tive in appearance, that has done more mischief throughout
the Union than any system yet devised. New York is the
door through which the vast produce of the great west must

pass to reach the commercial world. She stands there as a tax-gatherer, levying in direct and undenied violation of the Constitution of the United States toll upon the industry, and this it is, which has made her system of internal improvements successful. The false glare of that success deceived her weaker sisters, and I hesitate not to say had each never possessed a dollar's worth of credit, as intended by the framers of the Constitution, their people would have been happier and this day possessed better internal improvements than they have received under the debt-contracting policy.[1]

We have quoted at length from these remarks because they represented the views of a large body of delegates, who exerted considerable influence upon the provisions which were adopted. The stock of turnpike, bridge and manufacturing companies had been exempted from taxation for a term of years, but the constitution, as adopted, provided for the taxation of the property of such corporations. One delegate expressed the view "that capital would soon send the iron horse along the lines of every canal and that the too expensive canals would soon be useless as transportation routes."[2] This delegate was however from a county along the Ohio River and did not appreciate the difficulties of transportation for those who were distant from any routes; such for example as the producers of Wayne County, who hauled their wheat seventy miles to Cleveland in order to reach a market and to secure such necessities as salt and groceries. Complaint was very generally made in the debates concerning the great injury which transportation companies inflicted in locating their rights of way. The

---

[1] *Constitutional Debates, op. cit.* "Remarks of Mr. Reemelin of Hamilton County."

[2] *Ibid.* "Remarks of Mr. Archbold of Monroe County."

company generally assumed that the benefit from having a railway through the land was of greater value than the land occupied and damages resulting. The right of way was in the early period almost invariably donated, but the abuses had become so great that some remedy was demanded. A law was later passed which provided for an appraisement by disinterested parties. Corporations for both transportation and industrial purposes had become numerous, and since the shortcomings of the railway and turnpike companies were assigned by some delegates to all corporations, some restrictions seemed wise. The views of those favoring a liberal treatment were well expressed by one who said:

> What have corporations done? They have built your churches; they have bridged impassable streams; they have erected colleges; they have made roads, railways and telegraph lines. With the little wealth we have in Ohio, there would have been no other way of carrying out those great objects of public necessity and convenience than by the means of corporate associations.[1]

There was a long debate upon the question of general *versus* special incorporation of companies. Notwithstanding the unfortunate experience of the people with the transportation corporations, there was very little desire expressed by the delegates to curtail the organization of corporations. In fact one of the arguments against a general incorporation law was that it would tend to discourage organization, since it was thought that no general law could confer the particular privileges needed for different kinds of corporations. The major-

[1] *Constitutional Debates, op. cit.,* "Remarks of Mr. Stanberry of Franklin County."

ity, however, favored a general law for the following reasons: (a) it would economize the time of the legislature, which had in many sessions devoted most of its time to debating and granting special charters for transportation and industrial companies; (b) it would prevent the granting of undue privileges and powers, which were often concealed by innocent titles or hidden in appended clauses. Still others thought that under a general act corporations would unduly multiply and "railroad companies would start up like mushrooms and prejudice the earnings of other companies and the internal improvements of the state."[1] All agreed that the legislature should retain the power of regulating the charge for transportation. Some thought that this could be done best by fixing a maximum charge, while others held that the earnings should be regulated by fixing a maximum dividend. As a result of all this discussion the following provisions were agreed upon and placed in the new constitution:

(a) The credit of the state shall not in any manner be given or loaned to or in aid of any individual association or corporation whatever; nor shall the state hereafter become a joint owner or stockholder in any company or association in this state or elsewhere formed for any purpose whatever.

(b) The General Assembly shall never authorize any county, city, town or township by vote of its citizens or otherwise to become a stockholder in any joint stock company, corporation or association whatever; or to raise money for or loan its credit to or in the aid of any such company, corporation or association.[2]

---

[1] *Constitutional Debates, op. cit.*, "Remarks of Mr. Nash of Ross County."

[2] This did not in fact prevent the local governments from building transportation routes.

(c) The General Assembly shall pass no special act conferring corporate powers.

(d) Laws shall be passed taxing by a uniform rule all moneys, credits, investments in bonds, stocks and joint stock companies.

(e) The property of corporations now existing or hereafter created shall forever be subject to taxation, the same as the property of individuals.[1]

However, by later decisions of the Supreme Court of Ohio the clause in regard to special legislation was practically made inoperative, and a mass of legislation, special in application but general in form, was passed until by a later reversal of the court a great part of this was declared unconstitutional and the general-law clause became operative.

Many of the local governments, as we shall later notice, did engage in the building of transportation routes. The most extraordinary example was the construction of an interstate railway by the city of Cincinnati.

---

[1] *Laws of Ohio*, 1851. "Constitution of Ohio."

CHAPTER X

The Development of Railways

From the time of the earliest settlement and organization of Ohio, the people of the region were actively interested in internal improvement. Not only was the state the gateway between the East and the West but it also possessed a fertile soil and a variety of natural resources. Although the first important settlements were along the natural waterways, the fertility and resources of the interior region soon attracted settlers, and a demand for transportation routes was made when the possibility of abundant production was realized. The subject of transportation thus assuming such importance led to a fostering attitude on the part of the state toward canals and highways, and finally toward railways. For this reason and the additional one that the state would gain much from the movement of the traffic of other regions through her borders, there was an absence of that radicalism which at certain periods characterized the railway legislation of other states. The people of the state in their sovereign capacity and as individuals subscribed liberally from their limited means to the stock of transportation companies and donated their lands freely to such companies. Facility of transportation was the one necessary thing to bring wealth to the people of Ohio. So rapid was the increase of wealth and population, which resulted from the highways and canals already constructed, that a spirit of enterprise was developed in the people, peculiarly favorable to the adoption of the next improved system of transportation,—the railroad. Although the enthusiasm for means of transportation had in no sense abated, yet because the state was undertaking such large financial obligations for canal construction and because railways when first suggested were regarded as supplementary to canals, they became without any considerable discussion private enterprises.

The early interest of the people of Ohio in railroads is indicated by the fact that in 1830 a charter was granted to the Ohio and Steubenville Railroad Co. At this time there had not been opened a railway upon which steam was used as a motive power, and the celebrated trial of motive power in which George Stephenson's Rocket won the prize had been held in England but four months earlier. The progress of the Liverpool and Manchester Railway was closely followed in this country, and its success was used as an argument for the construction of railroads in the United States. Many, however, did not think that railroads would be of great value. The Pennsylvania Board of Public works reported that:[1]

While the Board avow themselves favorable to railroads, when it is impracticable to construct canals or under some peculiar circumstances, yet they cannot forbear expressing their opinion that the advocates of railways generally have greatly overrated their comparative value. It will be found that canals are from two to three and a half times better than railroads for the purpose required of them by Pennsylvania. Railroads can be made to carry the United States mail, passengers, and light valuable goods, when time is of more importance than cost of transportation.

[1] *Report of the Pennsylvania Board of Commissioners of Public Works*, quoted in *Ohio State Journal*, Jan. 2, 1832.

However, many people who thought they would not receive any direct benefit from the numerous canals which were being constructed by state funds, saw in the railroad a means of receiving equal benefits and urged the state to subscribe to the stock of railway companies, while they prepared at the same time to further the project by private aid.

The provisions of the first charter which are of especial interest were as follows:[1]

(a) The power "to transport, take and carry persons and property by the power and force of steam, of animals and any combination of them."

(b) The capital stock was limited to $500,000, with the provision that no part of the capital stock or the proceeds arising therefrom should be used in banking.

(c) The power was given to take public lands.

(d) The power "to regulate the time and manner in which goods and passengers shall be transported thereon and the manner of collecting tolls for such transportation and to erect and maintain toll houses and other buildings for the accommodation of their concern."

(e) The power "to demand and receive from all persons, using or traveling upon the railroad the following rates of toll, to wit: for every ton weight of goods or freight of any description three cents per mile for every mile the same shall pass upon the said road and at a ratable proportion for any greater or less quantity; for every pleasure carriage or carriages used for the conveyance of passengers three cents per mile in addition to the toll by weight upon the loading."

(f) All persons who should pay the prescribed toll might "with suitable and proper carriages use and travel upon the said railroad subject to such rules and regulations as the corporations are authorized to make."

[1] This was the first charter issued in Ohio and the second one in the United States.

(g) "Any person who willfully injured the railroad, buildings, or machines of the company should pay to the corporation three times the amount of the damage sustained."[1]

This railroad, like many others chartered from 1830 to 1850, was not constructed, but the charter formed the basis for the later ones, that were granted. However, the ten charters granted in 1832 introduced some new features. Provision was made that the appraisers in valuing the damages which resulted from taking the land should set off against this the increased value resulting to the land; the state was permitted in some cases to become a stockholder, and provisions were inserted to regulate tolls in harmony with canal tolls. Although at first few supposed that the railroad would be a direct competitor of canals, competition did soon appear, and whenever a proposed railway promised to compete with canals, the large obligations of the state, incurred for canal construction, were used as an argument against granting such a charter. This argument was not often successfully used, but it did result in a submission by some of the railway companies to a provision in their charter, whereby they agreed to pay to the state "such amounts annually as in the opinion of the Board of Public Works would be equivalent to one-half the tolls charged by the state at the time upon like property transported by canals during the season of navigation but for the existence of the railroad." Even as late as 1847 the Cincinnati, Hamilton and Dayton Railroad agreed to a provision in its charter that:

Whenever the revenues derived by the state from the Miami Canal shall be diminished by the operation of said road below

---

[1] *Cf. Laws of Ohio*, 1830, for the charter in full.

what it now is, it shall be lawful for the Board of Public Works to impose upon all property transported upon said road such tolls as will be sufficient to replace the revenues so diminished, which tolls so imposed said company shall pay to the members of the Board of Public Works.[1]

These provisions were, as will be shown later, observed only in part by the railways. At every session of the legislature there was a great deal of lobbying for the purpose of securing favorable charters, although little difficulty was experienced in obtaining any number of charters. The following table shows the freedom with which companies were incorporated and at the same time the difficulty of procuring the means with which to build the roads:[2]

Year	Number of companies incorporated	Number of companies which built their road
1830–1840	24	1
1840–1850	23	8
1850–1865	67	16
1865–1870	73	9

The people were anxious to obtain transportation facilities, and, while many of these companies were organized in good faith by those who thought them warranted by the industrial conditions, other companies were organized purely for personal gain. Organizers knew that the people of the state were enthusiastic over railways and would purchase the stock. These speculators were able

[1] *Laws of Ohio*, 1847.

[2] *Files of incorporated companies in the office of Secretary of State.* The following years are not given because they would be no evidence of the increase of transportation routes, since many of the articles of incorporation after this date were to combine two or more roads or for a large road to acquire a short line.

for many years to capitalize the zeal of the people, and one reason assigned for the establishment of the Railroad Commission in 1867 was to "diffuse such information as would enable the people to intelligently invest in railroad securities."[1] Exaggeration of profits to be derived, extensive advertising and desire for means of transportation led the people to subscribe liberally to the stock of the companies. Some of the earlier charters provided that when the authorized stock was over-subscribed, the directors should reduce the same by striking off from the largest number of shares in succession until the subscription should be reduced to the proper number composed of subscriptions to one share, and that if there should still be an excess, then lots should be drawn to determine who were to be excluded.[2] There is no case on record when it was necessary to resort to this provision, but on the contrary no original subscription as applied was sufficient to place the road in operation. Railroad conventions during the thirties became very numerous, and the first good effects of the canals only increased the enthusiasm of those who were receiving their benefits and heightened the desire for some adequate means of transportation on the part of those who had no canals. In the northeastern section of the state there was much railway agitation, since this region had benefited very largely from the Erie and the Ohio canals and had early perceived its advantageous position on the route of east and west trade. Sandusky was the pioneer city of Ohio in actual railroad building, and its enterprise was cited by the agitators in the other sections of Ohio as worthy of emulation. No other class did more to further popular subscriptions to railways than the editors

[1] *Laws of Ohio*, 1867.   [2] *Ibid.*, 1838.

of newspapers, who incited local pride by describing what other sections were doing, by the argument that railroads would make work, by holding out the danger of the control of the railways by foreign capital and by minimizing the accidents upon the early roads.[1]

In the East, stock subscriptions were at first solicited from house to house for some of the roads to the West, and no hope was held out of a direct return. It was expected however that the people of New York, Philadelphia and Baltimore would indirectly derive such benefits from the Western trade that all might well contribute. When individuals subscribed to the stock, mortgages on their property were frequently given, as is shown by the report of the Bellefontaine and Indiana Railroad in 1852, which exhibits a list of town lots and farms conveyed to the road. These properties were offered as security for a loan of $200,000 and comprised 213 lots in different towns in several counties and 57 farms, almost all of which contained less than one hundred acres. This indicates that it was the small property holder who probably suffered most from this method of subscription. The right of way was not only usually donated but a subscription was also frequently made from which but a small per cent of the donors ever realized a dollar on the investment as such. In most cases the subscription of each individual was small as compared to the total amount subscribed, but it fre-

---

[1] The newspapers were careful to explain that the accidents were not due to the nature of the railroad. Later they did make much of the "horrible accident," but this was after railways had become powerful and some of their abuses had developed. In fact, the accidents were one of the important reasons advanced for a railroad commission in 1867. In this early period many of the people had strange ideas of railroads, for few of them had ever seen a railroad and could be made to believe almost anything about it.

quently represented a large sum from the point of view of the subscriber's possessions. It is true that some value resulted to the landowners along the way, yet many gave without any fair return. Since the original stock subscriptions proved inadequate to build the railroads, provisions were inserted in the old charters or attached to the new ones which gave the companies power to borrow money, and to pledge their income and stock for its payment. Soon every available method was used to increase the capital stock and bonds, although this was supposed to be carefully provided for by the charters and laws. Only ten per cent of the capital stock was required to be paid in before the election of the directors, who were then authorized to "borrow money on the credit of the corporation not exceeding its authorized capitalization." This capital stock could be then increased "to such amounts as may be decided to be necessary or required," and bonds could be issued to two-thirds of the authorized capitalization. As a result of such liberal terms, the inducements to credit railroad building were very great and naturally enough "the public were deceived by boards of directors who falsified their accounts and presented reports which were not true. Subscriptions were obtained until the parties behind the scenes stepped out, leaving the innocent and deluded outsiders suffering to bear the burdens placed upon them by dishonest and stupid managers."[1] In many cases dividends were paid in stock, for this was an easy way to save present cash, if there was any, and to capitalize future earnings. Thus nearly all the early railroads in Ohio were built on an extended system of credit and a temporizing policy. Failure and insolvency

[1] *Report of Railroad Commissioner*, 1875.

of some companies resulted before the temporary completion of the roads. Insolvent companies were carried through financial periods by individual exertions only to be swallowed up and overwhelmed by the next crisis, and "out of this insolvent condition grew extravagance, speculation, gambling and stock jobbing in every department of railroad management."[1]

If the state and local governments and the people, by popular subscription, had not come to the aid of the companies, some of the most important roads would not have been built for may years, and the rapid extension of the system would have been delayed. During the decade from 1830 to 1840 very little was done in actual construction, and whatever progress had been made was checked by the panic of 1837.

Partly because popular stock subscriptions could not be secured in sufficient amounts, partly because the companies were not able to borrow enough money without having something tangible to offer as security, and partly because of the people's impatience to secure railroads, the law of 1837 was passed. It authorized a loan of credit by the state to railroad companies, and a subscription to the stock of turnpike, canal and slack water navigation companies. Under this law the following loans were made to railway companies:

> To the Mad River and Lake Railroad Company.. $270,000
> To the Little Miami Railroad Company 115,000
> To the Mansfield and Sandusky City Company... 33,333
> To the Ohio Railroad Company................. 249,000
> To the Painesville and Fairport Railroad........ 6,182
> To the Ashland and Vermillion Railroad 44,000
>
> Total..................................... $717,515

[1] *Report of Railroad Commissioner*, 1868.

The legislature thought this a large sum, but it did not prove enough to build seventy miles of road, for the cost of all the early roads was underestimated, notwithstanding the fact that they were cheaply built with light rails and little or no ballast. This fact of actual overestimated cost, with the additional financial difficulties of the periods of inflation and depreciation of the currency, led to a demand for higher rates, and most of the roads openly disregarded the charters and laws which limited the rates. The loans made by the state to the last three of the above companies were entire losses; par was realized on the little Miami loan, but most of the amount in the remaining cases was lost.[1] Owing to the numerous accusations of fraud and extravagance the loan act was repealed in 1840. The bank troubles of the forties were responsible for a considerable opposition to railroads, for they were also corporations against which much criticism was made. As a result a law very objectionable to railroads was passed in 1842, which until its repeal in 1845 discouraged investments in railway stock. The continual attempts of the railroad companies to have damages to the land written off by the benefits resulting from the existence of the road, led to a law in the same year which required a deposit for damages which might occur from the construction of the railways. The state debt had reached the enormous sum of $18,668,321.61 by 1844, and there was little prospect that the state would grant further aid in building railways. Yet the demand for such

[1] When the Board of Public Works was authorized to sell the personal property of the Ohio R. R. Co. in 1844 in order to realize something from the State's loan, subscription of stock, gift of land and labor, which as a total amounted to $557,756, it was reported that this property had disappeared at the dissolution sale in 1842, and they were able to find only one set of car wheels, one locomotive and one saw-mill.

roads was none the less pressing, and by 1846, when prosperity returned, this demand secured expression in a law which permitted the local governments to aid private companies in building railroads. Although the state's experience had admittedly been a failure, the people needed transportation means and felt that public aid in some form was necessary to secure them. They also believed that the local governments could and would protect better the investments of the public money, since the local community would directly receive the benefit. Although most of the special acts empowering such subscriptions by the local governments specified the amount to be subscribed, it was not uncommon to find an act empowering the county commissioners of X county "to subscribe to the stock of any railroad that passed through or terminated in the county." Most of the subscriptions were made only upon vote of the people. There was practically no opposition to these bills in the legislature, for it came to be regarded as largely a local question whether such an obligation was to be assumed, and, if so, in what amounts. When it became fairly evident in 1850 that the new constitutional convention would prohibit this power, many such bills were introduced. From a careful examination of laws passed during this period a total authorized subscription of $6,878,000 has been found. This, however, did not by any means include the whole sum, since in some cases the subscription was not specified, nor does it include the subscriptions of the later period. Estimating all these subscriptions, a conservative sum for the direct subscription by the state and local governments would be $40,000,000. The constitution of 1851 prevented the state from further loaning its credit to railroad companies, and the effect as considered by many is expressed as follows :[1]

Many of the roads are needed at the proposed points of termini and along their routes, yet it is found almost impossible to secure a stock subscription from the citizens sufficient to build the road, and in many cases not sufficient to commence the road. The constitution and laws of the state prohibit subscription by the counties and municipalities, and the liability of every stockholder for an equal amount in addition to his stock amounts to so great a barrier as to defeat every effort to raise stock subscriptions sufficient to do the grading and masonry. In addition to this is the experience of a large majority of the companies, and especially of the short lines which depend upon local traffic, that the roads will not pay. The aid and coöperation of towns and cities to whose growth and prosperity the roads so largely contribute should be given. In this way can we alone hope to compete with those states and territories where liberal subsidies are granted, and where municipal and other corporations are authorized to aid in the construction of railways by subscribing to the capital stock.[2]

A summary of the financial condition of the railways in Ohio in the year 1868 shows that there were thirty-five corporations in the state with 3200 miles of track. Of these thirty-five corporations only seven had ever paid a dividend and these represented only 540 miles of track ; that is to say, less than seventeen per cent of the total state mileage had ever paid any dividend. There had been paid into these thirty-five companies in stock $172,047,542.38 ; the average amount of stock per mile

---

[1] *Cf.* chap. ix for changes made by this constitution in transportation and industrial organization.

[2] *Report of Commissioner of Railways*, 1868.

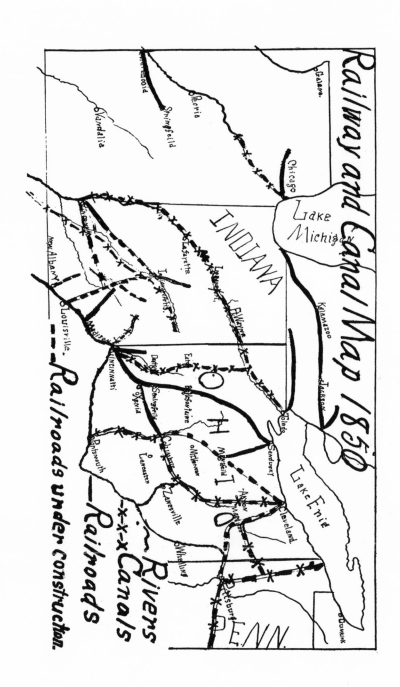

Railway and Canal Map 1850

Galena.
Chicago
Peoria
Springfeild
Vandalia
Lake Michigan
INDIANA
Lafayette
Kalamazoo
Jackson
Fort Wayne
New Albany
Louisville.
Lincinnatti
Cincinnatti
Madison
Toledo
Sandusky
Lake Erie
Springfield
Cleveland
Dayton
Bellsville
Columbus
Millersour
Mansfield
Akron
Lancaster
Zanesville
Wheeling
Pittsburg
Dunkirk
PENN.

~ Rivers
-x-x-x Canals
— Railroads
- - - Railroads under construction.

was $31,740; the total debt was $41,605,769.61 and the average amount of debt and stock per mile was $56,309.23.

The local desire for railroads led to the act of 1871 which permitted local governments to aid in railway construction. The law was however declared unconstitutional. Yet the willingness to aid in such construction is shown by the fact that although the law was in operation only six months, $6,000,000 in bonds, as required by the act, had been deposited with the treasurer of the state. Nothing further was done toward securing government aid until 1880 when a law was passed which authorized certain local governments to build and operate railroads. Under this act four roads were built but none was of importance except the Cincinnati Southern Railway.

The presidents of the early railway companies were often men skilled in law or politics, selected with the expectation that their social position or personal success in other pursuits would go far toward popularizing the enterprise and securing the necessary means to carry forward the work. High premiums were paid for men and means to meet temporary emergencies, without knowing or regarding what the future effects would be on the interests of the company. Much was also done to create a favorable attitude among the people by selecting courteous employees who would care for the comfort of the traveller.[1] The cost of the early railroads was greatly underestimated, for in addition to knowing little about railroads, the people were anxious to build them

[1] *Cleveland Herald*, Oct. 7, 1850. A traveler from Sandusky to Cincinnati in 1850 comments favorably upon "the excellent management of the road, the competency and carefulness of the engineers, the attention and politeness of the conductors, the freedom from rowdyism and the excellent language of subordinates and the frequent distribution of cold water through the train."

with the comparatively small means which they possessed. In preparing the road-bed the dirt was usually thrown up enough to receive the ties, for most of the roads were not ballasted until long after construction, and then at first only poorly, since equipment was light. The bridges in many cases were substantial as compared with the remainder of the way, but in time proved too weak to support the heavier locomotives which came in response to the demand for a heavier load. They were usually built of wood, although stone in some cases was employed, and iron came into general use after the civil war. In 1868 there were in Ohio 746 wooden, 65 stone, and 18 iron bridges. The contractors for the construction work often took stock in part payment, and in fact the securing of a contract sometimes hinged on the amount of stock which one or the other contractor was willing to take. Many of the incorporators had exaggerated ideas of what railways would accomplish in the carrying business and laid double tracks. The iron rails were frequently secured in England. Those for the Cincinnati, Columbus and Cleveland Railway were shipped from England via Montreal.[1] A traveler over this road complains that the greatest inconvenience " is the lack of the T rail on a considerable portion of the road. The flat-rail and the rough condition of the track gives a motion to the cars at times as unsteady as the bouncing of the lumbering stage over the early corduroy roads of the West.[2] The Cincinnati, Hamilton and Dayton secured its rails from England via New Orleans. These rails cost fifty dollars per ton at Cincinnati and were T rails weighing sixty-five pounds to the yard. By 1870 steel rails were being used and " the policy of using these

---

[1] *Cleveland Herald*, May 21, 1849.   [2] *Ibid.*, Oct. 7, 1850.

rails in renewals was already showing results in reducing the expense of maintenance."[1]   Locomotives were built at the Cuyahoga Iron works by 1850 and the first one in Ohio is described as "exceeding in power any other engine of the same weight and as a specimen of beauty and complete finish, surpassing that of any other engine that has been constructed in this country or in England."[2] Wood was used as a fuel in all the early engines.   Coal was not generally used until after 1870 when the great coal-fields of the southeastern part of the state were reached by railroads.

In the early period of railroads the passenger business was of greater relative importance than freight, for it was much easier to attract passengers than freight, and moreover the road was not built substantially enough to transport large amounts of the latter.   It required years of continual improvement to make the railways competitors of the waterways in transporting the bulky products long distances.   Most of the freight which was carried in the early period consisted either of raw products originating near the line and carried to canal and river points or merchandise distributed from these points. The advocates of canals were fond of saying that a railroad occupied a middle ground between a canal and a good turnpike, and the fact that a railway could be built anywhere was a disadvantage in that it would lead to insecurity of property values, because as soon as the railroad was built and had proven a success, another competitor would be built along the side of it.   Extensive sales of surplus products in 1840 were practically confined to wheat, corn, flour, pork, whiskey and tobacco,

[1] *Fourth Report of Cleveland, Columbus and Indianapolis Railroad Company*, 1871.

[2] *Cincinnati Gazette*, Oct. 13, 1837.

and the bulk of this moved to New Orleans via river. In October, 1831, the Baltimore and Ohio railroad had carried only 593 tons of freight but had carried 81,905 passengers. The novelty and rapidity of travel by railroad as compared with all other previous methods attracted many passengers. When the Cincinnati, Hamilton and Dayton was opened in 1852, only passenger trains were operated; but when freight trains were placed on the road at the end of the second year, the receipts, notwithstanding the fact that this road ran along the canal, showed that the following products had been carried: flour, 100,000 barrels; apples, eggs and clover seed, 21,702 barrels; whiskey, 45,000 barrels; meats, 28,-000 barrels; grain, 500,000 barrels; merchandise, 74,000 tons.[1] The extent of east and west-bound traffic is seen from the Pennsylvania and New York Central reports in 1859. The east-bound freight on the Pennsylvania was 353,164 tons and on the New York Central 570,927 tons. The west-bound was 190,705 tons on the former and 263,392 tons on the latter.

After the Central West had been settled and thus made a source of supply of raw products, as well as a market for the finished goods of the East, each seaboard city endeavored to secure a through route to the West. New York sought its route at first by the Erie Canal and Great Lakes; Philadelphia at first by turnpike, later by canals and still later by rail; Baltimore by turnpike, canals, and then by rail, while New Orleans had to rely upon improvements in the river and boats. All the early roads were short lines, and one of a hundred miles was decidedly the exception. The task of consolidating these required many years and various devices with

[1] *Report of Cincinnati, Hamilton and Dayton Railroad Company*, 1853.

which much complaint and frequent scandal were connected. The people of Ohio at first favored for obvious reasons these consolidations and furthered them by enacting favorable legislation. The first important act in reference to consolidations was passed in 1851 and permitted any two companies to consolidate by filing with the secretary of state the agreement. Any stockholder who opposed such consolidation could be paid par for his stock. This law also permitted a road to aid any other road in construction work with a view to future consolidation, and in this way many lines were undoubtedly completed which otherwise would have failed for want of funds. Sometimes a more prosperous road would take advantage of a poorer road lying in the way of its progress to some desired commercial point by a policy of exclusion and of non-intercourse, until the income of the weaker road was so reduced as to render it valueless to stockholders, a burden to its creditors and inefficient in its service. This contest for the Ohio railroads soon assumed large proportions, the three chief contestants being the New York Central, the Erie, and the Pennsylvania. The Erie attempted to purchase control of the Columbus, Chicago and Indiana Railroad, but the Pennsylvania secured it first, and then in revenge the Erie endeavored to get control of the Pittsburgh, Ft. Wayne and Chicago R. R., which was closely affiliated with the Pennsylvania. The latter company, however, obtained a special act from the legislature of Pennsylvania which retained in office three-fourths of the Board of Directors of the Ft. Wayne Railroad. The Erie with equal success used the New York legislature. In 1869 the railroad lobby assembled for the first time in the halls of the Ohio legislature. Notwithstanding the clause in the Ohio constitution that forbade the legislature to pass any act conferring special corporate powers, which it was thought would be sufficient to save the state from the disgraces of Pennsylvania and New York, a host of bills fathered by the railroad lobby was introduced. One permitted the lease of any Ohio railroad without any of the restrictions of the previous act, while another forbade the lease of any Ohio railroad unless such road would file a sworn statement with the auditor of the state showing that it was solvent, a condition which was prohibitive in many cases, and particularly so in the case that it was designed to cover. The New York Central R. R. refused to sell tickets or send freight over certain roads friendly to the Erie. The Erie placed on Lake Erie a line of boats from Cleveland to Dunkirk to compete with the New York Central.[1] In addition to the above causes of complaint, representatives of various roads began to hold conventions for fixing rates and deciding on what increase of rates should be made when the navigation of the river, canals and lakes should close. Expressions of opposition to consolidations and rate agreements were not lacking:

The tens of thousands of merchants in the country cannot enter into a convention and combine against the railroad. The contest is unequal, and will lead to results which will demand the attention of the public. In the case of railroads we are especially opposed to combinations because we know that nine-tenths of the stock in these great corporations is not held by the original subscribers, but by speculators in stocks who have little claim on public sympathy. If four great companies can agree upon rates, why not all in the country try? The last would be more difficult to effect, but more dangerous in principle.[2]

[1] *Cleveland Herald*, Aug. 2, 1858.
[2] *Cincinnati Gazette*, Sept. 23, 1859.

The truth is that the majority of the directors in our corporations are dummies. If the history and inside workings
of corporations could be exposed not only would the world
come to the conclusion that corporations have no soul, but
that all the brains lie in one head.   Those who hold stock in
any railroad at all liable to attack, fear to hold shares, the
value of which may at any time be held at the mercy of a
gang of Wall Street sharpers, who rob friend and foe alike
without pity and without remorse.[1]

Cincinnati, the chief commercial center of Ohio, was
unfriendly at first to consolidations but when she realized
that they were to be an accomplished fact and, that the
great through lines were passing to the north of her, she
endeavored to secure connection with the routes to the
east.

Can our trade with the northwest be sustained while the
railroads to the north of us carry freight cheaper than the
Cincinnati roads? We need not tell our merchants that the
trade which existed not many years ago between Cincinnati
and Pittsburgh has been largely destroyed, and that the trade
with the west from Cincinnati in manufactures of iron and
glassware has been entirely diverted from us by competing
routes.   Chicago supplies Pittsburgh with her manufactures.[2]

The New Orleans trade had been a decreasing one as
compared with New York, but after the extension of the
Pennsylvania, the New York Central and other lines
from Ohio into the regions northwest of Cincinnati, this
city confined herself largely to the cultivation of the
southern trade in which she had always predominated

---

[1] *Cleveland Herald*, June 22, 1867. This complaint was largely due
to the fact that a law required a certain proportion of the stockholders
and directors of Ohio railroads to be residents of the state.

[2] *Cincinnati Gazette*, March 15, 1861.

and upon which her real greatness has always rested.
After the consolidation had progressed to some extent,
fast freight lines were formed. Other causes leading to
their formation were the Civil War, which closed southern
ports to the products of the North except at great risk,
and the growing demand in Europe for American products, especially breadstuffs. Owing to the high prices
and the fear that the opening of the Mississippi would
cause a part of their traffic to move by way of the river,
the railroad companies hesitated to build the extra cars
necessary to carry this produce. Notwithstanding the
evils connected with the operations of these fast freight
companies, they rendered, at a time when companies were
numerous, a valuable service by insuring the continuous
movement and security of goods, as well as the payment
of damages that were received in transit. Their agents
stimulated the traffic. They did not wait for business;
they went after it; and it was chiefly the anxiety of these
agents to secure business which led to favoritism in rates
and the numerous rate wars. They were the real soldiers
in the battles of railroad *versus* railroad and railroad *versus*
waterways. Express and sleeping car companies developed later. Although there are those who argue that
all this business should have been done by the railroad
company, the latter had a sufficient problem in securing
capital for building, operating and maintaining the railroads and assuming the risks thereof. Whatever the intention of the legislature was in first encouraging and
then discouraging consolidation, the fact is that it went
on in one form or another. The formation of the through
lines was not wholly a gain to Ohio, for it brought her
agricultural industry into competition with that of the
western states with their cheap and fertile land. In the
second place although the through lines gave her pro-

ducers better facilities to market their goods, the producers were brought into more direct competition with
those of the eastern centers of production in supplying
the central and western population. Pennsylvania coal
was carried as a return load at cheap rates, and this
affected the coal mining and manufacturing industries of
Ohio. The cheap rates made to western producers of
grain and provisions affected Ohio agriculture, and lastly,
the cheap transportation of eastern manufactured goods
to the West at the time when Ohio was trying to manufacture for the western market made it more difficult for
her to compete with the East. On the whole, with the
natural resources, Ohio producers could compete more
easily with the eastern manufacturers, and as a result
there was a proportionate decrease in the agricultural
industry and a great increase in manufacturing and the
mechanical arts. In the following table a list will be
found of those consolidations for which it was necessary
to receive official recognition. The list does not include
those numerous combinations which came about by a
purchase of the majority of the capital stock or by agreements for operation.[1]

[1] *Files of the record of the Incorporated Companies in the Office of the
Secretary of State of Ohio.*

Year	Lease	Sale	Consolidations[1]	Total Combinations
1830–1845......	1	—	—	1
1845–1850......	1	—	—	1
1850–1855......	7	—	3	10
1855–1860......	2	2	6	10
1860–1865......	10	10	29	29
1865–1870......	24	7	12	43
1870–1875......	7	1	7	15
1875–1880......	9	5	4	18
1880–1885......	7	7	22	36
1885–1890......	8	9	23	40
1890–1895......	4	8	12	24
1895–1900......	5	11	4	20

These numerous consolidations in one form or another made it possible for the overland routes to compete more strongly with the water routes. It is to be noticed that the waterways not only held the field at the beginning of the contest, but also that the natural conditions were decidedly favorable for water transportation in the territory which was the chief center of the contest. The Great Lakes with the St. Lawrence and Erie Canal afforded an eastern outlet, the Ohio and Mississippi Rivers a southern one. The projectors of the combinations realized that if the land routes were to be real factors in the carrying trade, they must reach these great water routes where trade was already established. Local trade was disregarded in favor of the through traffic, and although Ohio occupied a central position in this movement of traffic, she was in no position to protect herself except as the water routes on the north and south secured at certain seasons a lower rate for her through trade. The Ohio railroads in the midst of the period of

[1] By consolidation is meant the uniting of two or more companies into one by taking out articles of incorporation as one.

competition were receiving on fourth-class freight, which
included wheat, corn, pork, whiskey, iron, etc., about
one cent per ton mile for the through business, while
the local charges on the same products were about two
and one-third cents per ton mile.   Through rates could
not be advanced because the water routes stood ready to
make a lower rate.   In many cases the local rates were
not exorbitant, but only seemed to be so in comparison
with the abnormally low through rates.   The local roads
could not afford to refuse to carry the through traffic,
even if it had been possible for them to do so, for the
local business would not sustain the road.   While the
through rate often did not equal the cost of moving the
goods, yet since the road-bed and rolling stock existed,
almost anything was better than nothing in the period
in which traffic was developing; moreover, this through
traffic would be a valuable source of revenue when happier times came.   The reports of the presidents of Ohio
railroads during this period abound in regrets at the
necessity of carrying the through freight at such low
rates, but they emphasize the importance of sharing in
the through business.   There was introduced in the legislature of New York in 1860 a bill to compel all railroads to equalize their tariffs of way and through rates,
and although intended primarily to protect the Erie
Canal, the West took much interest in it, since it affected
its through business.   Rate cutting had been practiced
to such an extent that business was becoming unprofit-
able.   Petitions were circulated to have the Ohio legislature pass a similar bill.   It was, however, discovered
that the pro-rate principle had been inserted in a former
law which permitted railways to build bridges over
canals; but this, like many other railroad laws, had not
been observed.   In fact, conditions during this period

seemed to make it almost impossible to observe many of the transportation laws and principles. One president reports that "railroads should offer equal facilities to all travelers and for all business to pass over any particular line, and if the railroad companies do not voluntarily do this, the legislature should compel them to do it."[1] Yet a few months later we find this road engaged with another road in a fierce rate war, which violated every principle of equality and justice.

The legislature by charter provision and numerous laws sought to protect the canals of the state against railroad competition, but whenever the railways came into competition with the canals the latter gradually secured the business. A general law which superseded the former acts provided that

every railroad that extended to any place in the vicinity of, or to a point of intersection with any navigable canals of this state or other works of internal improvement belonging to this state shall establish a tariff of rates for the transportation of merchandise, produce and other property consigned to a point of intersection, and it shall be illegal for the railroad to charge or receive a higher rate for transporting similar merchandise, produce, or property over a shorter distance of its road, than is charged or received according to such fixed tariffs for transporting to and from such places of intersection as aforesaid.[2]

However, the railroads paid little attention to these laws. The surrounding circumstances of the hour regulated the rates.[3] The railways built many elevators in Ohio and used their cars on the side tracks to receive the grain.

[1] *Report of President of the C. H. & D. R. R.*, 1865.
[1] *Laws of Ohio*, 1852.
[3] *Cf. Report of Ohio Railroad Commissioner*, 1868.

Thus by better organization of their business, by continued operation throughout the year, and by greater rapidity in transportation, together with minor contributing causes, they secured the ascendency over canals.[1] It was much easier for the railways to secure the traffic of the canals than that of the Great Lakes and the Ohio and Mississippi Rivers. The Great Lakes were not only in immediate proximity to a region which produced large quantities of bulky raw farm produce, but the large iron-ore deposits of the Lake Superior district also supplied another product peculiarly suited for water transportation.[2] By 1870 the practicability of railroads as carriers of western produce was established. The charges at this time were at a point that permitted a profit to the railroad. The increase in the movement of traffic by rail as compared with that by water is shown by the wheat and flour traffic from Chicago to the seaboard:

In 1863 wheat from Chicago via Lake was 10,646,552 bushels.
"   "   "   "   " R. R. "   89,861   "
In 1873 "   "   "   " Lake " 13,429,069   "
"   "   "   "   " R. R. "   2,902,953   "
In 1863 flour "   "   " Lake "   1,207,345 barrels.
"   "   "   "   " R. R. "   311,844   "
In 1873 "   "   "   " Lake "   574,393   "
"   "   "   "   " R. R. "   1,129,074   "

When the Pennsylvania Railroad reached Pittsburgh it was for some years largely dependent for its prosperity upon the condition of navigation on the Ohio River, since this was its only western connection. Low water did not so much affect the Baltimore and Ohio, since it

[1] Cf. chapter vii for a more detailed statement of railway and canal competition.

[2] In 1867 the average freight rate from Escanoba to Lake Erie was on a ton of iron ore $4.25 in 1870; $2.50 in 1896.

reached the river below Pittsburgh, where low water did not so quickly affect navigation. The New York Central reached the Great Lakes at Buffalo. It was, therefore, more necessary for the Pennsylvania to secure through connections to the western lakes than for any other road except the Erie, and thus it was with this road that the contest for the control of Ohio roads was most active.

The Civil War also accelerated the movement of the through traffic to the trunk line. Not only was the market for provisions to the south affected by the war, but the dangers incident to the reaching of the markets were also so great, that at the close of the war practically all the traffic which had gone down the rivers now moved east over the railroads or over the lake route. Coal and the cotton traffic of the lower Mississippi were exceptions.

However, the cities along the Ohio were unwilling to have the river cease to be a transportation agent and began an agitation for river improvement, which at the present time promises considerable results. The total annual value of the Ohio River trade was estimated in 1873 at $694,000,000, but this was probably overestimated, for most of the statistics were supplied by those commercially interested in the traffic to an investigating committee whose report would affect the question of national aid for the improvement of the river.[1] When the Portland Canal around the falls at Louisville was completed, the river trade was materially affected, for whereas boats had been limited to a maximum tonnage of nine hundred tons, they could now carry seventeen

---

[1] Cf. *Report of Senate Committee on Transportation Routes to the Seaboard*, 43d Congress, vol. i, *passim*.

hundred tons. Freight was carried to New Orleans for as low as twelve and a half cents per hundred pounds. Coal was moving by towed barges, which had taken the place of floated barges by 1860, at a cost of less than one cent per ton mile.[1] Notwithstanding the numerous appropriations by the national government for river improvement and despite the activity of the commercial interests of the Ohio Valley, the river trade declined in favor of the railroad routes.

The preponderance in influence of railways in matters of transportation together with other evils which appeared as the railroads grew in mileage, led to a demand for some measure of control over their operation and management. The first expressions of this sentiment were due to the disappointment of the people at the result of their aid to railroads, but this sentiment was not strong enough to secure expression in legal enactment. The auditor of the state in 1851 gave expression to this growing sentiment for control by stating "that there is another class of corporations which is rapidly growing up and will soon control a large amount of property and capital. The railroads are deservedly objects of popular favor, but this only requires that greater care should be exercised in the adoption and enforcement of an effective system for their government and taxation.[2]

When consolidation became more frequent, the apprehension of the people was further increased.

No one can but notice the propensity now raging for the organization of great railway companies. It is to be feared that our dangerous inclination towards extremes will lead legislatures to favor too much the consolidation of railroad

---

[1] *Report of Chamber of Commerce of Cincinnati*, 1876.
[2] *Report of Auditor of State*, 1851.

companies so as to ultimately overshadow the country with monopolizing and overbearing corporations. The legislature will find that it will commit a grave error if it does not keep the several corporations within as narrow compass as possible, where they can be easily influenced by public opinion, and where the proximity of the people, the rights and feelings of the masses, will receive sympathy, and the interests of the local districts will be studied.[1]

The above quotation and numerous others which might be given show that some of the people foresaw what was to happen later, and, at the same time, they further show how firmly the idea of competition was adhered to. The numerous accidents were also beginning to be noticed, for this was a good point at which to attack railways, since tangible evidence of their shortcomings could be given. The roads were beginning to be less solicitous about satisfying local business and were looking more to the through trade. It must be understood, however, that all these complaints and criticisms were due primarily to the industrial changes and adjustments which were taking place. The Western states were being settled, and industrial life in Ohio was undergoing a change with the friction that is always incident to such changes.

The decade 1850 to 1860 was one of great activity in railroad building, and this activity was due in a great part to the dazzling effects of the gold discoveries in California and the opening of the region west of the Mississippi. The number of railroad employees had increased from 4831 in 1850 to 35,567 in 1860. The mileage center of railways had moved from near Mauch Chunk, Pennsylvania, in 1840, to near Williamsport, Pennsylvania, in 1850, and in 1860, it was sixty miles

[1] *Cleveland Herald*, Aug. 10, 1853.

south of Mansfield Ohio.[1]   The expenditure for railways in Ohio during this decade was given as $11,896,351.[2] This intense activity was checked by the panic of 1857, which many believed the railways had caused, and a disposition was shown to subject them to greater control. Governor Chase in his message of 1857 recommended the establishment of a railway commission because

the railway system had grown to its present magnitude without system, without general organization, and in some important respects without due responsibility.   The benefits of railroads are such and their safety and prosperity are so identified with the safety and prosperity of the people that no proper protection or support could be withheld from them, while the dangers from mismanagement are so great that no reasonable precaution against it should be omitted.[3]

This recommendation was not enacted into law, although in 1861 a law was passed which regulated the interchange of freight and passengers.   Any agent who refused to accept traffic from another road or diverted it was subject to a fine of one hundred dollars or imprisonment for not more than thirty days or both.[4]   Governor Anderson in his message of 1866 again recommended a railway commission and urged

legislation to protect the lives and limbs, property and other rights from the encroachment or neglect of these powerful

[1] In 1870 it had traveled away from the direct line to Cincinnati toward Chicago.   In 1880 it was thirty miles northwest of Logansport, Indiana, and in 1890 it was ninety miles northwest of Chicago.

[2] *Report of Commissioner of Statistics*, 1861.

[3] *Exec. Doc.*, 1857; New York had established a commission in 1855, and this was used as an argument for Ohio to do likewise.

[4] This law was due to the effects of consolidation and through route competition.

corporations. The subject of railroads has many and intrinsic difficulties: the principle of combination; their unsleeping vigilance; their great power of seducing all, from the county auditor who taxes them, up to the Congress of the United States which ought to regulate them.[1]

In obedience to this growing sentiment a committee was appointed by the Senate to investigate the management, charges and workings of railroad, telegraph and and express companies.[2]

The report was the first systematic inquiry that had been made of the railroad problem, and although it was by no means a comprehensive investigation, it was quite ample enough to show the urgent need of legislation to reform abuses, to protect railroad property, and to maintain the rights of the public. There had been constant and very wide discriminations, and although both through and local tariffs had been published, these were but a mere guide. Whenever the obtaining of business seemed to require it the tariffs were not observed. The vigor of the competition, and the shrewdness and persistence of the shipper were the dominant factors in determining rates. In some cases the charges were not even sufficient to pay for unloading the goods. Goods were often carried from New York to Cincinnati for less than from Columbus to Cincinnati. There were at this time four trunk lines from Ohio to the seaboard, two from the headwaters of the Ohio river region and two from the Lake Erie region. South of Ohio there was

---

[1] *Exec. Doc.*, 1866.

[2] A law was passed in the same year which forbade an officer or stockholder of an express or freight company to be an officer of a railroad company, and provided a fine of sixty dollars a day for any one who acted as an agent of any two of the above companies.

no railroad connecting the Mississippi Valley with the Atlantic until the Charleston and Memphis was reached. Ohio was thus an isthmus through which the immense volume of rail commerce between the East and the West moved most conveniently, and economically. These railroads competed on widely different terms, for some led directly from the principal commercial centers of the state, such as the Baltimore and Ohio from Cincinnati and the New York Central from Cleveland. Some had low grades; some had permanent traffic arrangements with local Ohio railroads and received the through business at less expense; some had to build connecting lines; others came into direct competition with water routes and spent large sums in getting the business away from these routes. However, dividends were expected to be paid, and security in possession of the local trade led to indifference toward its claim and interests. At the same time the uncertainty of the possession of the through trade produced sensitiveness and constant concessions. This condition led the committee to report that

railroads ought not to be used as charities for the benefit of shippers remote from the market. It is wrong to give prefer⁘ ence to regular over irregular shippers, for it leads to favoritism and oppression in the hands of weak, passionate or corrupt officers, with no rule to protect the officers or guide the public except the rule of real or pretended judgment as to the interests of the public. The period of competition has been a ruinous contest, producing confusion in railroad affairs, trickery and empiricism in their management, and a confusion and distrust to be found in no other branch of business.

The introduction and improvement of the railroad, es-

[1] *Report of the Senate Committee on Railroads*, 1867.

pecially as regards speed, had led to a change in the methods of conducting the mercantile business in Ohio. For now instead of stocking up for long periods, the merchant would buy in small quantities and thus have the use of his capital, and also take advantage of favorable changes in the market, since he had quick connections with the primary markets in New York, Philadelphia and Baltimore. But so many delays in forwarding goods, and damages from shipment resulted, for many of the so-called through lines were made up of a number of different lines with accidental connections, that these merchants with other capitalists and some railway officials had organized freight companies which, as has been shown, were responsible for many of the evils of which complaint was made. These companies issued their own bills of lading, kept goods moving and collected damages.[1] However much the above conditions needed legislation, the committee but expressed a general desire, when it warned the people against doing anything to interfere with investments in railways. The people were still anxious to secure greater railway development and had hesitated about attempting any control for fear the injury wrought would be greater than the good received.[2] As the result of the investigations the committee recommended legislation on the following points:

(a) No greater charge should be permitted for a short haul than for a longer one;

---

[1] During the war the government used considerable of the equipment of the Baltimore and Ohio and the Pennsylvania Railroads; in this and in many other cases these freight companies were of great value.

[2] *Cf. Senate Report on Railways, op. cit.*, 1867. "The state ought to deal with indulgent liberality with railroad investments, for they have been of incalcuable value to the state in developing its resources, augmenting its population and opening a way to markets."

(b) Every railroad company should publish its tariffs and be prevented from rebating;

(c) Preference, except for live stock, perishable freight and certain other commodities should be prohibited, and undue advantages of all kinds whether to classes of freight or to individuals should be forbidden;

(d) Private freight companies should be discouraged in favor of companies formed by the railways.

As a result of this report and of agitation for ten years, the law of 1867 provided for the appointment by the Governor of a railway commissioner whose powers were:

(a) To investigate upon complaint or otherwise any violation of the railroad laws and prosecute all such violations;

(b) To examine all defective tracks, bridges and dangerous places, and notify the railroad company of their existence, and by a later amendment compel them to make the repairs;

(c) To collect statistics on railways and telegraph lines and issue a report to the governor for the information of the legislature.[1]

The first commissioner did much at a very critical time to point the way to more intelligent legislation, for legislation had followed and not anticipated the wants and conditions of the railroad business. No careful record had been collected and preserved by which the experience of one period might be compared with another. The greatest need of the law-making power was, what in a large way it is even yet, information derived from experience upon which legislation might be based. The practice and policy of the railroad were then as now to conceal from the public the conditions and workings of their roads. The first movements toward the building of railways were regarded as private enterprises with

[1] *Laws of Ohio*, 1867.

which the public had no right to interfere except in so far as it was necessary to give the corporation the right of appropriating land, crossing highways and watercourses. It required a decade or more to determine the cost of building and equipping the first railroad, and by that time many other companies had been organized and were using every means to secure funds to complete their roads. As their numbers increased, competition, jealousy and opposition, combined with the disappointment of the people at the result of their public and private subscriptions, gave character to the legislation, although such legislation in Ohio was kept somewhat conservative by the great gains to the people from having railroads to transport not only state, but also interstate products. The first commissioner reports:

It is undoubtedly for the interests of the people that as many lines of railroad as will be necessary for our highest development and prosperity be built and maintained in the state. We should remove from the statute books all unjust and impracticable laws. Much needed legislation has been prevented by a fear or anxiety lest more evil than good would be done or that wholesome and judicial provisions would be coupled with others of so doubtful or prejudicial a character as to defeat the desired object.

He also recommended a maximum rate, but one high enough fairly to compensate any company in the state. This meant, in actual practice, latitude for the rate wars to continue, and hence did not touch the real evil, for there was not any considerable complaint that rates were too high, but that they were irregular and disproportionate.[1]

[1] *Report of Commissioner of Railroads*, 1868. "The local shipper should not complain if his transportation costs him more than the one who lives at the competing point. It is simply the misfortune of his

Railroads completed in 1875

The influence of this first commissioner did much to prevent extremely radical legislation, although the peculiar interests of the people of Ohio were a larger factor in the prevention. Owing to the general prosperity, the development of manufacturing, and the opening of coal lands on an extensive scale, the mania of the people for internal improvements at public expense again broke out in 1871 and resulted in the enactment of the Boesel law. This permitted counties, cities, incorporated villages, and townships to build, lease and operate railroads.[1] It was taken advantage of at once but was declared unconstitutional soon after its enactment. Consolidations were proceeding rapidly, but both on this subject and on that of rates the various commissioners of the period took a conservative position. " The only certain road to cheaper rates is through consolidation in some form within proper limits and control, and it is as well to attempt to dam the Mississippi or St. Lawrence as to try to prevent by legislation this union of railway interests,"— an expression of the old principle laid down by the first great authority on railroads, Stephenson, but one which the people have been slow to learn.[2]

location. These principles apply to every class of business and must be controlled by supply and demand and the laws of commerce, and not by legislation, provided that all companies are held strictly within a fair and maximum rate."

[1] *Laws of Ohio*, 1871.

[2] *Report of Railroad Commissioner*, 1872. "The impropriety and impracticability of fixing unyielding and inflexible rates on transportation by general law applicable to all railroads, or by special law to particular railroads or classes of railroads, seem too apparent to need comment." *Report of Railroad Commissioner*, 1873. The Baltimore and Ohio at this time was hauling coke from Connelsville to Columbus and Zanesville in competition with the Pennsylvania. The Hocking Valley was carrying iron ore instead of empty cars from Toledo to the growing industrial centers of the state, and the quoted arguments of the Commissioner strongly appealed to the people.

There were many industrial centers in Ohio by 1873 which were benefiting from abnormally low rates, and in view of their interests and the fact that Ohio had five hundred Granges with a membership of twenty thousand, the commissioner warns the people "against the hasty and inconsiderate legislation of Illinois," and urges them to investigate the question carefully, and to collect data upon which to base intelligent legislation, for the depression which began this year was in danger of causing extreme opposition to railways.

During the succeeding years laws were passed to regulate the hours of employment, to require the use of safety devices, to regulate rates, to permit certain local governments to build railroads and to tax railroads. No act of major importance was passed until the two-cent rate law and the act providing for a Railway Commission in 1906 were enacted.

The act which established a Railway Commission provides for a bipartisan board of three members appointed by the governor. The chief powers of the commission are as follows:

(a) to compel the railroad to furnish adequate service;

(b) to require a schedule of rates to be posted and a notice of ten days to be given before any change in the schedule is made;

(c) to require the railway to furnish sufficient cars, or, in case of an insufficient number, to make an equal distribution among the applicants;

(d) to require a prompt forwarding and interchange of traffic;

(e) to investigate complaints formally or informally made, or on its own initiative;

(f) to fix a reasonable rate with the right of appeal from the decision to the courts, but no injunction can be issued during the time of the trial and the burden of proof must rest upon the plaintiff;

(g) to inquire into the management and business of the company with the right to inspect all books;

(h) to investigate all accidents and violations of the railroad laws of the state;

(i) to compel the companies to file full statements of their business.

The railroad is made liable for three times the amount of the damages sustained for the violation of any of the provisions of this act.

In summarizing the railway legislation of Ohio, we may divide it roughly into three periods. The period extending to 1848, during which the legislation was based upon the hope of what railroads were to accomplish for the state. The people were anxious to secure means of transportation and were willing to grant almost any terms which the builders asked. They aided railways by both public and private subscriptions, but their disappointment at the results which accrued led to the second period, extending from 1848 to 1867, in which the state ceased to aid railways. The intense desire for transportation routes induced the people to aid railways through their local governments, but some of the evils had become so apparent as to lead to enactment of such restrictive legislation as would not seriously hinder the development of railroads. This culminated in the establishment of the weak commission of 1867, which was not followed by any marked restrictive legislation until the rate wars and discriminations against local business in favor of through traffic led to the attempts at further control. The industrial development of the state, and particularly the variety of its industries, and its position as regards the east and west trade still prevented extremely radical legislation. For several years after the establishment of the commissions, bills were annually introduced either to abolish the office or to curtail the work of the commissioners, and as late as 1874 the commissioner complained that these continued attacks impaired the efficiency of the office [1] and recommended that either the powers of the commissioner be strengthened or the office be abolished.[2] It was supposed that the commissioner would be able to make public such information as the investor in railroad securities would wish; but as a matter of fact, one of the last places where an intelligent investor would seek for such information would be in one of these state reports. There were more people then than now who argued that a railroad bore much the same relation to the public that any other kind of a business did, and that the state should confine its activity to the exercise of the police power. Yet an increasing number were adopting the view that the state had created these corporations in order to erect great public highways to be operated for the benefit of the people, in the safest and most economical manner, and that the companies, so-called, were individuals in the position of trustees, who had voluntarily invested their capital in a property designed for, and held to, the public use with the right to receive no more than a reasonable compensation. Many of the railroad officials had come to consider railroads as instrumentalities to produce dividends, regardless of the industrial and social effects upon the people served. The bond between the

---

[1] In 1874 the legislature refused to make any appropriation for the inspector of bridges, the chief officer under the commissioner.

[2] In 1880 the commissioner complains that "in no state has the commissioner been furnished with less power and fewer means to execute this power than in Ohio."

people and the railroads was broken when the projectors found that they could not depend upon popular subscriptions to finance the road; there was thenceforth a strong incentive to emphasize the interests of the capitalists. Water routes had ceased to be transportation agencies of any great importance except on the Great Lakes, and along the coast. Even these were controlled in many cases by the railroads. Discriminations and consolidations continued and were believed by many to be the real source of the power of the trusts. The popular agitation for greater control of railroads arose and in Ohio expressed itself in the strong railway commission of 1906 and the two-cent law of the same year.

The beginning of the taxation of railroads in Ohio was made by an act of the legislature in 1836, which incorporated the Akron and Pennsylvania Railroad and provided that when the dividends of the company exceeded six per cent, the legislature might impose a tax.[1] In 1844 an act referring to the Little Miami Railroad classed it with banks, insurance and bridge companies as corporations subject to taxation. In 1848 the legislature passed a law reserving the right to tax all railroad companies created under its authority. Railroads had seemed such an all-desirable asset for the state to secure that it was not thought wise to tax them until they could pay dividends. An act of 1851 provided that the companies should report to the auditor of the state their financial condition, and if the dividends exceeded the per cent fixed by their charters, when such a limit was inserted, the auditor should draw upon the company for six per cent of their dividends, and if such a company failed to report or pay its assessment the auditor levied

[1] *Laws of Ohio*, 1836.

one per cent on the capital stock. This was secured by an action of debt.[1] Railroads were not taxed on their general property until 1852, when the railway officials were directed to report the value of their property to the auditor of each county through which the line passed. This self-valuation did not work successfully, and in 1862 the present plan was adopted.[2] This method makes the auditors of the county through which the line passes a board of valuation. The right of way is valued as personal property. Yet this board cannot see the property, and if it did see it the motive power and rolling stock could not be accurately valued. The state is therefore largely dependent upon the valuation of the railway officials.

The value of railroads as assessed for taxes was as follows:

In 1853	$8,945,571
In 1873	84,789,794
In 1880	77,848,180
In 1885	90,884,010
In 1890	101,662,221
In 1895	105,824,592
In 1900	108,228,120
In 1905	138,858,945 [3]

Such a system of taxation is far from satisfactory, and in actual practice there has often been no fair relation between the amount of the tax and the value of the property. This is indicated by comparing the following table with the preceding one:

[1] This radical law as a matter of fact applied only to those railroads which were the chief competitors for canal traffic, and is but another expression of the feeling of the canal interests which were then suffering very much from railway competition.

[2] *Laws of Ohio*, 1862.

[3] *Reports of Auditor of State.*

Year	Number of miles at close of decade
1840	36
1850	299
1860	2,974
1870	3,374
1880	5,154
1890	7,091
1900	8,691
1905	8,922

In the development of the Ohio railway system the commercial centers of the Atlantic seaboard played an important rôle, each claiming that it was the natural market for the western trade.   The West lent a willing ear to each claimant in order to secure the benefits of the several markets.   New York State had in 1837 spent ten millions of dollars on her canals, Pennsylvania twenty millions, and two millions had been invested in the Baltimore and Ohio railway.   But the Erie Canal found enough business in western New York to justify its construction, and when the Ohio canals were opened, traffic on the Erie Canal became so congested that other routes to Eastern markets for Western produce were needed.   Railroads were then planned to the West by New York, Philadelphia, and Baltimore.   Philadelphia had been so secure in her position as a market for the West, that it seemed somewhat presumptuous to her for another city to make efforts to secure this trade.   Thus we read :

New York has projected and is actually making in addition to her great canal a grand railroad, which is to seize the Mississippi by one of its fingers and compel it to be friendly to New York.   No matter if this railroad costs twenty million dollars, no matter if it makes a communication one hundred miles longer than by way of Philadelphia, no matter if it is obstructed by snow for months, it is, nevertheless, a New York railroad, and on its way west will avoid Philadelphia. Baltimore is also striving hard to extend her railroad to the Ohio River. The western trade will be satisfied if it is furnished with cheap and expeditious communication to the Atlantic seaboard, and by supplying such, these cities will reap an advantage, as they will encourage the trade to flow east instead of passing down the natural currents of the great western rivers to the Gulf of Mexico.[1]

It was recognized that the natural location of the commercial centers so far as waterways were concerned, would be modified by the locomotive, for in the middle of the century the improvement of highways and the building of railways had lessened the relative superiority of those cities, which had been considered the great natural depots of commerce. One of the papers stated :

When Baltimore and Philadelphia shall have locomotive connections with the west by the great central railroad, when Charleston, Savannah and other southern cities on the Atlantic shall have regular railroad connections with the fertile valleys of the Mississippi and Ohio, when Boston and Portland have their railroad connections with the St. Lawrence River at Montreal, and are united with the great west by a continuous line, when all these and many other unnatural routes for the western trade will be completed, then will new towns and new cities and great commercial depots spring into being, and then the direction of western traffic will depend more upon locomotive velocity, than the natural course of the sluggish currents of rivers and canals.[2]

Many of the commercial interests of the West became impatient with the attempts of the canal interests to preserve the traffic on the waterways by legislative enact-

---

[1] *Commercial List and Philadelphia Price Current*—quoted in *Cincinnati Gazette*, March 12, 1836.

[2] *Cincinnati Gazette*, Oct. 30, 1849.

ments. In 1844 a resolution of the Ohio legislature expressed this situation, when it asked the state of New York to repeal the clause of the charter of the Utica and Schenectady Railroad which prohibited this road from carrying freight.[1] This compelled the products of the West to reach New York either through the New York canals or by way of the long southern route, and as a result transportation ceased early in the autumn and began late in the spring.

This forced the produce business of the west into the hands of speculators and large capitalists, who are able to purchase in large quantities and keep on hand during the winter season the produce of the west, which at the opening of the canals was forced into the market. The glut is followed by a reduction of prices in western markets. This restriction further imposes upon the western merchants the necessity of purchasing in the autumn large quantities of goods and bringing them on before the close of the canal to the great injury not only of our merchants, but especially to our consumers, for the reason that of a necessity a large amount of capital must remain idle during a large part of the winter season. This causes the loss to be partly made up by an increase of the prices to the consumers.[2]

When the Baltimore and Ohio, the Pennsylvania, the New York Central and the Erie Railroads were being built to the West, they did not expect to secure all this trade, for New Orleans had been since the opening of the valleys an important market; but the spoiling in transit of large quantities of produce brought immediately much of the

---

[1] This provision had been inserted in the charter of this railroad, which was a link in the through overland route to the west, in order to protect the traffic of the Erie Canal.

[2] *Laws of Ohio*, 1844. Resolutions of the House.

grain, flour and provision traffic to the railroad. After
the Civil War produced its disastrous effects on south-
bound traffic, the railroads found in 1872 that they had
carried eighty-three per cent of the grain and provisions
from the West to a market. The railroad agreements of
the trunk lines in 1858 made a difference between the
water and the rail and the all-rail route to the East of
eight cents per hundred pounds on first and second class
and five cents per hundred pounds on third and fourth
class freight. On the Cleveland, Columbus, Cincinnati
and Indianapolis in 1875 the average price received for
east-bound freight was .757 cent per ton mile and the
"line is covered with trains and over-burdened with
traffic, and while it is impossible to obtain actual cost in
much of the transportation business, yet this low priced
traffic cannot be abandoned without imperishing the best
interests of the Railway."[1] The following table shows
the increase in tonnage and the rates received for transporting this traffic eastward to the seaboard:

Year	Tons moving East through Ohio	Average freight rate per T. Mile.
1870	1,673,000,000	1.993 cents.
1871	1,773,000,000	2.215 "
1872	2,223,000,000	1.569 "
1874	3,717,000,000	1.344 "
1876	3,779,000,000	1.117 "
1878	4,286,000,000	.961 "
1880	6,665,000,000	.815 "
1881	7,609,000,000	.895 "
1891	11,856,000,000	.682 "
1907	21,385,000,000	.276 " [2]

Not only was there competition among the commercial centers of the East in building routes to the West,

[1] *Fifth Report of the Cleveland, Columbus, Cincinnati & Indianapolis
R. R. Co.*   [2] *Reports of Railroad Commissioner.*

but there was also considerable rivalry among Ohio cities to secure these routes.[1] Sandusky and Cleveland contested for the primacy in the northern part of the state, but because the latter was nearer Buffalo, the terminus of the Erie Canal, and had mineral resources nearby, it secured the Ohio Canal as well as the terminus of the C. C. C. & I. The fact that Cleveland was in direct line from Columbus and Cincinnati also aided her in this last case. This city soon began to secure results from her railways,[2] and her development excited the jealousy of the metropolis of Ohio, Cincinnati. As a result this city began as early as 1835 an agitation for a railway to the South which, after more than fifty years of agitation and an expenditure of about twenty millions, she secured.[3] The importance of an overland route to the South was realized quite early, as the following indicates:

The most exciting subject now before the people in this city is the proposed railway to Charleston. The execution of this will make Cincinnati the rival of New York by giving

---

[1] *Cf. Cincinnati Gazette*, July 26, 1850. In 1850 the cost of traveling by water and rail from St. Louis to Fall River was as follows: from St. Louis to Louisville, $7.00; from Louisville to Cincinnati, $2.50; from Cincinnati to Buffalo, $10.00; from Buffalo to Oswego, $5.00; from Oswego to Albany, $4.25; from Albany to New York, $0.75; from New York to Fall River, $4.00. Total from St. Louis to Fall River, $33.50.

[2] *Cleveland Herald*, December 6, 1858. "Our forest city has been waked up this spring with renewed energy, zeal and enterprise. We feel the effects of our railroads in the activity they have given to trade. Railroads create business; they pick it up all along the road. The farmer who lives ten miles from Cleveland gets seventy-five cents for his wheat, which in the primary markets is selling for eighty cents." *Cincinnati Commercial*, April 7, 1851. "A new trade has sprung up in the line of roads through this place to New York, and one which bids to be of importance. The four eastern lines of railroad have agreed to put wheat in bags or barrels at the same rates as flour."

[3] *Report of Trustees of the Sinking Fund of Cincinnati*, 1906.

her the advantage of the climate for the trade of the west. It will free us from the dependence of New Orleans and free the south from dependence on New York and New England. We shall manufacture in the west all that is now manufactured in the east. From the Lakes to Charleston there will be a continuous and eternal stream of commerce.[1]

This might not have been an exaggerated prophecy if the industrial development of the South could have proceeded without the interruption and the destruction caused by the Civil War.[2] Louisville opposed the granting of a charter to a company to build this road through Kentucky, since it would divert some of the river traffic and with it the transfers, delay and storage from which she derived considerable revenue. Louisville threatened "to reduce Cincinnati to a mere grass plot by taking away all her business except that of swine slaying."[3] The people of central Kentucky however wanted a market and the bill passed. Louisville also disputed with Cincinnati and Cleveland for the trade of the productive Wabash Valley and to this end built a railway into the valley. Cleveland reached the valley first by a railroad, and when the Baltimore and

[1] *The Western Monthly Magazine*, June, 1835.

[2] *Cf. Ohio State Journal and Columbus Gazette*, December 23, 1835. The political and social value of such a railroad was not lost sight of, for this was soon after the Nullification trouble with South Carolina. "What is now the amount of personal intercourse between the millions of American citizens of North Carolina, South Carolina and Georgia on the one hand, and Ohio, Indiana, Illinois on the other? Do they not live and die in ignorance of each other; and, perhaps, with wrong opinions and prejudices which the intercourse of a few years would annihilate? The people of the two great valleys would meet, exchange their opinions, compare their sentiments, blend their feelings, and yield up their political and social enmity."

[3] *Cincinnati Gazette*, Jan. 7, 1836.

Ohio was extended from Cincinnati into this region, Cincinnati was able to retain a part of this trade, which she had formerly controlled completely.[1] The building of the East and West lines to the north of Cincinnati into this region excited her protests for "all these lines lie north of us and tend to divert trade and travel from us."[2] Yet her self-assurance began to return when the Baltimore and Ohio reached Cincinnati. This sentiment was expressed in the following words:

Seven hundred miles of new railroad that perfects the direct route between the central east and the central west and re-stores to its ancient channels the stream of trade and travel temporarily diverted to the extreme north is this day publicly opened after the expenditure of thirty million dollars. We all know that long before there was either steamboat or stage route along Lake Erie, emigration and traffic was across the mountains from Baltimore and Philadelphia to and through Cincinnati to the Mississippi. But just as temporary tracks or Ws are made to carry the cars around the mountains during the construction of tunnels, so the east and west has turned the Alleghenies by the long circuit of the Lakes, while the engineers have been leveling the mountains and filling up the valleys in the air line between Baltimore and Cincinnati.[3]

The advantage of distance, however, was over-empha-sized, and Cincinnati continued to lose her position of leadership, although her volume of trade continued to increase.

[1] *Cincinnati Gazette*, Dec. 18, 1847. The question of the right of the national government to undertake improvements for commercial pur-poses was occupying a great amount of attention, and a resolution of 1847 expressing this right was adopted in the lower house by a vote of 138 to 54. An analysis of this vote shows that the South contributed 34 of the negative votes, and the Loco Foco members of the west 10.

[2] *Ibid.*, June 14, 1850.

[3] *Cincinnati Commercial*, Sept. 12, 1851.

Toledo derived but little benefit from railways until after the Civil War, when the rich agricultural section of the northwestern part of the state began to produce largely. The interior cities, especially those on the direct lines between the commercial centers, soon benefited from railway development. Columbus became a railway center, owing to the fact that it was: (a) The capital of the state; (b) on almost a direct line from Cleveland to Cincinnati, and from Pittsburgh to Indianapolis; (c) in a rich producing center of raw products and near a coal supply. A railroad from Xenia reached Columbus in 1850, but it was not until the opening of the Hocking Valley R. R. that the city had any importance as an industrial center. The first through train on this railroad arrived in Columbus, August 17, 1869, and was made up of a coal train of fifteen cars destined for Chicago.[1] This was the beginning of that coal trade from this valley to Chicago and the lake ports[2] which formed the basis of the manufacturing industries in many centers of the Middle West.[3]

The present railway system of Ohio is made up of 9121 miles of main track and a total mileage of 16,123 miles. There are $119,531,084 of preferred stock and $240,127,696 of common stock upon which $11,230,164 was paid in dividends, or a dividend of 3.12 per cent. The bonded indebtedness is $465,810,363. In 1907 the

---

[1] *Ohio State Journal*, Aug. 18, 1869.

[2] In 1860 it took two weeks to get a boat load of coal from this valley to Columbus, but now it could be secured in one day.

[3] The road was extended to Athens in 1870, and the earnings of the road in 1871 were $549,000, of which coal contributed $298,000, but this was exceeded by that of 1872, when of a total earnings of $846,000, coal contributed $298,000. Reports of Hocking Valley Railroad Company, 1871 and 1872.

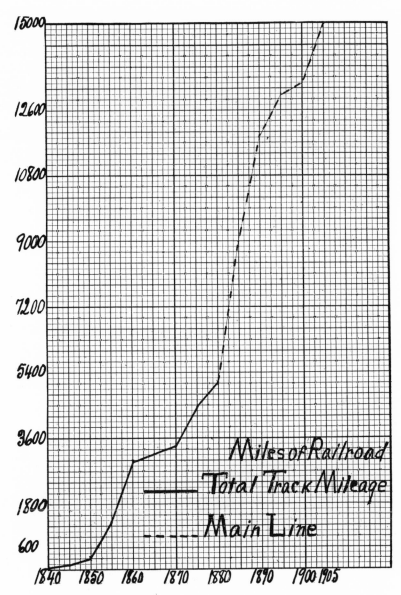

Along the perpendicular line on the left the number of miles is represented. The change from total track to main line mileage was made because nowhere can the exact number of miles of main line before 1880 be found.

cost of equipment was reported as $79,018,216, and the cost of the road at $773.129,037, which made a total cost per mile of $93,430.00. The total earnings from all sources in 1907 were $153,901,607, an increase over 1906 of $15,190,037. Passenger earning increased $1,161,728, in 1907, which with the lower fare collected under the two-cent law then in operation meant a decided increase in the number traveling, for it would hardly be reasonable to explain this on the ground of an increase in the number of trips. Again, statistics show that the amount received per passenger mile in 1907 was the same as in 1906, while the passenger earnings per mile were $3325, an increase per mile of $128.40. The total number of passengers transported in 1907 was 37,069,582, as compared with 36,666,206 in 1966. The average distance that each was carried was 34.69 miles, an increase of 7.77 miles over 1906, but the average amount received from each customer was three and one hundredths cents less than in 1906. Extreme care should be used, however, in making any deductions from the above statistics as to the workings of the two-cent law, for these statistics are for only one year and a very prosperous year on the whole. Nor do they give any reference to the earnings of particular lines, where the injustice, if any resulted, would appear most clearly. Freight earnings were 77.89 per cent of the total earnings. The operating expenses were $106,294,441 and were divided as follows:

19.13 per cent. for maintenance of way and structure.
23.87 per cent. for maintenance of equipment.
54.30 per cent. for operating expenses.
2.70 per cent. for general expenses.

Taxes were paid to the amount of $4,338,510 on general

property, and $1,539,016 in excise taxes, the total of which represented 2.81 per cent of the total earnings of the road. The state has collected in excise taxes since the law was enacted in 1895, $9,087,352. The following table shows how expenditures were divided:

> 65.47 per cent. for operating expenses.
> 21.77 per cent. for fixed charges.
> 5.50 per cent. for rents.
> 4.45 per cent. for permanent improvements.
> 2.81 per cent. for taxes.

The average distance that freight was hauled was 105.92 miles, the average number of tons per loaded car was 23.43 tons and the average number of tons per load train was 401.47 tons. On the following roads the passenger receipts in Ohio exceeded $1,000,000:

Pennsylvania System	$4,000,000 [1]
Baltimore and Ohio.........................	3,333,000
Lake Shore and Michigan Southern	2,750,000
Pittsburgh, Cincinnati, Chicago & St. Louis..	2,500,000
Cleveland, Cincinnati, Chicago & St. Louis...	2,250,000
Erie (N. Y. Pan)............................	1,133,000
Cincinnati, Hamilton & Dayton..............	1,166,000

The table on the following page represents in order of importance the characteristics of the freight traffic of the leading roads.[2]

[1] Figures are given in round numbers.

[2] Statistics for these and the preceding tables are from the *Report of the Railroad Commission, 1907.*

Grain	Anthracite Coal	Bituminous Coal	Coke	Iron Ore
B. & O.[1]	Erie.[2] Penn.[2]	Penn.[3]	Penn.[5]	Penn.
Lake Shore & Mich. So.[1]	N. Y., Chicago & St. Louis.[2]	Lake Shore & Mich. So.[4]	B. & O.[6]	B. & O.
Penn.[1]	P. C. C. &. St. Louis.[2]	B. & O.[4]	Lake Shore & Mich. So.[6]	Erie.
C. C. C. & St. Louis.[1]	Michigan Central.[2]	Hocking Valley.[4]	Erie.[6]	Cleveland, Lorain & Wheeling (B. & O.).
P. C. C. & St. Louis.[1]	B. & O.[2]	Toledo & Ohio Central.[4]	Norfolk & Western.[6]	Wheeling & Lake Erie.
N. Y., C. & St. Louis.[1]		Wheeling & Lake Erie.[4]		
		Cleveland, Lorain & Wheeling (B. & O.).[4]		
		Norfolk & Western.[4]		

[1] Each of these roads carried over 400,000 tons.

[2] Each of these roads carried over 170,000 tons, and one other carried as much as 50,000 tons.

[3] This road carried three times as much as any other railway.

[4] Each of which carried over 3,500,000 tons.

[5] This road carried twice as much as any other railway.

[6] Each of these roads carried 1,000,000 tons or over.

CHAPTER XI

IMPROVEMENT OF THE OHIO RIVERS AND HARBORS

THE improvement of the Ohio River is a subject which has been agitated for over a century, although the engineering difficulties are not great and the work does not call for an extraordinary outlay of money. The failure of this continued agitation to accomplish its purpose has been due largely to the fact that the national government has not, until very recently, had any systematic plans for the improvement of rivers and harbors. The haphazard appropriations which were made for the improvement of the Ohio River failed to keep the river an efficient means of transportation, for commercial demands made upon it increased rapidly. The river has its headwaters in the Appalachian mountains, where the rapid melting of the snow, the heavy rainfall and great fall of the streams emptying into the Ohio cause very sudden rises. Many logs and debris are carried down the stream by the swift currents of the flood-stage, and navigation at such times is exceedingly dangerous. During the period of a thaw, the floating ice is a source of much danger, and, during the dry season, the numerous sandbars cause great delay. Thus for a great part of the year the Ohio River was not a satisfactory commercial waterway. In addition to all these obstacles to navigation the falls of the river at Louisville seriously interfered with navigation for many years, although this single obstacle was not so great as the collective ones of snags, logs, rocks, bars and islands. The agitation for the removal of these obstructions was begun early but it was long in securing any results. It was argued that the removal of the bars should not be attempted, since they were the natural dams that prevented an excessive lowering of the water during the dry season. These bars made a series of pools in the Ohio River which were navigable for local purposes, however difficult it might be to carry on the through river traffic. Those who believed in the retention of the bars favored the construction of wing dams which, while retaining the water, would at the same time make a center channel for through river navigation. The bars shifted from season to season, and even when removed would often reappear after a freshet. Yet another class contended for making the river a slack-water stream by the construction of a series of locks and dams. Col. Long, an engineer in the employment of the national government, reported adversely on this plan in the following words: "By the introduction of locks and dams the natural navigation will be destroyed except during the time of high waters, when the boats could pass over the dams."[1] The dams, he thought, would destroy the flat boat trade, which at that time was very important. The people at large were urged to raise funds by subscription for the improvement of the rivers and then to secure aid through their representatives from the state and the national governments. The *Navigator* urged upon Pennsylvania the necessity of opening the Ohio to navigation because the Cumberland Road would draw the trade to the south of Pennsylvania, while on the other hand, the people of

---

[1] *Report on Internal Commerce of United States*, House of Representatives, 1884.

New York were agitating the building of roads and canals which would tend to direct the trade to the north.[1] It was proposed that a turnpike be constructed from Harrisburg to Pittsburgh and that the Ohio River be improved. Pennsylvania might control by these means the great highway to the West and secure the profits of the Western trade. In 1820 the Pennsylvania legislature did make an appropriation of $15,000 for the improvement of the Ohio River, but shortly thereafter the Erie Canal was completed, and Philadelphia lost in a large measure her Western trade to New York. After 1825 the people of Pennsylvania did not interest themselves so much in the improvement of the Ohio River, but attempted to recover the trade by building a railway to the West.

At Louisville a portage around the falls of two and a half miles to Shippingsport was used, until a canal from Louisville to Portland was constructed. The national government subscribed $235,000 of the $1,000,000 stock for its construction. Congress, at the session of 1824, appropriated $75,000 for the removal of sand-bars and snags in the Ohio and Mississippi Rivers and at various times appropriated other sums for similar purposes; for the losses to shipping on account of these obstructions to navigation were enormous, amounting, between the years 1822 and 1827, to $1,362,500. In 1819 the report of a commission appointed by the states bordering on the Ohio River to inquire into means of improving the navigation of the river was sent to the governors of the states, and, while the investigation was not made by engineers, the report contained much valuable information as to the state of trade and industry in the Ohio

[1] *The Navigator*, Pittsburgh, 1812.

Valley.[1]   The depth of water for purposes of navigation
naturally divided the river into three stages, viz.: New
Orleans to the mouth of the Ohio, from this point to
Louisville, and from Louisville to Pittsburgh.   The commissioners could not estimate the cost of removing bars,
snags and rocks, but they thought that this could be
done between Pittsburgh and Louisville for less than the
average annual loss to shipping.   They marvelled at the
fact that four states should hesitate to undertake the
clearing of the Ohio River of obstructions, when New
York alone was building a canal across the length of the
state.   The commissioners further urged that the James
and the Ohio Rivers should be connected, and the Kanawha river be improved in order to secure a cheaper supply
of salt, which, on account of the growing stock industry in
Kentucky and Ohio, was in greater demand.   The loss of
property due to the obstacles in the Ohio was great;
vessels were locked up for want of sufficient depth of
water; many boats were on bars, while the whole region
had a vast amount of products waiting to be transported
to market.   Notwithstanding all these facts the Ohio
Senate by resolution declared that it was not expedient
at that time to make any appropriation for river improvement.[2]   The state of Indiana about this time took
the then common method of raising funds by authorizing
a lottery for the purpose of building a canal around the
falls at Louisville.   Subscriptions to this lottery were
freely made by the people[3] of Ohio, until Kentucky
entered the field a few years later and asked for subscriptions for the same purpose.   Disputes then arose
as to the respective merits of the two routes.   Investi-

[1] *Liberty Hall and Cincinnati Gazette*, June 24, 1820.
[2] *Senate Doc.*, 1820.
[3] *Liberty Hall and Cincinnati Gazette*, Oct. 27, 1819.

gating commissions were appointed; some reporting in favor of one route, some in favor of another, until no one felt certain which was the better route. The people of Ohio accused the people of Louisville of attempting to prevent any canal from being built in order to secure profits incident to the delay of shipping and the transfer of goods around the falls. While the arguments and investigations were continuing, shipping in the meantime was suffering great loss and delay at Louisville. Finally the national government gave aid, and the Portland Canal was completed in 1828.

Cincinnati during these years was growing rapidly but was suffering greatly from inadequate transportation facilities. Projects of many kinds were advanced for the relief of the city. A Pittsburgh editor called it the city of projects and affirmed that one citizen could not meet another on the street without having handed to him a pencil and paper with the request that he subscribe to the stock of some projected improvement company. By 1830 the railroad had appeared and it offered such seemingly superior advantages to water transportation, that the thoughts and efforts of the people were directed to securing railroads. The interests demanding river improvements became less insistent, and it was easy for the national government to continue its careless and unsystematic plan of expenditures for internal waterways. In reference to the improvement of the smaller rivers, the state legislature in 1807 authorized a lottery for the improvement of the Cuyahoga and Muskingum Rivers, and commissioners were appointed in the same year to raise by lottery $12,250 for securing the banks of the Scioto River.[1]   After the war of 1812 numerous acts of the

[1] *Laws of Ohio,* 1807.

legislature were passed which referred to the navigation of the state rivers; for Ohio entered upon a period of great prosperity about 1815. Numerous Navigation Boards were appointed, which consisted of one representative from each county through which a river flowed. These boards were granted large powers by the legislature over the improvement and the commerce of the river. Among the chief obstacles to the navigation of the rivers were the many small dams which had been built for the use of the mills. So long as only small boats were used on the river, and so long as products were taken to market only when the rivers were high, these dams did not interfere to any appreciable extent with navigation; but when production became greater a demand arose for the removal of these hindrances to the continuous navigation of the rivers. These boards could remove any artificial obstruction or compel the owner of dams to remove them, or give bond to remove them within a specified time.[1] Acts were passed in 1808 requiring the owner of any mill dam to construct a lock or slope that would permit the safe passage of boats or crafts.[2] The mill owners, however, disregarded this act in many cases; for mills were so valuable to a community that, so long as they did not seriously interfere with navigation, the people did not object. There was thus a conflict of industrial and commercial interests, and, when the commercial needs became more important than the industrial, that is to say, when the possible production of the region was seriously limited by these commercial obstructions, the dams were removed. In the early history of the state all the larger rivers and many of the smaller and now insignificant streams were declared by the legisla-

---

[1] *Laws of Ohio*, 1816.   [2] *Ibid.*, 1808.

ture navigable, although as the importance of these smaller streams declined they were taken out of the class of navigable streams. These small streams, however, continued to be of great value to the people of the state during the time of high waters, and as late as 1816 the Adventurer, a seventy-five foot keel boat with a burden of sixteen tons, sailed down the little Walnut, an insignificant stream in the central part of the state, thence into the Scioto, down the Ohio, and up the Mississippi and the Missouri to a point in the present state of Missouri.[1] What occurred in this case happened in many other sections of the state, since the rivers in flood time afforded an easy and inexpensive means of transporting goods and persons. Governor Worthington, in his message of 1816, pointed out the necessity of improving the internal waterways of the state, "for roads and waterways determined the extent of the production of the state, since they solved the problem of the disposal of the surplus products."[2] The Governor suggested that a special tax for the improvement of navigable streams be levied on the people of those counties through which the streams passed, since he believed that the people along the stream derived the principal advantages from the rivers. This was largely true at this time, since the rivers were used chiefly for the transportation of those products which were raised by the people living in the valleys. There was no great number of improved highways, which enabled the distant producer to raise products for the general market.

The absence of bridges was a serious hindrance to the early producers, and those who undertook the building

[1] *Intelligencer*, May 30, 1816.
[2] *Senate Doc.*, 1816.

of bridges were considered as the ancient bridge builders of Rome, public benefactors. Liberal inducements were made to private individuals who would agree to undertake this work. The first important bridge in the state was one across Will's Creek, in the present county of Guernsey; but by 1811 [1] we find the legislature empowering private individuals to construct toll bridges across the Muskingum, Hocking and Scioto rivers, and by 1816 Ohio gave her permission to construct a toll bridge across the Ohio river at Wheeling. Careful provision was always made in these acts for the protection of the people; the toll was fixed for different kinds of travel; rates were ordered posted; provision was usually made for purchase by the county, and the legislature always reserved the right to change the rate of toll at the close of three or five year periods. Gradually these bridges were acquired by the counties and made free. There was generally strong competition between the localities for the placing of the bridges, but the very fact that they were constructed by private individuals was assurance that their location would be at the point of greatest traffic, since the returns to the builders depended directly upon the amount of traffic.

Little national aid for the improvement of inland streams and harbors was extended in the first thirty years of the national government. The right of the general government to undertake internal improvement for purely commercial purposes was denied by many, and when appropriations were made, they were justified under the military and post-road powers of the national government. However, the Western states insisted that Congress had this power, and, when national offices were to

---

[1] *Laws of Ohio*, 1811.

be filled, one of the first questions asked concerning a candidate was as to his position on the question of internal improvement by the national government. As the settlement and production of the West became greater, the question of transportation facilities became pressing, and aid was sought from the national government to deepen channels, dredge harbors, construct light-houses, breakwaters and piers. The West by 1852 argued that the commerce of that region amounted to more than the foreign commerce of the country, and it was therefore worthy of greater consideration. Thus we read :

The poor laborer, the industrious mechanic, the farmer more especially, are all subjected to a great loss by the unpardonable neglect of the national government to appropriate money to improve navigation. The rate of transportation of goods to the west is increased, for the more difficult and dangerous transportation is, the higher are the rates of insurance and freights. The losses of the merchants and traders are great from delay and disappointment in receiving their orders. The improvement of the western rivers and harbors would attract capital and develop industries.[1]

The following table shows the amounts appropriated by the national government for the various rivers and harbors from the beginning of the government until the present time.

[1] *Cincinnati Commercial*, Oct. 3, 1851.

Ohio River.[1]

Before 1830	$233,500.00
1830 to 1840	180,000.00
1840 to 1850	107,131.01
1850 to 1860	95,000.00
1860 to 1870	758,200.00
1870 to 1880	4,660,609.77
1880 to 1890	3,737,500.00
1890 to 1900	6,221,678.82
1900 to 1907	6,615,796.95
Total	$21,609,416.55

Cleveland Harbor.

Before 1830	$28,965.56
1830 to 1840	100,447.59
1840 to 1850	25,000.00
1850 to 1860	30,145.00
1860 to 1870	130,186.00
1870 to 1880	464,500.00
1880 to 1890	743,750.00
1890 to 1900	1,424,000.00
1900 to 1907	1,805,000.00
Total	$4,851,994.15

Toledo.

Before 1830	
1830 to 1860	
1860 to 1870	$119,700.00
1870 to 1880	482,000.00
1880 to 1890	607,500.00
1890 to 1900	474,250.00
1900 to 1907	494,250.00
Total	$2,177,700.00

[1] *House Doc.*, vol. 92, 57th congress, 2d session, 1902–03. Also *U. S. Statutes at Large*, 59th congress, 1905–07, vol. 34, pt. i. *Ibid.*, 58th congress, 1903–05, vol. 33, pt. i.

All Other Lake Ports.

Before 1830	$103,584.93
1830 to 1840	238,264.93
1840 to 1850	40,000.00
1850 to 1860	60,852.29
1860 to 1870	411,312.51
1870 to 1880	574,900.00
1880 to 1890	545,250.00
1890 to 1900	1,305,449.10
1900 to 1907	2,966,700.00
Total	$6,246,313.76
Total for rivers and harbors in Ohio since 1830	$32,394,324.56

Total Appropriation in Order of Amount from 1826 to 1907 for Ohio Rivers and Harbors.

Ohio River	$21,609,416.55
Cleveland Harbor	4,851,994.15
Toledo	2,177,700.00
Muskingum River	1,690,102.94
Sandusky	1,340,192.00
Ashtabula	1,281,269.31
Fairport	951,107.71
Conneaut	617,697.59
Huron Harbor	518,773.71
Vermillion	163,277.55
Black River and Lorain Harbor	161,000.00
Port Clinton	102,000.00
Rocky River	39,000.00
Cuningham Creek	19,781.12
Total	$35,523,312.63

The River and Harbor Appropriation Bill was for many years a source of accusations of fraud, for no systematic plan for the improvement of rivers and harbors was devised, and hence each congressman attempted to get the largest possible appropriation for his district. Those congressmen whose districts really needed appropriations were compelled to support the appropriation for

other districts which did not need them, in order to get
the votes of these congressmen, and thus it resulted that
millions of dollars were appropriated from which very
little commercial value was derived.[1]   Happily a new era
has arrived, and now there is a systematic plan for the
improvement of rivers and harbors that promises in
time to make the commercial facilities of our rivers and
harbors important factors in the future industrial development of the country.[2]

[1] In many cases these appropriations were said to form the small
change of political party financiering.

[2] *Cf. Moody's Magazine*, vol. 5, No. 1, for a fuller statement, by the
writer, of this phase of the subject.   The leaders of this systematic work
for the improvement of rivers and harbors have been Congressmen
Ransdell, of Louisiana, and Burton, of Ohio.

CHAPTER XII

The Development of Highways in Ohio, 1850–1908

The year 1851 marks a dividing point in the development of highways in Ohio. In that year a new constitution was adopted that established a different relation between the state government and the highway construction, although before this date the state had ceased officially to subscribe to the stock of turnpike companies.[1] Local governments henceforth became more active in road-building, although, for more than twenty-five years after 1850, private companies continued to construct roads. In accordance with the policy followed for several years before 1850 and in harmony with the provisions of the new constitution, the legislature passed a general act for the government of turnpike and plank road companies. The chief provisions of this law were as follows:

(a) Any five persons could incorporate such a company;

(b) the road must be 60 feet wide with 16 feet covered with stone, gravel or wood and with no ascent of over 5°;

(c) no toll gate could be erected within certain distances of incorporated towns and villages;

(d) companies must erect mile stones along their road and post their rates for public inspection;

---

[1] *Cf.* chap. 9 for the specific changes made by the constitution.

(e) a fine of twenty-five dollars was fixed for any violation of the toll laws.   If any company failed for five days to keep its road in repair, any person could complain to the Justice of the Peace, who was required to appoint viewers upon whose report it was decided whether the right to collect toll between the gates where the repairs were needed should be continued.[1]

It will be observed that the above terms tended to hasten the transfer of the turnpikes from private to public control, and by 1870 public construction had become very common.   Many of the toll roads were beginning to wear out, and opportunity for complaint was frequent. An act of 1853 regulated the public construction of highways just as the above act governed their private construction.[2]   This act was comprehensive in its terms and provided the manner of laying out, of opening and of vacating all public roads, including the township roads, which previous to this time had been of little consequence.   The extent of private highways is seen from the Auditor's Report of 1853, which for purposes of taxation valued turnpikes, plank roads and bridges at $919,496.   Of this total valuation turnpikes comprised $474,240, plank roads $302,939 and bridges $142,317. These were distributed among the counties in the following order of importance:

[1] *Laws of Ohio*, 1852.   [2] *Ibid.*, 1853.

Plank Roads	Turnpikes	Bridges
Cuyahoga.	Hamilton.	Muskingum.
Huron.	Butler.	Butler.
Ashtabula.	Franklin.	Lucas.
Franklin.	Miami.	Hamilton.
Seneca.	Fairfield.	Wood.
Lake.	Adams.	
Lucas.	Pickaway.	
Sandusky.	Warren.	

As might have been expected, roads were most numerous in those counties which either had large cities or were near centers of growing industrial importance. It will also be observed that plank roads were practically confined to the Lake region; for it was in Canada that plank roads originated, and from this region and from Michigan a cheap supply of lumber was secured for their construction,[1]

In 1854 the state held $1,853,365.21 of stock in turnpike companies.[2] The Sinking Fund Commissioners were authorized to sell it, but, as the sale could not then be satisfactorily made, these commissioners were authorized in 1865 to sell it for what they deemed its actual value.[3] In 1854 county commissioners and township

[1] The general absence of gravel in many sections also helps to explain the location of Plank Roads, just as the numerous turnpikes around Cincinnati and Columbus are explained by the presence of gravel.

[2] *Report of Auditor*, 1854.

[3] *Laws of Ohio*, 1854 and 1865.

trustees were authorized to levy a special tax for a road
and bridge fund, and in 1857 an act was passed, and
amended in 1861, which provided an easy method of
transferring private turnpikes and plank roads to
county commissioners. This movement to make roads
free public highways continued, and by 1885 the transfer
had in most cases been accomplished, although a few toll
roads are yet found in Ohio. Whereas in 1866 there
were 2539 miles of toll roads in Ohio, in 1873 there
were only 1502 miles. Free turnpikes had increased
from 1897 miles in 1869 to 4327 miles in 1873.[1] The act
of 1865 which increased the powers of the local officials to
acquire and construct highways marks the real beginning
of free public roads on an extensive scale, just as the act
of 1817 marked the beginning of the era of private turnpike construction. This act of 1865 was frequently
amended, as in 1867 when the county commissioners
were authorized to levy additional assessments on the
adjoining land until the road was completed, and in 1870
when the special road and bridge fund levy was increased.
In general, the legislation was getting away from the
narrow theory that a highway was to be constructed by
the abutting property owners and was taking the view
that the township and county might well be regarded
as the transportation unit on which costs should be
assessed.[2]

The long period of private construction which extended from 1817 to about 1870 did much to secure
highways for the people in the only possible way, since

[1] *Reports of Auditor*, 1869 and 1873.

[2] County commissioners were authorized to issue bonds in 1876 to pay
for the turnpikes purchased from the private companies. These private
turnpikes were in most cases well constructed, and even to-day are in
many counties the best roads.

this policy assessed the cost upon the traveling public and the moving freight. With the excellent laws governing the operation of private turnpike companies, it was doubtless a better way to secure roads than to attempt to secure them by the general property tax. The toll was an ability tax, equitably distributed, and the cost of these roads, thus placed on those best able to bear the charge, aided in the industrial development of the state. This method of securing roads also did much to supply bridges which for many years were constructed with private capital, sometimes supplied by the turnpike company, but often furnished by a separate company. If the few bridges which the public were willing and able to build in the early period had been a matter for official or popular decision, great difficulty would have been experienced in determining their location. When these bridges were built by private capital, business considerations alone entered into the question, and consequently the bridges were located at the points of maximum traffic. There is no better index of the development of the region than that of the change from fords to ferries, from ferries to wooden bridges and from wooden bridges to iron bridges. In colonial North America there was not to be found a bridge of any considerable importance. They appeared as soon as population increased, and in time bridge-building both as a science and as an art was far in advance of highway construction. This was due to the fact that bridges had to keep pace with the rapid development in railway construction and operation. If the progress of bridge-building had been measured by that of highways, we should to-day still be using the wooden bridge. It is to be noted also that in all the early laws, which were almost invariably passed to fix the rate of ferriage, no mention is made of a charge for wagons; their use as a means of transportation was delayed until the regions had been settled for some time.[1] Bridges in the West were contemporaneous with the privately constructed turnpikes, and while the excellent stone bridges of the National Road served in a way as models, most of the bridges were built for many years of wood. When the railways began to use heavier rolling stock, iron bridges took the place of the wooden ones, but the latter continued in use and are yet found on many of the highways of Ohio.

Since 1870 so much special legislation has been enacted empowering this or that board of county commissioners or township trustees to purchase a toll road, to levy a certain road or bridge tax, to divide the district into special road districts, to appoint road superintendents, to transfer the care of the roads to the county commissioners, that at present in many cases no one is quite certain even after a careful investigation what the road law really is. The legislation of the whole period has been based on the theory that each community should be permitted to do what it pleased in reference to constructing and repairing its highways. The year 1892 may be taken as marking the beginning of the present period of agitation for improved highways. The Governor in his message of this year[2] called the attention of the Legislature to this subject, and in response to his recommendation the Legislature empowered him to appoint a Good Roads Commission.[3] In the three ways of improving transportation, viz., improvement of the way, improvement of the motive power, and improvement of the

[1] *United States Census Reports.* There were in Ohio in 1840 only 13,321 wagons and carriages reported; in 1850, 95,000; in 1860, 270,000, and in 1870, 800,000.

[2] *Exec. Doc.*, 1892.   [3] *Laws of Ohio*, 1892.

vehicle, little had been done during the preceding fifty years to reduce the cost of transportation over highways. The vehicle had been improved, but there had been very little improvement in the way and practically none in the motive power, and the increased cost of labor had in part counteracted the improvement made in the vehicle. At a cost of twenty-five cents per ton-mile there can be no competition with railways except for very short distances, and the prevalence of the interurbans has materially reduced this distance. The present agitation for improved highways is one for good roads all over the particular area and not, as it was in the early period, an agitation for great thoroughfares through the state or between certain centers. The people of Franklin County, with Columbus as the industrial center, do not, in 1908, want, as they did in 1820, a road to the Lakes or to the Ohio River, but they demand improved roads for all the inhabitants of Franklin County. The appointment of the Highway Commission in 1892 was followed by many state and local Good Roads Meetings and resulted in the establishment of a State Highway Commission in 1900 with a commissioner appointed by the Governor.[1] The duties of this commissioner are to instruct, assist and co-operate in the building and improvement of the public roads, under the direction of the highway commissioner, in such counties and townships of the state of Ohio as shall comply with the provisions of this act. The highway commissioner may make inquiries in regard to systems of road-building and management throughout the United States, and make investigations and experiments in regard to the best methods of road-making and

---

[1] The commissioner must be a competent engineer. He is appointed for a term of four years.

the best kinds of road material, and investigate the
chemical and physical character of road materials.   He
has authority to prepare, publish and distribute bulletins
and reports on the subject of road improvement.   The
county commissioners or the township trustees may
apply for state aid in building roads, and, after an investigation by the state commissioner, the route is mapped
and the costs estimated under his direction.   The county
commissioners then vote to adopt or to reject the proposed improvement.   The cost is divided as follows : fifty
per cent upon the state, twenty-five per cent upon the
county, ten per cent upon the township and fifteen per
cent upon the land owners along the route.[1]   Any turnpike may be reconstructed under this act, but, in all cases,
a competent engineer must be employed to survey and
plan the road.   This supplies the one requisite, which
has been absent in most cases in past road-building and
which has been more responsible than any one other
thing for bad road building.   The roads thus constructed are called state highways but are to be kept in repair by the local governments.

The present roads in Ohio are classified as state, county
and township roads.   State roads are those originally
built by the state, such as those from the Three Per
Cent Fund and those of later construction, but in either
case they are kept in repair by the local governments.[2]

---

[1] *Laws of Ohio*, 1902, 1904, 1906 and 1908.   It will be observed that
the tendency is to recognize the general benefit of highways, and hence
to assess a less percentage of the cost upon the abutting property owners.

[2] In addition to the Three Per Cent Fund from the national government, public lands were given in specific cases for the construction of
roads.   The Maumee Road Lands, averaging two miles in width, lay
on each side of a road extending from the Maumee river at Perrysburg
to the western limit of the Western Reserve, and included about 60,000
acres.   These lands were originally granted by the Indians in 1808 to

County toads are those constructed or purchased by the county, while township roads are those opened under the authority of the township trustees.

Roads may be also classified as turnpikes, one-mile, two-Mile and three-mile assessment pikes and township roads. A general tax may be levied upon vote of the people by the county commissioners for turnpike construction. This plan does not entail any higher assessment on the abutting property owners whereas the construction of one, two and three-mile assessment pikes always does. A special levy is made in most townships for road purposes but in some cases all the roads are under the charge of the county commissioners. It is quite impossible to make any general statement that will answer the question of the manner in which roads in Ohio are kept in repair. That this is so results from two facts. In the first place, the state has such a variety of soils and materials for road building, and there is such a difference in the character of the industrial life in different sections, that no one law would be satisfactory to all sections. In the second place, many different agencies constructed the roads, and laws which were enacted to suit the work of each agency tended to create confusion.

To summarize briefly the different periods of highway development one finds the following periods: First, the period of state construction, either by applying the proceeds of the Three Per Cent Fund or by subscribing to the stock of private turnpike companies. This period

the national government, and made over by it to the state government in 1823 on the condition that the state would within four years construct and keep in repair a road between the above points.

The Turnpike Lands of 31,360 acres in Seneca, Crawford and Marion counties, granted to the state in 1827, were another example of grants by the national government for the purpose of state roads.

extended from 1804 to 1844, although the subscription period covered only the last decade of the period; second, the period of private turnpikes and plank roads, the former beginning in 1817 and extending to 1870, the latter beginning in 1850 and extending to 1865; third, the period of local assessment extending from 1845 to 1885, although from 1845 to 1851 many local governments subscribed to the stock of private turnpike companies and the practice of assessing abutting property is still followed to a limited extent; fourth, the period of construction by general assessment, extending from 1870 to the present, the first fifteen years of the period being characterized by a transfer of the private turnpikes to the public; fifth, the period of direct state aid, which began in 1900. These periods overlap and, in thus dividing them, it is intended only to designate the characteristics of each period.

The people of Ohio as well as those of other states are beginning to realize the need of good roads. The business of the country is becoming too extensive, and the establishment of world markets compels it to be conducted on too economical a basis for transportation to make up such a large part of the cost of production as it now does. Little organized and systematic effort has been made to master the details of the science of road-building, for the work has been considered an art which any one might practice. Enough time, effort and money have undoubtedly been spent in the state of Ohio during the past half century to supply every section of the state with the best of roads. Much of the energy and money has been unwisely expended, and, even when good roads were constructed, proper provision has not been made for their care and maintenance. The people have been piling up instead of building roads. Stone and gravel have been placed on the roads in the late summer with no foundation for support, so that when the autumn rains and freezes come and the movement of crops to the market begins, this wearing surface gradually disappears in the mud upon which it has been placed. Only recently has there been any real effort made to regulate the character of the vehicle and the weight of load which might be transported. There has been a system of supervision by those who knew little or nothing of what they supervised. The chief duty of such supervisors has been to see that every one worked an allotted time on the roads, regardless of when or where he worked. As a result the time has been, when it was most convenient for the worker, and the place where it would benefit the individual worker the most. When the improved road is a reality, an improvement in the motive power may be considered, but in the present state of highways it is useless to think of this. Probably within the next half century we shall see the horse disappear from many of our public highways for purposes of freight movement. Large freight companies may be formed to operate motor trains along the leading thoroughfares to which point the horse and wagon will haul the produce of the farm.

CHAPTER XIII[1]

The Interurban Railway in Ohio

The interurban railway has been developed in Ohio as in few other sections of the world. The numerous industrial centers, the variety of soil and resources and the topography of the greater part of the state has seemed to warrant this rapid development, which beginning about 1890 grew to 2633 miles in 1907.[2] Prior to 1890 there were incorporated in Ohio 163 companies for the building of street railways, but few of the lines were ever built and many of those constructed were only for one street.[3] The result was that all the large cities of Ohio had for a number of years many companies operating different lines and various kinds of vehicles for transporting the people about the city. Before this year a few short lines had been constructed beyond the city limits, but these attempts were not very ambitious. By this time, however, the feasibility of other lines had been established, for it had been proven that electric cars could be operated in all kinds of weather, that a considerable speed was possible and that, as a result of the improvement of

[1] Much of the data for this chapter has been secured from an unpublished paper by C. W. Reeder, Assistant Librarian at the Ohio State University.

[2] *Report of the Commissioners of Railways and Telegraphs*, 1907.

[3] *Reports of Secretary of State.* Just as Ohio became one of the leading states in the early period of railways, so she has become a leader in electric traction.

electrical mechanism, the cost of operation was comparatively low.   All of these facts promised to attract capital
for building interurban railways.[1]   The improvements
already made meant clean car barns instead of filthy
stables housing thousands of horses and depreciating
the value of the surrounding property, as well as cleaner
streets, more comfort and greater speed in traveling
about the city.   About 1890 the movement for roads to
connect the adjacent towns began, but the next five years
were on the whole a period of agitation, organization
and incorporation.   The incorporations for these years
were as follows:

1891	23	1894	18
1892	19	1895	30
1893	20		

Of the twenty-three cities named in the charters of
1895 all are now connected by interurbans, but the main
field of construction during this period was around
Cleveland.[2]   In Cincinnati the development had not gone
beyond the city proper, although the city lines had been
extended to the many suburbs north and east of the
city.   The next period, extending from 1895 to 1901,
shows a marked development of lines around the industrial centers of Dayton, Youngstown and Toledo.
This period was one of great progress, for, in addition to
the roads built around new centers, the lines around the

[1] In 1888 the Newark and Granville Electric Railway Company was
incorporated, which constructed the interurban railway between these
places. This was a road seven miles in length, and was the first interurban in Ohio.

[2] The first line to begin building was the Akron, Bedford and Cleveland, which ran through the populous section of the many small towns
in the Cleveland industrial district.

large cities of Cleveland and Cincinnati were extended to further outlying suburbs and districts. This paved the way for connecting the various detached systems and the formation of trunk lines. The period from 1900 to 1907 witnessed a further development along the lines of the preceding period, but the interurbans now attracted capital more readily. Franchises were easy to secure, the rural communities were taking an active interest in promoting the construction of lines, the increased speed reduced the danger of competition and great improvements were being made in the motive power. The characteristic feature of this period was the formation of syndicates and combinations of numerous kinds. In 1901 there were 868 miles of interurbans in Ohio, but in 1907 there were 2,633 miles divided among sixty-one companies.[1] The advantages of consolidation were soon realized. The saving in cost of power made by the substitution of one power-house for numerous small ones and by the use of the best methods of distributing the power amounted to almost fifty per cent.[2] Another source of saving came from using the common rolling stock. Each road had a certain reserve stock representing a margin of safety over the demand for cars during regular service, and when the roads were consolidated this reserve stock became common property to be used whenever and wherever it was most needed. This is especially important in handling the excursion business

---

[1] *Report of the Auditor*, 1904. The average cost per mile is reported as $52,542. The syndicates and combinations formed were so numerous and of such short duration that a description of them would not be pertinent to our purpose. Failure of companies, receiverships and other characteristic features were as frequently present as they were in the early railroad period.

[2] *Street Railway Journal*, 16, 448.

from which an important part of the passenger receipts are secured. The fact that a number of separate roads can be operated as a unit rather than as an aggregate is a powerful stimulus to traffic. This is especially true in securing the through passenger and freight business.

The process of development has been first, mutual distrust; second, friendly relations for mutual benefit, and third, consolidations for greater traffic and profits. The advantage of consolidation shows itself in three important ways: (a) economy in fixed charges; (b) economy in administration: (c) economy in maintenance and repair.[1] When a group of roads comes under a consolidated management, there is greater financial support for the enterprise, and funds are generally secured at a materially lower rate of interest than in the case of the single roads. Many roads were paying from five to six per cent on their funded debt before consolidation. Money was secured after consolidation for one-half of one per cent to one per cent less. Since most of the roads are operated upon a small margin of profit, this saving of interest on the funded debt is an important item. The average investor has a feeling of security in a well consolidated system that he seldom had in the case of a single road. In the administration of the business there are many savings through consolidation, such for example as in superintendence, office expenses and clerk hire. Although this may be only one or two per cent of the total operating expenses, the saving is pure gain. Two other large items of operating expenses, insurance and legal expenses, are also materially reduced. Other savings come in the bookkeeping and auditing departments. A large system can purchase its material on

---

[1] *Street Railway Journal*, 16, 823.

better terms, since it purchases in larger quantities. It can also do its repair work in one central shop at a lower expense.

The industrial effects of interurbans may be discussed under the heads of effects upon movement of population, rents and railways. The presence of a rapid and cheap means of transportation, such as the electric interurban, permits the widening of the area devoted to residential purposes and the concentration of business within a certain area. It is to be hoped (and there are some reasons for such a hope), that the concentrated area will include only the financial concerns, the large wholesale and retail business, and that the further development of electric traction will send the manufacturing plants and shops and many of the residences to the outlying districts. The development has probably progressed sufficiently far to answer the question asked in the early years of the traction, as to whether the electric cars would ruralize the city or urbanize the country, by the reply that it will do neither the one nor the other. What it has made possible is that the urban center can be extended over a much greater area. The increased speed permits the residence of certain classes at a greater distance from their work and the location of certain businesses at a greater distance from the financial center. The question of taxes has urged along this movement, for the heavy city tax is avoided both by the wealthy citizens who can have their country homes at a distance and by the man of moderate means who does not go so far out nor build in exclusive areas. The question of health has been a powerful influence in the movement to the outlying areas, where the city dweller exchanges the crowded space, unwholesome air and noise, for the quiet and healthful surroundings of country or semi-country life.

The claim has been advanced that the electric lines will solve the over-crowding in the cities; that they will move the working man from the physical and moral un-healthfulness of the congested tenement districts; but neither experience nor present prospects warrant a belief that this will be the easy solution of the problem. It is questionable whether the tenement class wants to remove from the crowded centers, although this desire may result from the fact that present industrial conditions and organization of business do not permit their removal.

Another phase of the population movement is the effect of the interurban upon the rural town. Much depends in this particular upon the size of the the town, its distance from the city with which it is connected by the interurban, the excellence of the business houses in the town and the general character of the rural population around it. While there is a tendency for the town citizen and a small part of the rural dwellers to patronize the city stores, the ease of reaching the town by the other rural dwellers probably more than compensates this loss and if the town store is progressive and caters to the changing wants of the people, its lower rents and lower costs of labor may retain its volume of trade.[1] However the city merchant by advertising in town papers, by paying the cost of transportation to the city

---

[1] It is not assumed that all town and rural dwellers have their incomes immediately increased by the appearance of the interurban, and that from some mysterious source they have more to spend, but that the interurban tends to increase their expenditures for comforts and conveniences. They no longer can be sold the left-over and out-of-style goods and second-grade products of the primary markets, since through the wonderful improvement of country life by the rural free mail delivery, rural telephone and better schools, they know more about conditions in large centers, and the interurban may afford them the opportunity of reaching the center at a low cost.

in return for a purchase of a definite amount, by sending purchases to the interurban station and by other means, is bidding strongly for the rural trade.[1]   Closely allied to the shifting of population is the rise in rentals and in the value of real estate near the interurban.   The facilities for transporting the produce of the land to the city, and the demands for such lands as residences have been one of the important causes in increasing their value from fifty to a hundred dollars per acre, according to their distance from the city.

At first the railroads strongly opposed the inter-urbans by attempting to prevent the granting of fran-chises to them, by hindering the work of construction and by refusing the interurbans permission to cross their tracks, but this attitude has greatly changed, although there is yet some opposition between them. The greatest inroad that the interurban has made upon the railroad's earnings is in the short-haul passen-ger business; for reduced rates, frequent service and direct transportation to the heart of the cities are power-ful attractions for this short-haul business.   Although some of the interurban systems have placed in operation limited trains between the larger cities, they have not been able as yet to attract much of the through business, for there are practically no interurbans that rival the steam roads in comfort of traveling.[2]   The report of the interurban railways in Ohio for 1907 shows that the average amount received from each passenger was eleven cents, while the passenger earnings per train mile were twenty-one cents.   In order to meet the competition of

---

[1] Many of the newspapers in country towns will not accept advertise-ments from the city merchants.

[2] Neither the road-bed is as good, nor the coach as comfortable as that of the steam road, and in most cases the speed is not as great.

the interurban the steam roads reduced the fare and placed faster and more numerous trains on their lines. This kept for them much of the suburban traffic. The interurban offered the traveler a clean, if not as comfortable and as quick a journey from a point near his home to one near his office. The interurbans have also begun to compete with the railways in the express and freight business, and this promises to develop into large proportions on many lines. Statistics of earnings do not convey the correct impression of the importance of the freight and express traffic, for many of the small centers depend almost wholly upon the interurban to supply many of their wants. Merchants, grocerymen and shopkeepers need no longer carry large stocks, for a demand can be supplied within a few hours.[1] The busiest place to be seen in many of the interurban centers is the interurban freight house. However, the total earnings from freight were in 1907 only $620,980, while total passenger earnings were $10,533,963. Freight cars numbered only 219, whereas there were 1,578 passenger cars. On some roads, however, the freight earnings are as high as sixty per cent of the total receipts, but as yet the freight business is largely outgoing, with the important exception of the milk trade. Poultry, eggs and fruits supply considerable traffic to some lines, but in no case has there been any considerable development in carrying the bulky products of the farm. It is entirely possible that, when the interurban is further developed especially if the steamroads are electrified, many side-tracks will be built along the farms and at convenient points to which will be

---

[1] Many of the wholesale houses in the cities have special arrangements for filling and delivering these orders for goods which are shipped via the interurban.

brought the raw produce either from the farms direct or in large loads over the future improved highways. Express companies operate over the interurbans and are, in some cases, the well-known companies of the steam roads. In other cases the interurban company has made forwarding arrangements with the regular express companies.[1] The latest development in the business is the carrying of baggage upon the same terms as those of the steam railroads. This practice has materially increased the passenger receipts. Still another feature of the interurban traffic is the transportation of the mails in special cars.

Not the least of the good results of the interurban is its effect upon the social life of the city and the country. The desire for recreation grounds has received a partial realization through the construction of interurbans, and the recreation traffic forms a very large source of revenue. The importance of this business is indicated by the fact that the sixty-one interurban companies in Ohio reach more than fifty recreation grounds, many of which they own and maintain.[2] Church societies, Sunday-schools and organizations of various kinds charter cars for trips to these places. In addition they carry to these grounds thousands of other individuals who are seeking recreation. The farmer and his family go to the neighboring town more frequently, more quickly and more cheaply than formerly. The contact with a more thoroughly organized town life contributes to the breadth of view of the family, to its culture and to its happiness. The accessibility to markets and shops improves the table and

[1] Cf. *Report of the Railway Commission*, 1907. There are 55 express cars in operation on the interurbans of Ohio.

[2] *Red Book*, 1904.

the dress and increases the comforts of the home. The social life and the amusements of the city are made possessions of the dweller in the country, who widens his circle of acquaintance by his numerous trips to the city and forms new ties of friendship. Scarcely less valuable has been the interurban to the city dweller by bringing him into more frequent social contact with his rural brother and with the invigorating rural life. One of the greatest social benefits has come to the rural women, who can now make numerous calls on their neighbors and frequent shopping trips to the city, thus enlarging the boundary of what had been for many of them a narrow world. To many country boys and girls the interurban has made possible the advantages of a high school and college education without sacrificing the advantages of the home life. The interurban with the rural mail delivery, the daily newspaper and the telephone have done more within the past decade to lessen the isolation of the country life than all the other agencies for the past fifty years.

Electric traction is yet in the formative period of its development, but certain tendencies are somewhat evident. There is now a distinction between urban and interurban railways in that each is owned, in most cases, by different corporations. However, there is some tendency for these interests to combine, and this tendency will be accelerated by a further standardization of way and equipment.[1] Although most of the interurbans have been constructed along the lines of densest traffic, there will undoubtedly be a greater extension into sections not immediately served by any railway where, with

[1] It is true that there is considerable opposition on the part of some cities to having the heavy interurban cars, especially the freight cars, run over the streets of the city.

a private right of way, great speed and frequent service traffic will be developed. The electric roads will act in a way as feeders to the steam lines, as collectors and distributors of traffic, in addition to their primary function of handling the strictly local business. They will handle the light-package and short-haul freight but will do little of the heavier business for some time at least, on account of the greater cost and because of its interference with time and speed. In the local and suburban business, where distances are short between the frequent stops and where there is a steady demand on the central power station, electric traction will take the place of steam by a partial electrification of the steam roads and the construction of wholly electric railways.[1] All in all, the application of electricity as a motive power, together with the motor engines, promises to increase that great contribution to industrial and social progress which transportation has been wont to supply during the past half century.

[1] There are numerous instances where steam roads for considerable distances from the urban center have been made electric roads, but the experience extends over too short a time to make any general deductions as to the ultimate consequences. The necessary safeguards for protecting the movement of heavy trains at short intervals on electrified trunk lines are at present very expensive and form one of the principal handicaps to the widening use of electricity.

CHAPTER XIV

INDUSTRIAL DEVELOPMENT

1830-1900

THE agricultural industry in the early history of the state, so far as any existed, was one largely for domestic consumption. It was not long after the settlement of the state before the inhabitants realized that markets must be found; for, while the rapidly increasing immigrasion afforded a limited temporary market, the new settlers soon became producers, and the pressure of production on consumption became still more pronounced. Not only was the distance to market great, but, as New Orleans afforded for many years the chief market for the agricultural products, the accessibility of the market depended upon the weather and the condition of the rivers. The costs of reaching the market were almost prohibitive for agricultural products during a greater part of the year, and hence, as far as possible, they were reduced in bulk by converting the corn into whiskey and hogs, and the wheat into flour. The low prices for wheat and corn, together with the difficulty of marketing them, gave a great impetus to the stock-raising industry. The Virginia settlers of the Scioto Valley understood the business of fattening cattle and hogs on corn, but they had hesitated to engage in it on account of the distance from the markets. They thought that the long drive to Baltimore and Philadelphia would greatly reduce the weight of the stock, and although this was disproved as early as 1805, comparatively few entered this industry during the following decade. The greater number of the hogs were packed in Ohio after 1830, but the cattle continued to be driven to Eastern markets until the latter half of the century, when the through railway lines took over this business. However as late as 1848 it was estimated that there were driven from the central part of the state to Eastern markets more than fifteen hundred head of fat cattle, although many cars of livestock were soon moving East by rail.[1] Livestock had increased in number from five and three-quarter million head in 1840 to seven and three-quarter million in 1850 and to eight and one-quarter million in 1860.[2] This development of the livestock industry brought a great improvement in the condition of the farmer, in as much as whiskey and livestock then competed on an extensive scale for his corn. When the railways were extended to the Western states, Ohio could no longer raise corn in competition with these states for fattening livestock, and the center of this industry followed the corn center to the West. The most active period of the packing industry in Ohio was from 1850 to 1860.[3]

Agriculture as an important commercial industry did not date back much farther than the opening of the canals, for it was the facility and certainty which these transportation routes offered to the agricultural sections of the interior which placed the industry on a firm basis. More attention was now given to the cultivation of the

---

[1] *Report of the Board of Agriculture,* 1848.

[2] *Report of the Commissioner of Statistics,* 1860.

[3] *Report of the Commissioner of Statistics,* 1860. The percentage of increase in the exports of animal products during this decade was much greater than the percentage of increase in grain exports.

soil and to agricultural machinery, and the fact that the
era of great inventions in agricultural machinery was contemporaneous with the canal period is not a mere coin-
cidence. Land had not been and was not, until many
years later, cultivated with any great degree of care, since
its abundance made it comparatively cheap. The practice was to secure a maximum of returns from the land
until it began to show signs of exhaustion, and then to
sell it and buy other lands in the West or in the less settled parts of Ohio. Most of the population was hence of
a migratory type.[1] In 1832 a law was passed which provided for the establishment of county agricultural societies, and these societies did much under the direction of
the State Board of Agriculture to encourage the development of agriculture. They held fairs and supplied
centers for the dissemination of information on improved
methods of soil culture, stock breeding and the use of
agricultural machinery.[2] The State Board not only held
annual fairs at different points in the state to which for
many years the railroads carried products and stock free,
and passengers at reduced rates, but it also offered
bonuses for the invention of agricultural machines and
prizes for model farms.[3] During the decade from 1850
to 1860 a change occurred in the agricultural products
of the different sections of the state; for the counties of
the Miami and Scioto valleys now became the most important in the production of wheat, instead of the north-

[1] *Report of Commissioner of Statistics*, 1860. Rotation of crops was
not practiced on an extensive scale until after 1850. During the decade
from 1850 to 1860 three million acres of land were improved.

[2] As early as 1836 the agitation for the scientific study of agriculture
in the public schools was begun, which after seventy years was to become an accomplished fact.

[3] These bonuses were awarded after public trials were held which
always attracted large numbers of farmers.

eastern counties which centered around Guernsey county. Farming throughout the state was becoming more diversified, although the ten counties which led in the production of grain were all in the Scioto and Miami valleys. The rank in this particular was as follows, Butler, Ross, Pickaway, Franklin, Greene, Warren, Miami, Fairfield, Fayette and Licking.[1] Ohio ranked third in wheat production in 1860, with Illinois and Indiana exceeding her, whereas in 1850 she was exceeded only by Pennsylvania. The position of Ohio in the production of corn during these decades also shows the importance of the agriculture industry. In 1840 Ohio was third in corn production, with Kentucky first and Tennessee second; in 1850 Ohio was first, and in 1860 she was second with Illinois first. It was estimated in 1860 that Ohio had produced during the past decade over 200,000,000 bushels of wheat, of which over one-half was exported.[2] In 1837 Baltimore had imported 50,000 bushels of wheat from Europe, although at that time much wheat might have been piled up in the West waiting for a rise in the river to carry it to market.[3] Such an event was not likely to recur after 1860 when the development of transportation routes had freed the West from its dependence on the Ohio and the Mississippi rivers for a market.

Harvesting and threshing machinery was introduced in 1831 in the chief grain-growing sections of the state, but it met with great opposition from the laborers, who could be employed for one dollar per day.[4] Although both harvesting and threshing machines were manufac-

---

[1] *Report of the Commissioner of Statistics*, 1860. During this decade there was an average yield of wheat per acre of 12.5 bushels, and of corn 33.9 bushels per acre.

[2] *Ibid.*   [3] *Cincinnati Gazette*, February 20, 1837.

[4] In many cases the first machines in a community were destroyed.

tured at Hamilton by 1846, it was estimated that there were not in 1850 in Ohio one hundred harvesting machines in use.[1]   The Civil War was a very great factor in hastening the invention and use of agricultural machinery; for, while many laborers had been drawn from the farms to the army, they were still consumers of farm products, and there was necessarily a large substitution of mechanical for muscular power in the agricultural industry.   The number of patents on agricultural implements, exclusive of reapers, hay-forks and rakes increased from 350 in 1860 to 502 in 1864.

Two other phases of the agricultural industry should be mentioned in this review of the later industrial development.   The dairy industry continued to be centered in the Western Reserve until the growth of large cities made it profitable to devote the areas immediately surrounding them to the production of such products.   In the thirties there were enacted the dog-tax laws, measures " to encourage the raising of sheep and the growing of wool."[2]   This industry was forced in many ways, and in time the tariff policy had no more ardent and consistent supporters than the wool growers of Ohio, who made their influence felt whenever a change was proposed in the tariff schedule on wool.   Resolution after resolution was passed by the Ohio legislature, asking Congress to enact legislation to protect wool growers of Ohio from foreign competition.[3]   While most of the

---

[1] *Report of the State Board of Agriculture*, 1850.   New York led in the manufacture of agricultural machinery for many years, for the Genesee valley was the first great center of a surplus wheat production. Gradually the center of manufacture followed the agricultural industry to the west.   [2] *Laws of Ohio*, 1830.

[3] *Journal of the Senate*, 1886.   In 1886 the Legislature instructed the Ohio congressmen to oppose the Morrison Tariff Bill for the reason that " it will cripple the industry of the country and in a great measure destroy the great wool-growing interest of this state."

wool produced was not made up in the state, woolen manufacture did develop to a considerable extent in the earlier period.   In 1870 Ohio had 230 woolen mills with 334 sets of machinery, as compared with 173 mills in 1860, 182 in 1880 and 104 in 1890.[1]

To understand properly the change which occurred in the character of the industrial life of Ohio about the middle of the century, attention must be given to the movement of population after 1825.   The growth in population and wealth of the state was very rapid during the second quarter of the century, for the state was not only a halting place for the wave of Western emigration, but by its location and natural resources it became also a center of distribution and gradually a center of supply of non-agricultural products.   It had taken New York 200 years to reach a population of 2,000,000, but Ohio had secured this number within 50 years; it took Illinois nearly 40 years to reach 1,000,000, but Ohio only 30 years.   Based upon the census of 1850 the distribution of laborers among the different occupations was as follows:

```
Agriculture ....................................... 297,398
Commerce, mechanical arts and mining .......... 156,955
Common laborers................................ 102,042
```

As late as 1850 not less than 140,000 people in Ohio were born in the slave states.   The great movement from Ohio to Iowa, Minnesota, Kansas and other Western states began in this year, although by 1850 there were 215,000 natives of Ohio in the three states to the West of it.[2]

[1] *United States Census Reports.*

[2] *Reports of Commissioner of Statistics and Board of Agriculture,* 1851.

A great rage for land speculation set in which was no less marked in Ohio than in the states further West. When land sold for thirty dollars per acre in Ohio, it was often of interest to the Ohio farmer to sell out and move to the West or to the less-settled sections of the state where land could be purchased for ten dollars per acre. Between 1850 to 1860 this process of selling out and moving to the West carried 300,000 people out of the state, and as a result most of the old agricultural counties showed no gain in population, and many showed an actual loss.[1] The new agricultural counties of the northwestern part of the state had increased as rapidly in population as the Western states, because they too had cheap and fertile land. The Toledo congressional district which comprised the ten northwestern counties of the state showed an increase in the decade of 85 per cent, and it was in this decade that Toledo began to grow as an industrial center. Notwithstanding all these losses of agricultural population, the value of industrial products increased 98 per cent during the decade, and property doubled in value.[2] One of the chief causes of this increase was the railways, for Ohio had in 1861 more miles of railroad than any other state. While they had proved of little profit as yet to the stockholders, they had added wonderfully to the value of property and products. Other causes of this increase were the opening of coal and iron mines, salt works and the rapidly growing lake commerce.

[1] The region around Steubenville, which for many years had been the chief wheat-producing section, showed an actual loss. The counties of the Western Reserve during the decade did increase its population 15 per cent., but most of this was contributed by industries other than agriculture.

[2] *Report of Commissioner of Statistics*, 1861. *Cf.* the valuation of property for purposes of taxation in Auditor's report.

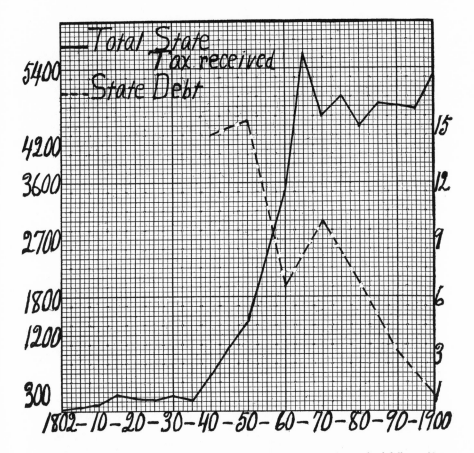

Along the perpendicular line on the left is represented the state tax in thousands of dollars. Along the perpendicular line on the right is represented the state debt in millions of dollars. The large tax raised between the years 1835 and 1865 was used in large part for the construction of internal improvements. This expenditure also explains the large debt in 1850. The increase in the debt between the years 1860 and 1870 was chiefly due to the Civil War. There was a deficit from 1826, but as the state was on the eve of large expenditures for canals and other internal improvements, this was not disclosed. The funds of the national government school lands and other public lands were counted as state funds.

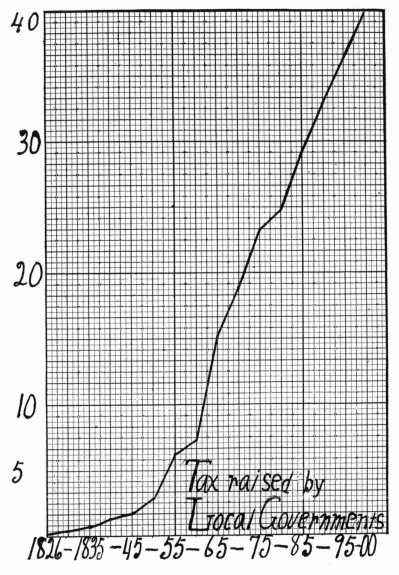

Along the perpendicular line on the left is represented in millions of dollars the amount of the tax raised. The great increase from 1860 to 1885 is partly explained by the expenditures for highways.

However, before there could be any considerable development of manufacturing and the mechanical arts, an adequate and certain source of power must be supplied. But this was furnished neither by the natural waterways nor by the canals nor by the early railroads, for the first two were closed a part of the year, either by low water or by ice, and the early railways were not constructed to carry such heavy commodities as coal even when they reached the mines. It is true that considerable quantities of coal were sent down the Ohio River at a very low cost, but so long as this was the only means of transporting this commodity, the prices fluctuated violently. Even when the railway began to carry coal in competition with waterways, the practice of the railway in abnormally increasing rates whenever the waterways were not navigable made the use of this kind of power very expensive. The geological survey had made known to the people by 1840 the coal resources of the state, but the sparsity of population and the competition of the East prevented any extensive development of coal mining in Ohio until after the Civil War, when the great coal fields of the southeastern part of the state were reached by railroads. The industrial development of Ohio cities was then made possible, although before this time the fact that Cincinnati and the lake cities had access to a limited coal supply, resulted in a respectable beginning of manufacturing at these places.[1] The natural waterway and canals were among the most im-

---

[1] Coal lands along the Ohio River had sold for $500 per acre by 1840, although much of the school land in the southeastern part of the state, which was underlaid with coal, had been sold on the basis of its surface value. Coke ovens were built as early as 1836, but the state geologist warned the people against erecting coke works, until further trials of coking Ohio coal had been made.

portant causes which contributed to the development of manufacturing in Ohio, for they brought the people into easy communication with the East, West and South. Although railroad building began in 1830 the waterways held the predominating influence in whatever there was of a manufacturing industry until the latter half of the century. The rapid settlement of the state and the character of many of the settlers also did much to establish manufacturing in the state, for many of the immigrants came from the New England states, New York and Pennsylvania, where the industry had attained some development. Their mechanical knowledge was soon applied in replacing the worn-out tools which they had brought with them and in supplying the increasing domestic need of tools. The legislature sought to encourage manufacturing by granting liberal charters to companies formed for this purpose. By a law of 1823 it exempted all such companies from taxation. While this general policy was followed for many years, the financial embarrassments of the period caused the auditor in 1845 to recommend the enactment of a law " to more effectually tax money and capital in trade and to provide for the incorporation of all manufacturing companies by a general law."[1] The development of manufacturing since 1850 is well shown by the following table:

[1] This exemption did not include all kinds of property in each case, and it was partly because each company had secured its charter by special laws, which often varied in the privileges granted, that the law of 1845 was enacted. Nor was this law in response to a demand for a relief from any of the evils of the modern trust methods. It was not until 1888 that we find an official expression of the disapproval of trust methods when the Legislature appointed a committee " to investigate combinations commonly called trusts, which have been and are now being formed throughout the country with the assumed purpose of maintaining inordinately remunerative prices by absorbing or controlling competitive interests." *Laws of Ohio*, 1888.

MANUFACTURING AND MECHANICAL INDUSTRIES IN OHIO.[1]

	Years						Per Cent. of Increase				
	1900	1890	1880	1870	186	1850	1850 to 1860	1860 to 1870	1870 to 1880	1880 to 1890	1890 to 1900
Number of establishments..	32,398	28,673	20,699	22,773	11,123	10,622	4.7	104.7	9.1[2]	38.5	13
Capital invested	$605,792,266	$402,793,019	$188,939,614	$141,923,964	$57,295,303	$29,019,538	97.4	147.7	33.1	113.2	50.4
Average number of wage-earners	345,869	292,982	183,609	137,202	75,602	51,491	46.8	81.5	33.8	59.6	18.1
Value of product...........	$832,438,113	$641,688,064	$348,298,390	$269,713,610	$121,671,148	$62,692,279	94.1	121.6	29.1	84.2	29.7
Per cent. of wage-earners employed on total population	8.3	8.	5.7	5.1	3.2	2.6					

[1] *Twelfth Census*, vol. VIII. [2] Decrease.

The rapidity with which artificial routes of transportation were developed determined in a large way the rapidity of the industrial development, although the fundamental conditions which warranted the building of these media of transport formed the basis for the industrial development.   However it must not be forgotten that the peculiar position of Ohio with reference to other industrial regions caused her industrial development to be influenced by numerous internal and external factors. The valuation of taxable property from 1825 to 1835 had increased from forty-five to seventy-five millions, and to one hundred and eleven millions in 1845.   The auditor was on the whole right when he said that " the increase has arisen mainly if not exclusively from the unprecedented rapidity of the settlement and the important changes effected through the instrumentality of our admirable system of internal improvements."[1]   Among these internal improvements, highways and canals had been most important; but by 1851 it was said that railways were taking the place of canals for transporting all light and valuable goods and were also hauling more of the heavy products, such as coal and grains.[2]   Notwithstanding the early manufacture of steam engines in the state, water power was for many years the chief source of power for manufacturing purposes, and as late as 1875 this power was one-quarter of the whole.   After the

[1] *Report of Auditor of State*, 1835.   The auditor recommended the further encouragement of canals, railroads and roads, and remarks that while in the execution of this purpose a diversity of private and local interests mingle, yet it is the purpose of government to look to the general good.

[2] In 1855 the Sault Saint Marie Canal was opened, and the Lake Superior iron ore was brought in large quantities to Cleveland and other lake ports to meet the Ohio coal and limestone.

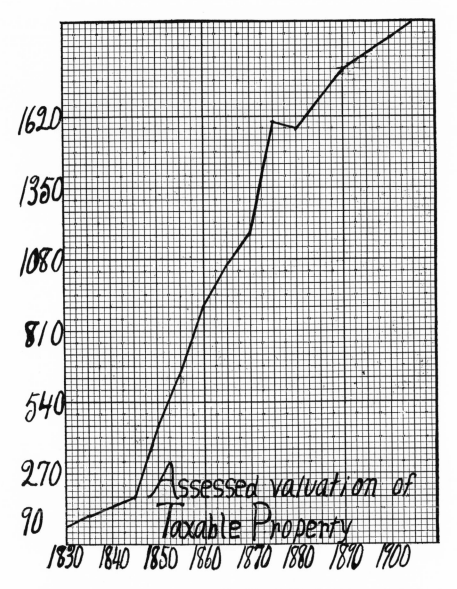

Along the perpendicular line is represented in millions of dollars the total assessed valuation of taxable property. There were re-valuations in 1826, 1835, 1841, 1847, 1854, 1861, 1871, 1881, 1891, and 1901. The apparent decrease in 1872 results from a new basis of valuation in 1871.

canals began to decay less water power was used, and in 1880 steam power made up eighty-five per cent of the total.[1]

In 1860 of all the grain products exported from the Middle West, sixty per cent moved by rail, and efforts were made to prove that the low rates on such products enhanced the price of them for the producer. There were in Ohio at this time about 3000 miles of railways, 3000 miles of turnpikes and 6000 miles of common roads.[2] After the Civil War the development of manufacturing and of the mechanical arts progressed rapidly at many centers. In fact the wonderfully harmonious industrial development of the state has been due to the variety of resources and to the keen rivalry of the numerous industrial centers. After this general survey it will be of value to note the causes of the development of these particular industrial centers.

Cincinnati grew into the metropolis of the West (the Queen City of the West, as she was wont to be called) because she was located on the Ohio river in a region rich in resources, and had a good market to the South. In the struggle to maintain her leadership she took part in many transportation schemes and furnished capital to many transportation projects which promised to aid her in retaining the Southern trade. When the national road, state roads, canals and railways were constructed, other industrial centers began to intrench upon Cincinnati's territory, and this led her to hasten the construction of the railway to the South. The enterprising merchants of Cincinnati had called a commercial convention of

[1] *Tenth Census of United States*, 1880. Natural gas was for a time used in certain sections, but the supply of it decreased rapidly.

[2] *Report of the Commissioner of Statistics*, 1858.

Southern merchants as early as 1837 at Atlanta " to devise ways and means of doing away with New York merchants as middlemen and establishing a direct trade between southern cities and Cincinnati."[1]   Efforts were also made to secure the completion of the Baltimore and Ohio Railroad because, by virtue of her position on an air line from Baltimore to St. Louis, Cincinnati seemed to have a great advantage in the growing East-and-West trade.   The packing industry began as early as 1810 in Cincinnati and in time earned for her the first right to the title, Porkopolis.   In 1850 eighty per cent of all the packing in the state, which then led all other states in this industry, was done at Cincinnati.   After the period of depression from 1874 to 1877, Cincinnati never recovered her former position and the center followed the livestock to the corn area of the West.   In the first half of the century Cincinnati held a commanding position in the trade of the West, and it was said in 1841 that

its commerce is coextensive with the navigation of the west, and its interior trade is spread over the whole extent of country between the river Ohio and the Lakes north and south, and the Scioto and Wabash rivers east and west ; the eastern half of Indiana and southern Ohio are the most important customers for the foreign goods from this market, and the lower Mississippi country for our various manufactured articles and the provisions sold through this market.[2]

Into Cincinnati from Ohio, Indiana and Kentucky came immense quantities of products from fields and forest, which were exchanged for the products of the South, such as sugar, molasses, tobacco and cotton, and for the

[1] *Cincinnati Gazette*, August 30, 1837.
[2] Charles Gist, *Cincinnati As It Is*.

manufactures of Cincinnati or other goods brought to
this place from the East or from foreign lands. Cincinnati
had become a great store-house of goods, a warehouse of
grain, a manufacturer of tools, machines and furniture.[1]
For reasons elsewhere described, the industries of Cincinnati suffered greatly during the war, but she soon recovered her prosperity, although the trade after the war
tended to flow to the East.[2] New Orleans complained
that

> Cincinnati not only has the trade that takes the quickest
> transportation by rail, but it is the money center and the mer-
> chandise distributing point. The shipper of flour either along
> the Ohio or Mississippi sells exchange in Cincinnati against it,
> and either he or someone else buys goods in Cincinnati and
> pays for them in values shipped to New Orleans.[3]

Time was becoming a more important element in production, and the city made renewed efforts to complete
the railway to the South, which upon the recovery of this
section from the devastations of the war promised " to
them opportunities of commercial and industrial expan-
sion only limited by the enterprise which we may use to
secure it. On the natural line from the south and southwest to the east and northeast, this city promises in the
near future to be on the great national thoroughfare of

---

[1] *Cincinnati Gazette*, January 23, 1850. There were in 1850 forty
wholesale dry-goods establishments in Cincinnati. By 1860 Cincinnati
claimed as tributary two-thirds of Ohio, Indiana and Illinois, western
Pennsylvania and Virginia, and all of Kentucky and Tennessee.

[2] *Cf.* chap. 10.

[3] Whereas New Orleans had imported some 260,000 bags of coffee before the war, she imported only 78,000 in 1868. Flour was being sent
to Rio Janeiro for which coffee was sent back as payment by way of the
eastern cities.

trade."[1]   Not all these expectations have been realized, but she is still struggling to retain her position in respect to Southern trade, and in the agitation for making the Ohio river a great commercial waterway Cincinnati has taken a very active part.

The growth of Cleveland as an industrial center was due to her position on the lake in the direct line of trade from the East to the West, the opening of the Erie Canal and later the Ohio canals, the supply of iron and coal to the South, the discovery and use of the Lake Superior ores and the early railway lines from Cleveland to the East and to different points within the state.   The first real impetus came from the canals, and we find her exports growing from 1020 tons in 1830, to 3002 tons in 1835, to 9504 tons in 1840 and 13,500 in 1846.   These exports were valued in this year at $5,500,000 and consisted principally of wheat, flour, corn, coal, pork, whiskey, butter, cheese, lard and wool.[2]   The opening of railroads into the regions to the South and to northern Indiana greatly increased Cleveland's trade and she began to compete successfully with Cincinnati as a market from which dealers were supplied with merchandise.[3] After the opening of the canals and railways Cleveland became the second coal market of Ohio, the receipts of which increased from 178 tons in 1830, to 6028 tons in 1840, to 83,000 tons in 1850 and 225,000 tons in 1858. However, it was the development of the lake trade which made Cleveland a great industrial center, and this trade

---

[1] *Cf. Report of the Chamber of Commerce of Cincinnati*, 1878.

[2] *Cleveland Herald*, July 6, 1847.

[3] The people of Cleveland, when they were contesting with Cincinnati for the trade of Indiana, accused the brokers of Cincinnati of holding out inducements for this trade by sharp bargaining in Indiana Bank Bills.

increased very rapidly after it was once started. " Trade between Cleveland and the Lake Superior region has assumed such proportions that it must be treated as a distinct one in the future. It is but a few years since this business was considered of little importance and a few broken-down steamers were sufficient to carry on this trade. Now this trade has the strongest, largest and fastest vessels." [1] In 1858 there were 241 vessels which cleared from Cleveland for points to the west and north with cargoes valued at $2,000,000, and these vessels brought back cargoes valued at $3,000,000. Cleveland had at this time rolling mills, furnaces, car-wheel and locomotive factories, paper mills and many other manufacturing establishments.

The industrial development of Columbus has been due to its proximity to an abundant coal supply, to its location in a rich agricultural section, to the canals, to the numerous railways, which make it a good distributing center and in part to its being the capital of the state. Previous to the opening of the coal fields to the southeast, the manufacturing industry of Columbus was confined to crude products such as soaps, candles and leather goods, but by 1870 her citizens were preparing to make more of her opportunities. [2] It was said " that Columbus needs a Board of Trade to build up the wholesale trade, for agents of foreign houses sell by sample in our stores goods which we should distribute." [3]   The Columbus

[1] *Cleveland Herald*, April 29, 1856.

[2] The fact that Columbus was the state capital tended to retard the development of industries, since undue emphasis was laid upon this asset and the citizens were not so aggressive in developing manufacturing.

[3] *Cf. Ohio State Journal*, Dec. 4, 1870. About this time Boards of Trade and Chambers of Commerce were being organized in many cities to further the trade interest of the city.

Iron Works were completed in 1870 and "iron was relied upon to change the destiny of Columbus from an ordinary state capital to that of an important manufacturing center" and this with the aid of coal it did.[1]

The development of Toledo as an industrial center has been of more recent date and has been due to her position on the lake, to the opening of the Miami Canal and the Wabash Canal of Indiana, to the development of the rich agricultural region in the northwestern section of the state and to her railway connections with the coal fields of the southeastern portion of the state. Toledo became early in her history a leading grain center, but her manufacturing industry had to wait for its development until the last quarter of the nineteenth century, when railway connections had been made with a coal supply.

The Zanesville district was a more important industrial center in the first half of the century than it has been since that time. This was due to the neighboring coal and iron and to the water power and transportation facilities of the Muskingum river. When the canals were opened, and especially after railways were built in other sections, this point declined as an industrial center. The growth of such centers as Dayton, Springfield and Hamilton was affected largely by the same causes which influenced the development of Cincinnati, although the Ohio river was of less importance in the case of these cities. As early as 1870 there was probably no other state, which had more centers of population, varied industry, trade and transportation than Ohio. For this very reason the undue increase of Cleveland and Cincinnati as great centers was prevented, for unlike Chicago

---

[1] *Cf. Ohio State Journal, op. cit.*

and New York they had no preponderating advantages over the other centers of the state.   The facts that the railway system of Ohio was at first largely one for east and west trade, that the state had natural commercial waterways to the north and south, that the state was for the most part level thus making the construction of north and south as well as east and west lines of communication comparatively low in cost, and that the variety of soil and natural resources warranted this construction,—all these facts prevented any one section from abnormally developing to the exclusion of other sections. Thus population and wealth became generally distributed over the state.   The comparative growth in population of the four leading industrial centers is shown by the following table.[1]

[1] *Twelfth Census of United States.*

City	1830	Per cent. of Increase	1840	Per cent. of Increase	1850	Per cent. of Increase	1860	Per cent. of Increase
Cincinnati ...	24,831	157.5 [1]	46,338	86.6	115,435	149.1 [2]	161,044	39.5
Cleveland ...	1,076	......	6,071	464.2 [3]	17,034	180.6 [4]	43,417	154.9
Columbus....	2,435	......	6,048	148.4	17,882	195.7 [5]	18,554	3.8
Toledo.......	......	......	1,222	......	3,829	213.3	13,768	259.6

City	1870	Per cent. of Increase	1880	Per cent. of Increase	1890	Per cent. of Increase	1900	Per cent. of Increase
Cincinnati ...	216,239	24.3	255,139	18	296,908	16.4	325,902	9.8
Cleveland ...	92,829	113.8	160,146	72.5	261,353	63.2	381,768	46.1
Columbus....	31,274	68.6	51,647	65.1	88,150	70.7	125,560	42.4
Toledo	31,584	129.4	50,137	58.7	81,434	62.4	131,822	61.9

After this review of the industrial development of Ohio, we may briefly characterize her position at the close of the nineteenth century. The iron industry was almost contemporaneous with the admission of the state into the union, and before 1815 the centers around Niles, in Adams and Muskingum counties, had developed to some

[1] Miami Canal to Dayton opened.
[2] Railway to Columbus, Cleveland and the East opened.
[3] Canals opened.
[4] Railways to East and South opened.
[5] Canal and railways opened.

extent, although the low grade of ore, the difficulty of transporting the product and the increasing cost of fuel for smelting made many of these early attempts unsuccessful and limited most of them to production for local purposes.[1] In 1825 the comparatively rich ores of the Hanging Rock district were discovered, and the chief center of the iron industry was transferred hither from Niles until the rich Superior ores restored the leadership to the Cleveland-Niles district, where it has since remained.[2] The legislature encouraged the industry by exempting iron mills for a time from taxation and by fixing low tolls on the canals for the ore and its manufactured products. In 1840 there were sixteen iron furnaces in the state, and while this number had increased to fifty-two in 1860, fifty per cent of these had been built since 1850. This shows that in the period of canal transportation the iron industry had but little development.[3] However, Ohio has always led all other states west of the Alleghanies in the manufacture of iron and steel products and, since 1870, has ranked second in the United States. This has been due to her location with respect to the ore and fuel, together with her advantages with respect to transporting the products to the regions of consumption.[4]

In the manufacture of foundry and machine-shop products, Ohio ranks second in the United States, with Cleveland and Cincinnati as the chief centers; but these

[1] Charcoal was used for many years for smelting purposes, and the attempts in 1836 to use Ohio coal for this purpose were a failure.

[2] Eighty-six iron works were built in the Hanging Rock district, and all except seventeen were built before 1855.

[3] *Report of the Commissioner of Statistics*, 1860. Of the ten Bessemer Steel establishments in the United States in 1878, Pennsylvania had five, New York one, Ohio one and Illinois three.

[4] The location of coke has become of late years a factor of increasing importance in determining the location of the iron industry.

products have always been important in Ohio on account of the supply of the raw material and the central position of the state within the consuming area.[1] Flouring and grist mill products rank third in materials manufactured, and this is due to the large corn and wheat area within and near the state. Closely related to this is the distilling industry, which has throughout the history of the state been important. Ohio has always been the largest boot and shoe manufacturing state west of the Alleghanies and, in 1900, ranked fourth in the United States, with the chief centers at Cincinnati, Columbus and Portsmouth.[2] Cincinnati also early became a center for the manufacture of men's clothing, for the trade of the Ohio River brought great numbers of customers to this center. Cleveland after 1880 likewise became an important center for men and women's clothing. Both centers were materially aided in this industry by the immigration of the Hebrews to these cities. Ohio ranked first in 1900 in the manufacture of carriages and wagons, the center having gradually moved westward from New York and tending to move still farther west with the center of the population. In pottery and clay products Ohio is taking a high rank and this industry, on account of the great supply of clay, is destined to be even more important. Ohio in 1900 ranked first in these products and supplied 28.8 per cent of the total product of the United States.[3]

[1] Cincinnati began as early as 1825 to manufacture steam engines, and in 1835 its shops had turned out 100 steam engines, 240 cotton gins, 20 sugar mills and 22 boilers.

[2] *Twelfth Census of United States*, 1900.

[3] The industry centers around East Liverpool, Roseville and Cincinnati. At the first named place 87.4 per cent. of all laborers employed in the city are engaged in this industry. The leadership of this city is due to the abundant clays found near it and to the skilled workmen, who were early attracted to this place from England. Of the total amount of yellow ware manufactured in the United States 49.1 per cent. is produced at East Liverpool.

She also produces more than 33 per cent of all the sewer pipe in the United States. The manufacture of rubber goods secured an early beginning at Akron, which produced 75 per cent of the total state product in 1900. Extensive paper and pulp factories are scattered throughout the state, but the chief center is the Miami Valley.

In 1900 the rank of industries in Cleveland according to value of product were iron and steel products, foundry and machine, slaughtering and meat products, women's clothing, malt liquors. In Cincinnati the order in importance of industrial products was men's clothing, foundry and machine products, slaughtering and meat products, distilled liquors, boots and shoes. The manufactured products of Columbus rank third in value, Toledo fourth and Dayton fifth.

Below is given a table of the value of manufactures and of the products of mechanical industries, together with those of the other leading Ohio industries.[1]

Year	Wheat Bushel	Corn Bushel	Coal[2]	Iron Ore[3]	Value of the Product of manufacturies and mechanical industries.
1840..	16,571,661	....	140,535	29,950	
1850..	31,500,000	56,619,608	640,000	52,658	$62,692,279
1860..	23,640,350	91,588,704	1,133,596	105,500	121,691,148
1870..	18,726,341	88,565,299	2,830,559	309,033	269,713,610
1880..	48,540,307	105,414,594	7,000,000	488,753	348,298,390
1890..	31,509,676	63,694,215	11,494,506	254,294	641,688,064
1900..	41,469,703	143,161,675	18,988,150	22,657	832,438,113

[1] *Reports of the Commissioner of Statistics.*
[2] Bituminous tons.   [3] Short tons.

To accompany this table there is appended in graphic form a statement of the prices of two leading export and import products for each year since 1830. This chart should be studied in connection with the preceding chapters upon the development of the means of transportation, inasmuch as the fluctuation of prices tended to decrease as added means of transportation were supplied.[1]

ANNUAL PRICES OF WHEAT, CORN, SUGAR AND COFFEE IN OHIO
MARKETS FROM 1830 TO 1902

Year	Wheat	Corn	Sugar	Coffee
1830	.56	.20	.095	.15
1832	.75	.37	.065	.14
1835	1.06	.32	.10	.145
1838	1.15	.625	.125	.15
1840	.60	.60	.075	.13
1843	.60	.20	.0625	.08
1845	.90	.31	.063	.087
1847	1.00	.33	.05	.085
1850	.70	.33	.06	.12
1853	1.00	.37	.05	.122
1855	1.62	.43	.075	.12
1858	1.03	.70	.075	.12
1860	.90	.32	.065	.14
1862	1.03	.31	.12	.33
1863	1.04	.53	.12	.304
1864	1.41	1.03	.18	.46
1865	1.78	.73	.20	.382
1866	2.27	.54	.16	.306
1867	2.29	.78	.14	.287
1868	2.31	.92	.14	.255
1869	1.57	.73	.13	.246
1870	1.14	.83	.13	.226
1871	1.27	.56	.11	.192

[1] These prices are wholesale prices and were taken from the Reports of the Commissioner of Statistics and of the Chamber of Commerce of Cincinnati.

The graph for prices during the past fifty years was secured by taking ten year annual averages, and thus the general trend of prices is indicated.

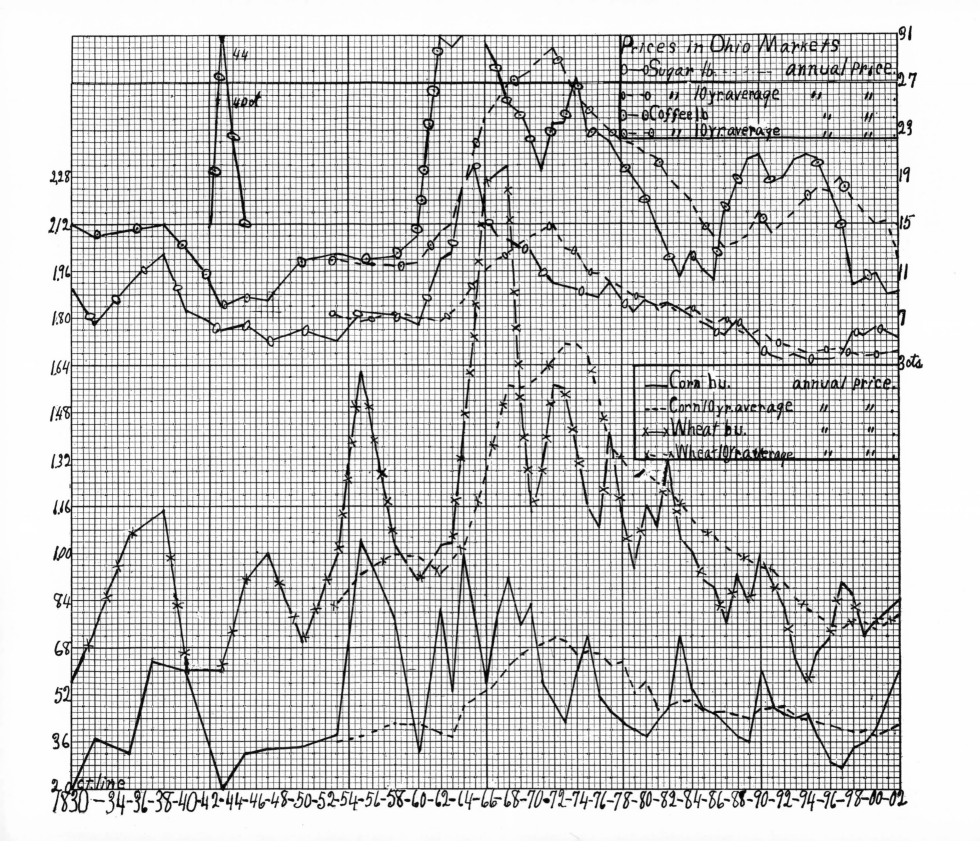

Prices in Ohio Markets

o──o Sugar lb. ----- annual Price.
o──o " 10 yr average " "
o──o Coffee lb " "
o──o " 10 yr average " "

──── Corn bu. annual price.
----- Corn 10 yr average " "
x──x Wheat bu. " "
x──x Wheat 10 yr average " "

2.28
2.12
1.96
1.80
1.64
1.48
1.32
1.16
1.00
.84
.68
.52
.36
.20 ct. line

31
27
23
19
15
11
7
3 cts

44
4 dot

1830—34-36-38-40-42-44-46-48-50-52-54-56-58-60-62-64-66-68-70-72-74-76-78-80-82-84-86-88-90-92-94-96-98-00-02

1872 .... 1.57	...... .49	...... .10	...... .236
1873 .... 1.56	...... .42	...... .10	...... .236
1874 .... 1.37	...... .60	...... .097	...... .277
1875 .... 1.16	...... .72	...... .09	...... .230
1876 .... 1.10	...... .51	...... .089	...... .231
1877 .... 1.41	...... .46	...... .10	...... .221
1878 .... 1.11	...... .42	...... .084	...... .20
1879 .... .95	...... .37	...... .077	...... .18
1880 .... 1.16	...... .376	...... .084	...... .177
1881 .... 1.09	...... .423	...... .081	...... .146
1882 .... 1.32	...... .488	...... .082	...... .123
1883 .... 1.05	...... .723	...... .078	...... .105
1884 .... 1.01	...... .532	...... .071	...... .128
1885 .... .886	...... .471	...... .063	...... .108
1886 .... .884	...... .39	...... .061	...... .102
1887 .... .796	...... .44	...... .054	...... .167
1888 .... .93	...... .37	...... .058	...... .183
1889 .... .83	...... .36	...... .049	...... .208
1890 .... .99	...... .60	...... .037	...... .208
1891 .... .90	...... .48	...... .035	...... .185
1892 .... .81	...... .45	...... .028	...... .187
1893 .... .64	...... .44	...... .034	...... .205
1894 .... .54	...... .45	...... .035	...... .207
1895 .... .66	...... .41	...... .036	...... .203
1896 .... .72	...... .27	...... .036	...... .185
1897 .... .89	...... .26	...... .057	...... .152
1898 .... .86	...... .34	...... .055	...... .097
1899 .... .72	...... .36	...... .061	...... .096
1900 .... .75	...... .41	...... .058	...... .107
1901 .... .77	...... .52	...... .052	...... .091
1902 .... .80	...... .61	...... .055	...... .083
1903 .... .81	...... .47	...... .054	...... .076

BIBLIOGRAPHY

PUBLIC DOCUMENTS.

Annual Reports of the Auditor of Ohio, 1802 to 1905.

Annual Reports of the Commissioner of Railways and Telegraphs of Ohio, 1867 to 1905.

Annual Reports of the Secretary of State of Ohio, 1825 to 1905.

Annual Reports of the Treasurer of State of Ohio, 1802 to 1905.

American Agriculture in Report of the U. S. Commissioner of Agriculture, 1892.

Cranch's Reports, Seventh, State of New Jersey versus Wilson.

Census Reports of United States for 1850, 1860, 1870, 1880, 1890 and 1900.

Canals, Public Documents Concerning, 1835.

Canal Reports, 1823 to 1836.

Canal Fund, Report of Commissioner Concerning, 1826.

Commerce, Internal, of U. S., House of Representatives, June 30, 1888.

Canals, Ohio, in Report of the Ohio State Archeological and Historical Society, 1905.

Files of Charters of Incorporated Companies, in Office of the Secretary of State of Ohio, 1830 to 1870.

Executive Documents of Ohio, 1830 to 1905.

Globe, Congressional, Part 4, 1861-1862, Appendix.

Journal of the Senate of Ohio, 1808 to 1905.

Journal of the House of Representatives of Ohio, 1808 to 1905.

Laws of the North-West Territory, 1787 to 1802.

Laws of Ohio, 1802 to 1908.

Land Laws, A Compilation of the Laws, Treatises, Resolutions and Ordinances of the General Assembly and State Governments, which Relate to Lands in the State of Ohio. Published by the General Assembly in 1825.

Ohio Railway Laws and Charters, George B. Wright, Commissioner of Railways and Telegraphs, 1870.

Ohio Reports, Sixth, Chapman versus The Mad River and Lake Erie R. R. and Sandusky City and Indiana R. R. Company.

Ohio Reports, Randall, 66.

Ohio Agriculture Reports, 1850 to 1905.
Publications of the Ohio State Archeological and Historical Society,
14 volumes.
Report of the Ohio Board of Public Works, 1836 to 1906.
Report of the Commissioner of Statistics of Ohio, 1855 to 1905.
Report of the Chief of the Engineers of the U. S. Army, 1896, Part 4.
Report of the Geological Survey of Ohio, 1836 to 1883.
Report of the Proceedings and Debates of the Convention for the Re-
vising of the Ohio Constitution, 1851. Two volumes.
Report of the Ohio Highway Department, 1905 to 1908.
Report of the Ohio Road Commission, 1893.
Report of the Ohio Turnpike Convention, 1844.
Report of the Trustees of the Sinking Fund of Cincinnati, 1906.
Senate Reports, Transportation Routes to the Seaboard, First Session,
43d Congress, volume 1.
Wheaton, Ninth, Reports of the U. S. Supreme Court.

NEWSPAPERS.

American Pioneer, The. A monthly Periodical devoted to the object
of the Logan Historical Society or to the collection and publica-
tion of facts relative to the Early Settlement and Successive Im-
provement of the Country. Vols. 1 and 2, 1842-1843, Chillicothe.
Advertiser, Cincinnati, January, 1823 to February, 1826.
Centinel of the North-west Territory, Cincinnati, Nov. 9, 1793 to Nov.
17, 1794.
Courier, Western and Public Advertiser, Ravenna, April, 1825 to June,
1830.
Freedonia, Chillicothe and Circleville, Sept., 1811 to Oct., 1813.
Gazette, Cincinnati, June 22, 1833 to Jan. 3, 1883.
Gazette, Cincinnati Literary, vols. 1 and 2, Jan. to Dec., 1824.
Gazette, St. Clairsville, Sept., 1826 to July, 1829.
Hesperian, The, or Western Monthly Magazine, Cincinnati, vols. 1
and 2, 1838 and 1839.
Hall, Liberty, and Cincinnati Gazette, Mar., 1816 to June, 1830.
Herald, Cleveland, Feb., 1841 to Mar., 1885.
Journal, Ohio State, Sept. 22, 1825 to Jan. 1, 1908.
Journal, Historical and Philosophical Society, Cincinnati, 1839.
Mercury, Cincinnati, Dec., 1805 to Nov. 1808.
Patron, Delaware, The, April, 1823 to May, 1830.
Spy, Western, The, Cincinnati, May, 1816 to April, 1820.
Supporter, Chillicothe, The, Dec., 1808 to Oct., 1825.
Spirit of the Lake and Boatman's Magazine, Cleveland, 1849.
Statesman, Ohio, The, Columbus, July, 1837 to Mar. 1877.

Street Railway Journal, vol. 16.

Time, Olden, The, a monthly publication, devoted to the preservation of Documents and other Authentic Information in relation to the Early Exploration and Settlement and Improvement of the Country around the Head of the Ohio, Cincinnati, 2 volumes, 1846 to 1848.

JOURNALS OF TOURS AND TRAVELS.

Ashe, Thomas. *Travels in America, performed in 1806 for the purpose of exploring the Rivers Allegheny, Monongahela, Ohio and Mississippi, and ascertaining the Produce and the Condition of their Banks and Vicinity.* Three volumes, Liverpool, 1808.

Bradbury, John. *Travels in the Interior of North America in the years 1809, 1810 and 1811, including a description of Upper Louisiana together with the States of Ohio, Kentucky, Indiana and Tennessee, etc.* London, 1817.

Bailey, Francis. *Journal of a Tour in the Unsettled Parts of North America in 1796 and 1797.* London, 1800.

Bullock, W. *Sketch of a Journey through the Western States of North America from New Orleans by the Mississippi, Ohio, City of Cincinnati and Falls of the Niagara to New York in 1827.* London, 1822.

Cuming, F. *Sketches of a Tour to the Western Country through the States of Ohio and Kentucky, a Voyage down the Ohio and Mississippi commenced in the winter of 1807 and concluded in 1809.* Pittsburg, 1810.

Dana, E. *Description of the Principal Roads and Routes by Land and Water through the Territory of the United States extending from the Province of New Brunswick in Nova Scotia to the Pacific Ocean.* Cincinnati, 1819.

Doddridge, Joseph. *Notes on the Settlement and Indian Wars of the Western Parts of Virginia and Pennsylvania for the years 1763 until 1783 inclusive, together with a view of the state of society and manners of the first settlers of the Western Country.* Albany, N. Y., 1786.

Espy, Josiah. *Memorandum of a Tour made in the States of Ohio and Kentucky and Indiana Territory in 1805.* Cincinnati, 1870.

Flint, Timothy. *Recollection of the Last Ten Years passed in occasional Residences and Journeyings in the valley of the Mississippi from Pittsburg and the Missouri to the Gulf of Mexico, etc.* Boston, 1825.

Gist, Christopher. *A Journal of Christopher Gist's Journey begun from Col. Cresap's at the old town on Potomack River, Maryland,*

Oct. 31, 1750, continued down the Ohio within 15 miles of the Falls thereof, etc.

Gordon, Harry. *Extracts from the Journal of Captain Harry Gordon, Chief Engineer in the Western of North America, who was sent from Fort Pitt on the River Ohio, down the said River, etc., to Illinois in 1766.* London, 1789.

Harris, Thaddeus. *The Journal of a Tour into the Territory North-West of the Alleghany Mountains made in the Spring of the year 1803.* Boston, 1805.

Hildreth, S. P. *Journal of some Emigrants from New England to the Muskingum in 1788.*

Hutchins, Thomas. *A Topographical Description of Virginia, Pennsylvania, Maryland and North Carolina, comprehending the rivers Ohio, Kenahwa, Scioto.* Boston, 1787.

May, John. *Journal and Letters of Col. John May of Boston, Relative to two Journeys to the Ohio Country in 1788 and 1789.* Cincinnati, 1875.

Michaux, F. A. *Travels to the Westward of the Alleghany in the State of Ohio, Kentucky and Tennessee, etc., in 1801.* London, 1805.

Palmer, John. *Journal of Travels in the United States of America and in Lower Canada, performed in the year 1817; containing particulars relating to the prices of Lands and Provinces, etc.* London, 1818.

Patterson, A. W. *History of the Backwoods or The Region of the Ohio, etc.* Pittsburg, 1843.

Schultz, Christian. *Travels on an Inland Voyage through the States of New York, Pennsylvania, Virginia, Ohio, etc., performed in the years 1807 and 1808.* New York, 1814.

Trent, William. *Journal of Captain William Trent from Logtown to Pickawillany, 1752.* Edited with Notes by Alfred T. Goodman, Secretary of The Western Reserve Historical Society, 1871.

Weld, Isaac. *Travels through North America and Upper and Lower Canada from 1795 to 1797.* Philadelphia, 1800.

MISCELLANEOUS.

Bliss, Eugene P. *Zeisbarger's (David) Diary.* Cleveland, 1872.

Brown, Samuel S. *The Western Gazetteer; or, Emigrants' Directory containing a Geographical description of the Western States and Territories, viz., the States of Kentucky, Louisiana, Indiana, Ohio and Tennessee and Mississippi, etc.* London, 1817.

Burnet, Jacob. *Notes on the Early Settlement of the North-West Territory.*

Cincinnati Directory, 1819 and 1829.

Cist, Charles. *Cincinnati Miscellany or Antiquities of the West.* Cincinnati, 1846.

Cist, Charles. *Cincinnati in 1841, 1851 and 1859.*

Conclin, George. *New River Guide, 1848.*

Cramer, Zadock. *The Navigator; or, the Traders Useful Guide in navigating the Monongahela, Allegheny, Ohio and Mississippi Rivers. A description of the Towns, Settlements, Villages, Harbors, etc.* Twelfth Edition, 1824.

Dana, E. *Geographical Sketches of the Western Country, designed for Emigrants and Settlers.* Cincinnati, 1819.

Depew, C. M. (Editor). *One Hundred Years of American Commerce.*

De Schweintz, Edmund. *The Life and Times of David Zeisberger, The Pioneer and Apostle of the Indians.* Philadelphia, 1871.

Dickens, Charles. *American Notes for General Circulation.* London, 1848.

Dodge, Martin. *Better Roads and Larger Profits, 1893.*

Ellet, Charles. *The Mississippi and Ohio Rivers; containing plans for the protection of the Delta from inundation, and investigations of the practicability and cost of improving the navigation of the Ohio and other Rivers by means of Reservoirs.* Philadelphia, 1873.

Evans, Nelson W. *Taxation in Ohio.* 1906.

Giauque, Florien. *Ohio Road and Bridge Laws.* 1895.

Huntington, C. C., and McClelland, C. P. *Ohio Canals, Their Construction, Cost, etc.* Columbus, 1905.

Hall, Harvey. *The Cincinnati Directory for 1825.*

Hall, James. *Statistics of the West at the close of the year 1836.*
          The West, its commerce and navigation, 1848.
          The West, its soil and production, 1847.

Hulbert, Archer Butler. *Historic Highways.* 16 vols., Cleveland, 1902.

Imlay, Gilbert. *A Topographical Description of the Western Territory of North America, etc.* Two Volumes. London, 1790.

Jenkins, Warren. *The Ohio Gazetteer and Travelers' Guide, containing a description of the several Towns, Townships and Counties with their Water Courses, Roads, Improvements, Mineral Resources, etc.* Columbus, 1837.

Kilbourne, John. *The Ohio Gazetteer or Topographical Dictionary.* Fifth and Sixth Editions, 1818 and 1819, Columbus.

Latrobe, H. B. *The First Steamboat on the Western Waters.* Baltimore, 1871.

Lloyd, James T. *Steamboat Directory and Disasters on the Western Waters.* Cincinnati, 1866.

McCain, C. C. *Compendium of Transportation Theories; Ohio Railroad Guide from Cincinnati to Erie in 1854.*

Railroad Reports.
> Reports of the Cincinnati, Hamilton and Dayton Railroad, 1850-1881.
>
> Reports of the Cleveland, Columbus, Cincinnati and Indianapolis Railroad, 1870-1880.
>
> Reports of the Detroit and Michigan Central Railroad, 1850-1870.
>
> Reports of the Lake Shore and Michigan Southern Railroad, 1870-1880.

Report of the Chamber of Commerce, Cincinnati, 1857 to 1905.

Report of the Proceedings of the Ohio River Valley Improvement Association, 1895 to 1906.

Ringwalt, J. R. *Development of Transportation Systems, 1888.*

Roundthaler, Edward. *Life of John Heckwelder.* Philadelphia, 1845.

Searight, Thomas B. *Old Pike.*

Smith, W. P. *The Great Railway Celebration of 1857.*

St. Clair Papers. Edited by William Henry Smith. Two Volumes, Cincinnati, 1882.

Stockdale, Percival. *Commerce of the Western Waters.* Pittsburg, 1807.

Whittlesey, Charles. *An Account of the First Mill in Ohio and the Massacre at Big Bottom.*

Wilson, W. B. *History of the Pennsylvania Railroad Company.*

LOCAL AND STATE HISTORY.

Albach, James R. *Annals of the West; Embracing a concise account of the Principal Events which have occurred in the Western States and Territories from the discovery of the Mississippi Valley to the year 1856.* Pittsburg, 1857.

Abbott, John S. C. *History of the State of Ohio from the discovery of the great valley to the present.* Detroit, 1875.

Andrews, Israel Ward. *Washington County and the Early Settlement of Ohio.* Marietta, 1876.

Atwater, Caleb. *A History of the State of Ohio, Natural and Civil.* Cincinnati, 1838.

Annals of the Early Settlers of Cuyahoga County. Tracts 3 to 9.

Bareis, George F. *History of Madison Township, Franklin County.*

Burnet, Jacob. *Cincinnati in 1800.*
> *History of the Upper Ohio Valley, 1891.*

Comley, W. J., and D'Eggville, W. *Ohio the Future Great State, Her Manufactures.*

Cist, Charles. *Cincinnati in 1841. Its Early Annals and Future Prospects.*

Drake, Benjamin, and Mansfield, E. *Cincinnati in 1826.*

Drake, Daniel. *Natural and Statistical View or Picture of Cincinnati and the Miami Country, etc.* Cincinnati, 1815.

Ford, Henry A., and Mrs. Kate B. *History of Cincinnati, 1789 to 1881.*

Hunt, W. E. *Coshocton County Historical Collections.* Cincinnati, 1875.

Hall, James. *Sketches of History, Life and Manners in the West.* Cincinnati, 1834.

Hildreth, S. P. *Pioneer History; Being an account of the First Examination of the Ohio Valley and the Early Settlements of the North-West Territory, etc.* Cincinnati, 1848.

Hinsdale, H. S. *The Old North-West with a view of the thirteen colonies as constituted by the royal charters.* New York, 1899.

Howe, Henry. *Historical Collections of Ohio.* Two volumes, Ohio Centennial Edition, Columbus, 1900.

Hosmer, H. S. *Early History of the Maumee Valley.* Toledo, 1858.

Jones, A. B. *Early Days of Cincinnati.* Cincinnati, 1888.

Knapp, H. S. *History of the Maumee Valley, commencing with its occupation by the French in 1680.* Toledo, 1872.

Lane, Samuel A. *Fifty Years and over of Akron and Summit County.*

McBride, James. *Pioneer Biography, Sketches of the lives of some of the Early Settlers of Butler County, Ohio.* Two volumes, Cincinnati, 1809 and 1871.

McConnel, D. T., and Carrod, Frederick. *Steubenville, Past and Present and Future.* Steubenville, 1872.

Mahoning Valley, Historical Collections of. Youngstown, 1875.

Martin, William T. *History of Franklin County; A collection of Reminiscences of the early settlement of the county.* Columbus, 1858.

Mentelle, M. *On the Location and the Settlement of Gallipolis, Ohio.*

Miller, Francis W. *Cincinnati's Beginnings. Missing chapters on the Early History of the city and the Miami Purchase, etc.* Cincinnati, 1880.

Mitchener, C. H. *Ohio Annals. Historical Events in Tuscarawas and Muskingum Valley and in other portions of the State of Ohio.* 1876.

Perkins, James H. *Annals of the West. Embracing a concise account of the Principal Events which have occurred in the Western States from the Discovery of the Mississippi Valley to the year 1846.* Cincinnati, 1846.

Rice, Harvey. *Pioneers of the Western Reserve.* Second Edition, Boston, 1888.

Smucker, Isaac. *History of the Welsh Settlements in Licking County, etc.* Newark, 1869.

Studer, Jacob. *History of Columbus; its Resources and Progress.* 1873.

Steele, Robert W., and Mary Davies. *Early Dayton, 1796 to 1896.*

Thurston, George B. *Pittsburg as it is, or Facts and Figures exhibiting the past and present of Pittsburg, its advantages, manufactures and commerce.* Pittsburg, 1857.

Walker, Charles W. *History of Athens County, Ohio, and Incidentally of the Ohio Land Company and the First Settlement of the State at Marietta, etc.* Cincinnati, 1869.

Whittlesey, Charles. *Fugitive Essays upon Interesting and Useful Subjects relating to the Early History of Ohio. Its Geology and Agriculture.* Hudson, 1852.

Whittlesey, Charles. *Early History of Cleveland.* Cleveland, 1867.